...And there was
War in Heaven!
Surviving the End Times

Carmen Welker

And There Was War in Heaven!
Surviving the End Times

Printed in the United States of America

ISBN 978-1-934916-04-9

www.netzaripress.com

Dedication

This book is dedicated to my husband and soul mate, Bill Welker, who never wavers in his support of my "God projects"; and to my colleagues, authors Andrew Gabriel Roth and Baruch ben Daniel who have allowed me to freely use whatever I desire from their awesome work entitled the "Aramaic English New Testament," published by Netzari Press (see Appendix 6).

Foreword

The end times study on which you're about to embark is from the Netzari/Messianic viewpoint which uses the proper Names of YHWH (Yahweh = The Creator/God the Father) which was given to us in the Hebrew Bible; and His Son, Yeshua the Messiah, referred to as "Jesus" in the Christian world. (Netzarim, or Nazarenes, are the original followers of Yeshua who live according to Torah and the Ketuvim Netzarim - the writings of the Netzarim.) The terms "God" and "Jesus" are occasionally used whenever necessary to make a point, and scriptures borrowed from Stern's Complete Jewish Bible often contain the term "ADONAI". The Aramaic English New Testament phonetically spells Yeshua as "Y'shua".

This study, as you will see, pulls no punches, as it is designed to awaken the world from its collective slumber concerning the Scriptures, which amply warn us about the end times - those perilous days when YHWH's patience with mankind comes to an end.

B'rit Chadashah (New Testament) scripture quotations are from the Aramaic English New Testament (AENT), copyright 2008 by Andrew Gabriel Roth. Used with permission of Netzari Press. All rights reserved.

Tanach (Old Testament) scripture quotations are from the Complete Jewish Bible, copyright 1998 by David H. Stern. Published by Jewish New Testament Publications, Inc., 6120 Day Long Lane, Clarksville, Maryland 21029. www.messianicjewish.net/jntp. Used by permission.

Table of Contents

And There Was War in Heaven!
Surviving the End Times

Chapter 1

A Brief Overview

Most people, including atheists, have heard rumors about the prophesied "end times" outlined in that ancient document we call the Holy Bible. But how many are actually paying attention? How many can see the "end times" are upon us right now? How many know *why* we're in the end times, or have actually bothered to prepare for the end - or realize that the most important thing we can do is to prepare **spiritually**?

Whether you are among the many who have been frightened by this topic and done everything in your power to stock up on water and canned goods, or have chosen to dismiss it altogether, the fact remains that nearly 400 Bible prophecies have already come true, which means the last few will, as well! (Please see Appendix 1.) Here is an example from Zephaniah, which reveals the seriousness of this issue:

Zephaniah 1: 14 The great Day of ADONAI is near, near and coming very quickly; Hear the sound of the Day of ADONAI! When it's here, even a warrior will cry bitterly. 15 That Day is a Day of fury, a Day of trouble and distress, a Day of waste and desolation, a Day of darkness and gloom, a Day of clouds and thick fog, 16 a Day of the shofar and battle-cry against the fortified cities and against the high towers [on the city walls]. 17 "I will bring such distress on people that they will grope their way like the blind, because they have sinned against ADONAI. Their blood will be poured out like dust and their bowels like dung. 18 Neither their silver nor their gold will be able to save them. On the day of ADONAI's fury, the whole land will be destroyed in the fire of his

1

jealousy. For he will make an end, a horrible end, of all those living in the land."

Those who have an intimate relationship with YHWH and know the Bible, understand that "the Day of ADONAI" is indeed at hand; and those who choose to ignore the warnings will end up very surprised when it happens - because it will happen, whether they "believe" or not! The Bible brims with ample expansion on this topic and clearly reveals that life as we know it will one day come to an end.

Among the many reasons we are facing these difficult times described in Zephaniah is because mankind, as a collective whole, has turned away from God. We are, in effect, "as the in the days of Noah":

*Matthew 24: 37. **And as in the days of Nukh (Noah), thus will be the coming of the Son of man.** 38. For as they were before the deluge, eating and drinking and taking women and giving them in marriage to men up to the day that Nukh entered into the ark. 39. **And they did not know until the deluge came and took them all, thus will be the coming of the Son of man.** 40. Then two men will be in the field, one will be taken and one will be left. 41. And two women will be grinding at the mill. One will be taken and one will be left. 42. Therefore be alert, because you do not know in what hour your Master will come. 43. And know this, that if the master of the house had known, he would not have allowed his house to be plundered. 44. Because of this also, you should be prepared, because in an hour that you do not expect, the Son of man will come.*

In Noah's day (please see Genesis 6-7), people were godless, decadent and out of control, and YHWH had decided to destroy the entire earth by flood. The only people who survived this flood, we are clearly told, were Noah and his family because Noah was "righteous and wholehearted."

Genesis 6: 9 Here is the history of Noach. In his generation, Noach was a man righteous and wholehearted; Noach walked with God. 10 Noach fathered three sons, Shem, Ham and Yefet. 11 The earth was corrupt before God, the earth was filled with violence. 12 God saw the earth, and, yes, it was corrupt; for all living beings had corrupted their ways on the earth. God said to Noach, "The end of all living beings has come before me, for because of them the earth is filled with violence. I will destroy them along with the earth.

As we see in the Bible, time and time again (see, for instance, Genesis 18), YHWH protects those who are "righteous" - those who believe in Him, love Him and obey His Torah. ("Torah", for those who don't know it, consists of YHWH's divine instruction to mankind revealed in the first five Books of the Bible, without which we would have *no blueprint* for moral, holy living.)

"Protection" doesn't necessarily mean we will never experience hard times or sickness or death; it means YHWH "walks" with us and will use us for His glory as long as we live, and allow us to be in His Presence throughout eternity after our earthly bodies die.

Why concentrate on Torah in an end times study? Because our disobedience to YHWH is the main reason the world is in the mess it's in! If you read my book, "Should Christians be Torah Observant?" you already know the emphasis I place on Torah, to include the fact that it is *not* an option. All believers should be Torah observant. Why? Same God, same rules; we are all ONE in Messiah (Ephesians 2:15)! Contrary to popular opinion, no one ever said He had separate rules for His natural and adopted children….

Romans 10: 1. My Brothers, The desire of my heart, and my intercession with Elohim for them is that they might have life. 2.

3

For I bear them witness that there is in them a zeal for Elohim; but it is not according to knowledge. 3. For they do not know the righteousness of Elohim, but seek to establish their own righteousness: and therefore they have not submitted themselves to the righteousness of Elohim. 4. For Mashiyach is the goal of Torah for righteousness to everyone that believes in him. 5. For Moshe describes the righteousness which is by Torah, this way: Whoever will do these things will live by them.

Can most of us truly admit that we have submitted ourselves to Him and His way of "making people righteous"? The entire Bible speaks to man's disobedience since the Garden of Eden and the Grace YHWH has continuously exhibited, despite the fact that we have concocted for ourselves all kinds of religions and theologies and ideas designed to supposedly please Him. The Bible, when read in context, reveals exactly how to please Him; but *haSatan* (Satan), YHWH's enemy, has successfully managed to guide God's people in the opposite direction, away from His divine instructions. For instance, Christianity and Islam both borrowed their respective theologies from Torah and then somehow managed to twist the Scriptures in a way that totally detracted from YHWH's original Word. Both religions contain *some* Truth but not *THE* Truth....

Indeed, it seems (judging from the many existing religions and denominations) most have not grasped what Yeshua said when He came to "proclaim the Kingdom of YHWH":

Luke 4: 43. And Y'shua said to them that, It is necessary for me to preach to other cities the Kingdom of Elohim, for because this reason I have been sent.

John 12: 49. For I have not spoken from my soul, but the Father who sent me. He gave a Commandment to me what I should say and what I should speak. 50. And I know that His commands are eternal life. Therefore, these things that I speak just as my Father told me, thus I speak.

Does this sound like a "new, more tolerant god" or someone who came to abolish His Father's original Divine Teachings/Instruction?

John 7: 15. And the Yehudeans were marveling and saying, "How does this man know the scrolls since he has not learned them?" 16. Y'shua answered and said, My teaching is not mine, rather it is of He who has sent me. 17. He who desires to do His will can comprehend my teaching, if it is from Elohim, or if from my own will I speak. 18. He who speaks from his own mind seeks glory for himself, but he who seeks the glory of He who sent him is true and there is no iniquity in his heart. 19. Did not Moshe give you Torah, yet not a man among you kept Torah?

Please note in verse 16 Yeshua explains that His teachings are not His, but the Father's! This, in itself reveals that He did not come to replace YHWH or change YHWH's teachings. And then He goes on to rebuke the Pharisees for judging Him when they personally don't bother to practice what they preach. In other words, they don't bother to keep Torah themselves, and they are guilty of adding their own respective thoughts and ideas to their teachings about Torah, yet they have the audacity to try to correct Him....

So important was this declaration from Yeshua, that His teachings were not His own but the Father's, that the Apostle John captured it again, later in the unfolding of the events leading to Yeshua's capture and conviction in the days just before the Pesach when Yeshua was speaking to large crowds:

John 12: 49. *For I have not spoken from my soul, but the Father who sent me. He gave a Commandment to me what I should say and what I should speak. 50. And I know that His commands are eternal life. Therefore, these things that I speak just as my Father told me, thus I speak.*

Regardless of all the things Yeshua **personally** taught concerning the importance of Torah, Christians around the world keep insisting that "Jesus" is a god who came, among other things, to "abolish the Law" - and to prove their point, they are always ready to quote from the much-misunderstood writings of the Apostle Paul....

Muslims, on the other hand (although their scriptures are also borrowed from Torah), totally ignore the Names of YHWH and Yeshua, and are adamant that God's "final prophet" was some mere human named Mohammed. It seems neither religion has paid attention to the fact that **Torah revealed the Name of our Creator**, which YHWH Himself gave it to Moshe (Moses):

Exodus 3: 13 *Moshe said to God, "Look, when I appear before the people of Isra'el and say to them, 'The God of your ancestors has sent me to you'; and they ask me, 'What is his name?' what am I to tell them?" 14 God said to Moshe, "Ehyeh Asher Ehyeh [I am/will be what I am/will be]," and added, "Here is what to say to the people of Isra'el: 'Ehyeh [I Am or I Will Be] has sent me to you.'" 15 God said further to Moshe, "Say this to the people of Isra'el: 'Yud-Heh-Vav-Heh [ADONAI] (יהוה = YHWH), the God of your fathers, the God of Avraham, the God of Yitz'chak and the God of Ya'akov, has sent me to you. This is my name forever; this is how I am to be remembered generation after generation.*

Please take notice of the last sentence above which reads: *"This is my name forever; this is how I am to be remembered generation after generation."* Since it is His Name FOREVER, why are most ignoring it? As mentioned above, Muslims don't bother acknowledging the Father or the Son; they simply refer to "Allah" which is Arabic for "God" – a mere title. And Christians devote all their energies to "Jesus" who, according to their more than 33,000 denominations, somehow "replaced" YHWH and His Torah, offering a kinder, gentler view of God based on "grace"....

And even religious Jews who know inside-out both the Torah and the *Tanach* (Old Testament), refuse to speak His Name because they're terrified of mispronouncing it! These are the same people who refuse to add "a thread of blue" (Numbers 15:38) to their *tzit-tzit* because they're unsure about the **shade** of blue. It seems it's easier to just blatantly **disobey** a command than to recognize the fact that YHWH never mentioned the exact "shade" of blue or its source....

And so it goes. Most religions and religious institutions today seem to find it easier to simply ignore YHWH's Torah than to open their hearts and minds in order to discover just *what it is*.

Here is a shocker: In the Book of Micah we are told that, in the *olam haba* (world to come) Torah *will* be obeyed! And since this is the case, one has to wonder why it is being ignored today.

Micah 4: 1 But in the acharit-hayamin (End of Days, which means end of this world, *olam hazeh*) *it will come about that the mountain of ADONAI's house will be established as the most important mountain. It will be regarded more highly than the other hills, and peoples will stream there. 2 Many Gentiles will go and say, "Come, let's go up to the mountain of ADONAI, to the house of the God of Ya'akov! He will teach us about his ways, and we will walk in his paths." For out of Tziyon (Zion) will go forth Torah, the*

7

word of ADONAI from Yerushalayim (Jerusalem). 3 He will judge between many peoples and arbitrate for many nations far away. Then they will hammer their swords into plow-blades and their spears into pruning-knives; nations will not raise swords at each other, and they will no longer learn war. 4 Instead, each person will sit under his vine and fig tree, with no one to upset him, for the mouth of ADONAI-Tzva'ot has spoken.

Most Christians are under the mistaken impression that they don't have to observe YHWH's Torah today, because "Jesus paid it all, and all we have to do to gain eternal life is to believe in Him"....

While that is *partially* true, there *is* more to the story! Children "believe" in their *parents*, but that doesn't mean they no longer have to obey them! It's exactly the same thing when it comes to God - once we "believe" in Him, we need to obey His rules because "believing" includes an automatic agreement to adhere to the instructions and lessons of the parent. If you can't agree to obey His rules, then why bother "believing" in Him?

"But we keep the Ten Commandments!" Really? Let's do a quick check of just a few of the Commandments to see if this is true:

1. Exodus 20: 2 "I am ADONAI your God, who brought you out of the land of Egypt, out of the abode of slavery."

Did "Allah" or "Jesus" perform this task? Or Buddha or Krishna or any other man-concocted god? No...only YHWH did – the same Divine Entity who has caused nearly 400 Bible prophecies to come true so far! The Bible is completely clear about who God is and what He has done for us – yet most can't seem to grasp it!

2. *Exodus 20:3-6: "You are to have no other gods before me. 4 You are not to make for yourselves a carved image or any kind of representation of anything in heaven above, on the earth beneath or in the water below the shoreline. 5 You are not to bow down to them or serve them; for I, ADONAI your God, am a jealous God, punishing the children for the sins of the parents to the third and fourth generation of those who hate me, 6 but displaying grace to the thousandth generation of those who love me and obey my mitzvot."*

"Other gods" include not only entities such as Satan, Buddah or Enkhi and their ilk, but also the love of self or money or possessions. Examples: The world economy is collapsing because people, who were unable to afford to do so, wracked up major credit card debt in pursuit of their own interests or gain. Billions, for instance, are spent on new cars, new homes and other possessions; and on things such as cosmetics and/or cosmetic surgery for those who wish to glorify their appearance. Many "mega-churches" have automatic teller machines in their lobbies "for your convenience" while "televangelists" - each with their own theologies and agendas - are constantly bombarding you with requests for donations to their ministries, regardless as to whether or not you can afford it - more often than not, so they can maintain their extravagant lifestyles....Google on "televangelists" to see for yourselves!

The truth is, whenever it's "all about me," you have broken the above commandment, and God can find no place in your life.

Before I move on, I want to briefly draw your attention to: *"You are not to make for yourselves a carved image or any kind of representation of anything in heaven above, on the earth beneath or in the water below the shoreline."* This is further clarified in Deuteronomy 4:

Deuteronomy 4: 15 "Therefore, watch out for yourselves! Since you did not see a shape of any kind on the day ADONAI spoke to you in Horev from the fire, 16 do not become corrupt and make yourselves a carved image having the shape of any figure - not a representation of a human being, male or female, 17 or a representation of any animal on earth, or a representation of any bird that flies in the air, 18 or a representation of anything that creeps along on the ground, or a representation of any fish in the water below the shoreline. 19 For the same reason, do not look up at the sky, at the sun, moon, stars and everything in the sky, and be drawn away to worship and serve them; ADONAI your God has allotted these to all the peoples under the entire sky.

When and how did the death of "Jesus" abolish the idea of NOT making any graven images for ourselves? Since when are we allowed to paint pictures of Him to suggest what He looked like? YHWH had His reasons for bringing Yeshua into the world at a time when there were no cameras or voice recorders! We are to follow Him by faith (Romans 10, etc), not His supposed appearance.

3. Exodus 20: 7 "You are not to use lightly the name of ADONAI your God, because ADONAI will not leave unpunished someone who uses his name lightly."

How many times have you heard people use "Jesus Christ!" as a cussword, or exclaim, "Oh my God!" or "I swear to God!" to drive home a point during a regular conversation? How many religious kooks (i.e., the "prophets" who kidnapped and raped Elizabeth Smart and Jaycee Dugard) have maintained they were merely doing God's work? They were guilty of abusing His Name!

4. *Exodus 20:8-11:* *"Remember the day, Shabbat, (Sabbath) to set it apart for God."*

Throughout the entire Bible we never, ever see that YHWH commanded any other day besides the Seventh Day to be set apart for Him. He clearly said that the Seventh Day Sabbath would be a sign between Him and His people **permanently** (Exodus 31:13 Exodus 31:16; Leviticus 16:31; Ezekiel 20:11-12; Isaiah 66:23; Isaiah 58:13-14). Yet Catholicism and Christianity have changed the Seventh Day (Saturday) to Sunday (the First Day)....

Daniel 7: *25 He will speak words against the Most High and try to exhaust the holy ones of the Most High. He will attempt to* **alter the seasons and the law;** *and [the holy ones] will be handed over to him for a time, times and half a time.*

The rest of the Ten Commandments insist we honor our parents and to keep ourselves from committing murder and adultery, and from stealing, lying and coveting. You need only turn on your television to find supposed **believers** with big, shiny crosses around their necks, gossiping or speaking badly about a friend or relative, or admitting, unashamedly, to some adulterous affair. From the comfort of your living room sofa, you can watch the latest Muslim terrorist acts against people they don't know or have never met, or you can go to your computer and Google "Jewish anti-missionaries" to find websites and blogs that bash believers in Messiah Yeshua in the most disgusting and vile language possible...And all this by supposed people of God.

If people truly knew YHWH and obeyed His Torah, the world, contrary to the naysayers, would be a **better** place! Many suggest, however, that the "Old Testament stuff" is just for the Jews. The question is: "Who says?" According to the Bible, Torah was never meant for just for "the Jews." How do we know this? Well, Cain and Abel, for instance, offered sacrifices; Noah knew the difference between "clean" and "unclean" animals, and obeyed the command to bring seven pairs of "clean" animals, and one pair of each "unclean" animal into the post-flood world; and we know the patriarchs, Abraham, Isaac and Jacob were all Torah observant because YHWH made His covenants with them and they did as He commanded (see Genesis 15; 17; 25; 27 and 28; Matthew 1:2), and yet *none of them were "Jews"*! There were no "Jews" until Jacob begat the Tribe of Yehudah (Genesis 29:35; Matthew 1:1-2), where the term "Jews" originated and ultimately became a blanket term to describe anyone who descended from the Patriarchs, Abraham, Isaac and Jacob. The *Tanach* ("Old Testament") shows that YHWH's Chosen were called Hebrews, not "Jews" (Genesis 14:13).

HaSatan has been very busy deceiving everyone he can possibly reach, and this includes those believers who have never understood the Bible in context, and/or who have believed "every wind of doctrine" that comes along. Judging by what we can glean through electronic and print media and from the goings-on in our very own communities, it is obvious that most haven't a clue about YHWH, let alone the fact that He clearly emphasized that *everyone* who chooses to believe in Him is to observe His laws:

*Numbers 15: 13 "**Every citizen** is to do these things in this way when presenting an offering made by fire as a fragrant aroma for ADONAI. 14 **If a foreigner stays with you - or whoever may be with you, through all your generations** - and he wants to bring an offering made by fire as a fragrant aroma for ADONAI, he **is to do the same as you.** 15 For this community **there will be the same law for you as for the foreigner living with you; this is a permanent*** *regulation through all your generations; the foreigner is to be treated the same way before ADONAI as yourselves. 16 The same Torah and standard of judgment will apply to both you and the foreigner living with you."*

Please re-read this in case you missed it: Any non-Jew (Gentile) is an "alien"/foreigner, and if they wish to be accepted by Him, they are to do *exactly* as those who already belong to Him...Remember, YHWH made His New Covenant *NOT* with the Gentiles, but with the Torah observant Houses of Israel and Judah (Jeremiah 31:32). This idea continues into the New Testament where Rav Sha'ul (the Apostle Paul) tells us:

Romans 10: 12. And in this, it discriminates neither Jews nor Gentiles. For there is one, Master YHWH, over them all, who is abundantly generous towards every one that calls on him. 13. For everyone that will call on the name of Master YHWH, will have life.

In other words, same God, same rules.

Micah 6: 8 Human being, you have already been told what is good, what ADONAI demands of you - no more than to act justly, love grace and walk in purity with your God.

How does one walk in purity with YHWH? By keeping His Torah! He commanded ALL to do as His Torah observant "chosen people" do.

Psalm 147: 19 He reveals his words to Ya'akov, his laws and rulings to Isra'el. 20 He has not done this for other nations; they do not know his rulings.

"They" certainly began to know His rulings once "the Jews" were scattered into the nations! If they hadn't been, then YHWH and His Son would have remained the best-kept secret of tiny, little Israel….

The bottom line is, we humans have been instrumental in helping to usher in the end times because we have, for the most part, ignored YHWH's original Divine Instructions - a fact clearly outlined in the Books of Daniel and Revelation and elsewhere.

Given the willful disobedience described above, and the general lack of knowledge and understanding of the end times, it is high time to get prepared! Therefore, get ready to do an in-depth, common-sense study on what we can expect in the final days ahead - which features our Savior Yeshua's return to Earth when He will put an unceremonious end to man's nonsense.

This study, as you will see, reveals the following:

1. Judging from the numerous earth-shattering natural and economic disasters around the world, we are not only in the "end times" as outlined in the Books of Daniel and Revelation, but we're in the proverbial "Twelfth Hour." And NOBODY gets "raptured out" before the bad times come!

2. The "Mark of the Beast" (Revelation 13:17; 14:9-11; 16:2; 19:20) is nothing man-made, such as a microchip implant, etc. It is something much more complicated than that....

3. Although the word "rapture" is found nowhere in the Scriptures, we are told there will be a "catching up" of **believers only** upon Yeshua's Second Coming (1 Corinthians 6:14; 1 Thessalonians 4:13-17); not of the unbelievers who will only be called

up before God on Judgment Day at the end of the Millennium. This "catching up" will be when Yeshua returns to Earth; not before. It will occur at the end of that seven year period which will begin when the Antichrist makes a seven year peace treaty with Israel.

4. Yeshua will rule and reign for a thousand years, at which time there will be the resurrection of ALL (the people who became believers during the Millennium, and all the DEAD unbelievers since the beginning of time who had heretofore remained in their graves). (See Isaiah 13:6,9; Jeremiah 46:10; Joel 1:15; 2:11; Amos 5:18; Obadiah 1:15, Revelation 20:1-15 and Acts 24:15). This will happen after what the Bible describes as very tough times; "Jacob's Trouble" (Jeremiah 30:4-7, Daniel 12:1, Matthew 24:15-22).

5. The "Antichrist" is not necessarily one man, but a system or body of men animated by one spirit. There have been many "antichrists" (anyone who is against Messiah Yeshua) in the world over the last two millennia, and so that dubious honor cannot go to just one man.

6. The so-called "seven year tribulation" is a myth, as the Scriptures never suggest the tribulation lasts seven years. Man has endured "tribulation" since he was banished from the Garden of Eden - including disease, wars, famine, pestilence, etc. (Yeshua, our Savior, personally endured a Tribulation that resulted in a horrible death which included humiliation and torture at the hands of spiritually blinded people. What would one call that, if not "tribulation"?)

The seven year period referred to in the Scriptures starts on the day the "prince yet to come" (referring to some well-known, well-loved world leader at the time) will make a seven-year covenant/peace treaty with Israel (Daniel 9:26-27). This is when the "end times scenario" actually begins to unfold, with the horrendous events that lead to Armageddon (Revelation 16:12-20), starting at the halfway mark (after three and a half years) when the "prince" begins to "back-pedal" on his promises to allow the Jews to worship according to Torah. Believers will be here through those events (not "raptured") because, as the Scriptures reveal, Yeshua does NOT return until the *end* of those seven years.

Chapter 2

Dangerous Doctrine

No one has perfectly unlocked the mysteries of the prophetic Books of Daniel and Revelation, and those who attempt to say otherwise are deluding themselves and misleading others with their personal opinions. It is simply too difficult for the human mind to comprehend the often awkward verbiage, allegories, signs and symbols, and confusing time lines of Revelation. It is therefore imperative to stick with the things we *can* understand, and go from there because, whether we choose to believe it or not, we *are* in the end times, judging from the precarious world events, ever-worsening plagues, strange weather patterns, and horrific natural disasters with which we have been inundated in recent times, along with the growing decadence among supposed civilized human beings. These things are clearly foretold in the Bible (see for example, 2 Timothy 3).

Of course, there are many theories about how the end times will play out - ranging from total disbelief or apathy by those who suggest that the Bible is nothing but a myth; to those who argue that man has always suffered disease, famine, wars and natural disasters; to the misconception posited by Christians that they have nothing to worry about because they will be supernaturally "raptured out" before anything bad happens.

Unfortunately, all of these theories are dangerous, including the "pre-trib Rapture" which, according to the Scriptures, is an unsubstantiated myth perpetuated by many Christians who honestly believe "the church" is so holy that God wouldn't dare allow them to suffer punishment. Apparently it has never occurred to these "pre-tribbers" that mankind has suffered endlessly in "tribulations" since the day Adam and Eve were kicked out of the Garden of Eden!

> **NOTE:** The eviction from the Garden itself must have been a terrifying and mind-boggling event for Adam and Eve, who had up until then, enjoyed a life of leisure. On that fateful day when they, through their deliberate disobedience to Torah, incurred YHWH's wrath, were not only tossed into an unknown wilderness where hard work, hunger, pain, disease and death reigned; but they were also forced to witness the death of one of their beloved animal friends which died at the hands of YHWH Himself when He used blood to atone for *their* sins - an act solely designed to show mankind the dire consequences of sin. YHWH provided the animal's hide as Adam's and Eve's covering to remind them of the "Pandora's Box" they had opened once they tasted the "fruit" of tree of the knowledge of good and evil - where they surely had a glimpse into another dimension to which man was never supposed to be privy. YHWH didn't "rapture" the duo out of the tribulation they had brought on themselves; He caused them to go *through* it so they would know beyond the proverbial "shadow of a doubt" what their actions had wrought!

And let's not forget that YHWH didn't "rapture" Noah out of his tribulation, either. Nor Lot; nor Shadrach, Meshach and Abednego; nor our Savior, Yeshua who died a terrible death at the hands of evil human beings! Mankind has *always* undergone various tribulations including famine, disease, earth quakes, fires, floods and all types of natural disasters. So, those who suggest that "God won't make us endure the Great Tribulation" are deluding themselves.

Still, there are many Christians who insist on believing variations of the lie that they will be supernaturally "zapped" out of here *before* the presumed seven-year tribulation begins, and that those who didn't "get it right the first time" will get a second chance when Jesus (Yeshua) returns to Earth.

The problem with this theory is not that it is downright false; rather, it is dangerous doctrine. Why? Because, for one thing, the Bible is explicit about the fact that there will be no "rapture" before the human race has experienced a litany of unimaginable hardships and sorrows. For another, believers in a bogus hope of being "raptured" *before* some really hard times arise, will surely curse God when they discover they're still around when the world is experiencing so many disasters, we won't even be able to recover from one before the next one hits! They're going to be so disappointed that God didn't "rapture" them (as their pastor, beloved "televangelist" or some self-proclaimed "Bible scholar" with a blog had predicted), they might stop believing in Him altogether. To add insult to injury, not only will some who believe themselves to be "good, decent and holy" be forced to endure hard times, but many will also be very upset to discover they were left behind on that long-awaited day when large numbers of people are suddenly missing from Earth!

The other side of the coin is, perhaps the number of missing won't even be large enough to make the evening news, because most people who *think* themselves believers don't realize they're only "lukewarm" and will be "vomited" out of Yeshua's mouth on the day He returns....

Revelation 3: 15. I know your works, that you are neither hot, nor cold; I would desire that you would be either cold or hot. 16. So, because you are lukewarm, neither hot nor cold, I am about to vomit you from my mouth.

Matthew 7: 13. Enter by the straight door, for wide is the door and broad is the road that leads to destruction, and many are they, those that go in it. 14. How narrow the door and straight the road that leads to life, and few are they, those that find it.

Only YHWH Himself knows who will be "raptured" to ultimately receive eternal life. But you can bet that those who are among the "elite" will be the people who believed in His Messiah (who is our Final Sin Sacrifice) **and** kept His commands - and this doesn't refer to just the Ten Commandments; but, rather, the keeping of his "forever" commands (those that are tagged by, not only the word "forever" on many commands, but also includes wording such as, "This is to be a permanent ordinance throughout your generations," or "This is an everlasting covenant"), which include the Seventh Day Sabbath and the Biblical Feasts and the eating of "clean" foods. (Please see Appendix 2.)

*Revelation 12: 17. And the dragon was enraged against the woman; and he went to make war upon the remnant of her seed **who keep the Commandments of Elohim and have the testimony of Y'shua.***

*1 John 2: 3. **And by this we will be sensible that we know him, if we keep his Commandments. 4. For he that says I know him, and does not keep his Commandments, is a liar and the truth is not in him. 5. But he that keeps his Word, in him is the Love of Elohim truly completed: for by this we know that we are in him. 6. He that says I am in him, is bound to walk according to his halacha.***

John 12: 50. And I know that His commands are eternal life. Therefore, these things that I speak just as my Father told me, thus I speak.

Returning to the myriad end times theories:

Though only YHWH knows, earthly theories concerning God and the end times are numerous. For instance, the **traditional Christian eschatology** is that "Jesus" comes, takes His people and then basically lights a match to the powder keg and burns everything and everybody into oblivion, and then creates a garden of paradise (in the Millennium) to which the believers return. There are endless theories about when and how this will happen....

The traditional Jewish perspective is that the Mashiyach (Messiah) comes on a big, white horse with a Heavenly Host and deals with his enemies while everybody looks on. The kings/rulers of the earth then get a lesson much like Pharoah (Pharoah is a type of a king who hardens his heart toward YHWH and then YHWH hardens his heart further to show him and his subjects there is only One Elohim).

It's no secret that traditional Jews deny the existence of our Savior, Yeshua. (They definitely refuse to believe in "Jesus" – and for good reason: Jesus, according to Christian teachings, was someone who came to Earth as part of a "trinity" who abolished the need for Torah, the Seventh Day Sabbath and the Biblical Feasts. So, what Jew would want to believe in this "Jesus"? In fact, the Scriptures clearly reveal that the God of Abraham, Isaac and Jacob is ONE, not a "trinity" according to Deuteronomy 6:4-9.)

Also, one of the biggest reasons Jews do not accept Yeshua as Messiah is because YHWH never demanded *human*

21

sacrifices....They don't realize that Yeshua was an *arm* of YHWH (Isaiah 53:1-12), a human with a divine *qnoma* (nature) who – though He could have called upon legions of angels to help Him out on that fateful "crucifixion" day, chose instead to martyr Himself to become our Final **SIN** Sacrifice. The "human" flesh of Yeshua died, bearing the sins of all, but His Divine *qnoma* lives to be the Ruach to dwell in each of us. So there was a "sacrifice", yes, but a "human sacrifice", no.

Jews do, however, believe the Torah contains several references to "the End of Days" (*acharit ha-yamim*), which is the time when the Mashiyach (Messiah) will be anointed as king. According to Jewish writings, the word "mashiyach" does not mean "savior" nor do they entertain the notion of an innocent, divine or semi-divine being who will sacrifice himself to save them from the consequences sin. They, instead, see the (yet to come) Messiah as a mere human being who will be a great and charismatic political leader descended from King David (Jeremiah 23:5) who is well-versed in the teachings of YHWH and observant of His commandments (Isaiah 11:2-5). He will be a great judge (Jeremiah 33:15) winning many battles for Israel, and ushering in the co-existence of all people (Isaiah 2:4) in the *Olam Ha-Ba* ("the World to Come").

Here is where the Netzarim viewpoint differs from that of Christianity and Judaism:

- Yeshua returns to earth - perhaps, some say, as early as 2015 to 2020, judging by the events in the Middle East which seem to be leading up to that "seven year peace treaty" the "Antichrist" makes with Israel (Daniel 9:26-27). Simultaneously, all *believers* who ever lived and died up to that point, are resurrected to take part in the "Marriage Supper

22

of the Lamb" (Revelation 19:7–10) and then return with Him to rule and reign on Earth for a thousand years (referred to as the Millennium). Yeshua and the returned believers, at that point, already have their "eternal bodies."

- In the meantime: At the point of the Messiah's return another (or many) dimension(s) in the material world "open up", re-creation of the earth begins along with a major clean-up, restructuring everything based on Torah and righteousness. All who are alive and everyone in the resurrection reclaim all the earth for Mashiyach, and for 1,000 years on earth, the Government of Mashiyach rules and reigns.

- During the Millennium, those who *weren't* "caught up" in the air (1 Corinthians 6:14; 1 Thessalonians 4:13-17) because they weren't believers, or were considered "lukewarm" upon Yeshua's return (Revelation 3:16), continue to live, procreate and die (*if* they were lucky enough to have made it through the terrible disasters and events of those days). The only difference is that during the Millennium, from the day of Yeshua's return, all mankind will live under Yeshua's government instead of the horribly flawed political system of man.

- Satan is released from his prison sometime at the end of the Millennium to wreak havoc (Revelation 20:7-8).

- The Scriptures reveal a period of stress and strife referred to as "Jacob's Trouble" (Jeremiah 30:4-7, Daniel 12:1, Matthew 24:15-22).

(We'll let you decide whether you believe it's at the *beginning* or the *end* of the Millennium because there will be severe chaos on either end!) Yeshua's return will bring with it much distress (Revelation 19:11-16) - but there is also distress at the end of the Millennium when YHWH "looses" Satan for a while before tossing him into the Lake of Fire just before Judgment Day, and then giving us a "new heaven and a new earth" (Revelation 20:11-15). At that point, YHWH's patience and "long-suffering" (Exodus 34:6, Numbers 14:18, Colossians 1:11, 1 Timothy 1:16, etc.) will have come to and end, and He will no longer tolerate our disobedience and "religiosity," and let us know, in no uncertain terms, that Judgment Day has arrived. That is the day He will call up ALL the *dead and living believers* who lived and died during the Millennium, along with all the dead *unbelievers* who have been dead in their graves since the beginning of time. They will all stand before YHWH to give an account of their lives. Those who were believers will receive eternal life; while the unbelievers, though having been given the opportunity to believe, will realize (also in no uncertain terms) the huge mistake they have made, just before they are tossed with their father Satan into the Lake of Fire (Revelation 20:15).

- The Millennium is our ultimate period of "grace and mercy" on Earth where YHWH gives mankind a final chance to choose Him or Satan. (If an unbeliever was lucky enough to have survived the horrendous things that happen on Earth prior to and after Yeshua's arrival, and he/she realizes Yeshua IS the Messiah and our Final Sin Sacrifice, and have changed their life accordingly, that person might have a second chance to enter into eternal life at the end of the Millennium, on Judgment Day.) It is the opportunity for ONE FINAL decision for those who never knew the Name of YHWH, or were never taught about Mashiyach, and for those who didn't live a life of willful disobedience and rebellion against Him.

Of course, there are those who insist that all believers are crazy and argue the earth will forever continue onward, with man growing ever more intelligent and powerful to the point where he is smarter than God. (Some religions, such as Scientology, even suggest that we, each, are already "little gods"; while atheists totally dismiss the Creator and are under the impression that believers are all a bunch of wild-eyed kooks.) After all, man has built empires, conquered the land, seas and outer space, built the great pyramids of Giza/Abu-Simbel and the English Channel Tunnel, and developed vaccines to cure various diseases...Why, man is even at the stage where he can clone himself - so who needs God?

The problems with this type of reasoning, however, are manifold. Let's do a short history lesson of what modern man, in all his wisdom, has accomplished:

The first known murder, after Adam and Eve were kicked out of the Garden of Eden, was when Cain killed his brother, Abel (Genesis 4). Since then, murders have been occurring worldwide regularly, rising exponentially. A quick search of the Internet reveals endless numbers of cases where mothers kill their children; children kill their parents; lovers kill their partners; blacks kill whites; whites kill blacks; "White Supremacists" bomb synagogues in hopes of killing Jews; would-be mothers abort their unborn babies; religious zealots kill abortion doctors;

"drive-by" shooters don't care about "collateral damage" while targeting their intended victims; and short-tempered people on our freeways believe they have the right to shoot other drivers who get in their way....

History books (those that haven't been changed to reflect "political correctness") amply describe the depravity of man. They reveal myriads have been killed in various types of "hate crimes" and political agendas - the pogroms, the Crusades, both World Wars, the Korean War, the Vietnam "Conflict," all the way up to today where thousands upon thousands are being killed in the Middle East because of the jealousy that started between the half-brothers, Isaac and Ishmael (Genesis 16-17). And let's not forget that at least six million Jews along with countless other innocents in Europe were murdered on the command of one narcissistic lunatic who exalted himself above all others....

Hatred begets hatred; retaliation begets retaliation; evil begets evil - the end result of which is: Innocent people are killed, in direct violation of the Sixth Commandment. This is the state of our world today; nothing has changed over the millennia. And yet we have the audacity to call ourselves "civilized."

In Biblical times, YHWH, commanded **His** people to kill pagans and heathens - those who did NOT keep His Torah. The reason was so that HIS people would not become infected or defiled with pagan ways, or intermarry with those who worshiped other gods (Leviticus 18:3 and 20:23; Deuteronomy 12:30, etc.).

Deuteronomy 11: 26 "See, I am setting before you today a blessing and a curse - 27 the blessing, if you listen to the mitzvot of ADONAI your God that I am giving you today; 28 and the curse, if you don't listen to the mitzvot of ADONAI your God, but turn aside from the way I am ordering you today and follow other gods that you have not known.

Deuteronomy 12: 28 Obey and pay attention to everything I am ordering you to do, so that things will go well with you and with your descendants after you forever, as you do what ADONAI sees as good and right. 29 "When ADONAI your God has cut off ahead of you the nations you are entering in order to dispossess, and when you have dispossessed them and are living in their land; 30 be careful, after they have been destroyed ahead of you, not to be trapped into following them; so that you inquire after their gods and ask, 'How did these nations serve their gods? I want to do the same.' 31 You must not do this to ADONAI your God! For they have done to their gods all the abominations that ADONAI hates! They even burn up their sons and daughters in the fire for their gods!

Please notice that Deuteronomy 12:28 sums up the entire Torah! Torah is good and right, and obedience brings good. Also note how adamant YHWH was (and still is) concerning **obedience** to His "forever" commands.

Did you happen to catch the last sentence of Deuteronomy 12:31? *"They even burn up their sons and daughters in the fire for their gods."* How many people today (including some so-called believers) have sold their children in exchange for drugs, or pimped them out as prostitutes? How many people wait like vultures for their parents or other relatives to die, or take out high dollar insurance policies on a "loved one" and then devise a way to kill them - just to satisfy their money "god"? Deuteronomy 18:13 warns: *"You must be wholehearted with ADONAI your God."*

Take a look at the following scripture because it will surely bring to mind the very thing that happens every year at

Christmas time, a man-made "holy day" whose roots are steeped in paganism:

Jeremiah 10: 1 Hear the word ADONAI speaks to you, house of Isra'el! 2 Here is what ADONAI says: "Don't learn the way of the Goyim, don't be frightened by astrological signs, even if the Goyim are afraid of them; 3 for the customs of the peoples are nothing. They cut down a tree in the forest; a craftsman works it with his axe; 4 they deck it with silver and gold. They fix it with hammer and nails, so that it won't move. 5 Like a scarecrow in a cucumber patch, it cannot speak. It has to be carried, because it cannot walk. Do not be afraid of it it can do nothing bad; likewise it is unable to do anything good!" 6 There is no one like you, ADONAI! You are great, and your name is great and mighty. 7 Who would not fear you, king of the nations? For it is your due! - since among all the wise of the nations and among all their royalty, there is no one like you. 8 One and all they are boorish and stupid; the teaching of their nothings is a piece of wood! 9 Silver is beaten into plates, then imported from Tarshish. Gold from Ufaz is worked by a craftsman and shaped by the hands of a goldsmith. They are clothed in blue and purple, all the work of skillful men. 10 But ADONAI, God, is the true God, the living God, the everlasting king. At his anger, the earth trembles; the nations cannot endure his fury. 11 "This is what you must say to them: 'The gods that did not make heaven and earth will perish from earth and from under heaven.'" 12 God made the earth by his power, established the world by his wisdom spread out the sky by his understanding. 13 When he thunders, the waters in heaven roar, he raises clouds from the ends of the earth, he makes the lightning flash in the rain and brings the wind out from his storehouses. 14 At this, everyone is proved stupid, ignorant, every goldsmith put to shame by his idol! The figures he casts are a fraud; there is no breath in them; 15 they are nothings, ridiculous objects; when the day for their punishment comes, they will perish. 16 Ya'akov's portion is not like these, for he is the one who formed all things. Isra'el is the tribe he claims as his heritage; ADONAI-Tzva'ot is his name.

Yes, Christians don't "worship" the Christmas tree. But the fact is, YHWH told us *not* to become involved in these pagan traditions because we are to concentrate on what HE commanded, including the Seventh Day Sabbath rest and the Biblical Feasts! The Scriptures reiterate again and again that *man's traditions are worthless*, yet we keep right on ignoring the very Word of God:

Matthew 15: 3. Then Y'shua answered and said to them, Why also do you transgress against the Commandments of Elohim because of your traditions?

Please note, this verse is a key admonishment of the Pharisees by Yeshua showing how the written Torah was being set against the traditions of the Pharisees. Yeshua is expressing great concern that the Pharisees were abrogating the Word of YHWH by their tradition. It should be clear that He would certainly *not* instruct his followers to do likewise!

Throughout the ages, man hasn't bothered to pay attention to YHWH's commands at all. We have taken His Word and turned it into something unrecognizable, thus "putting God in a box" to make Him be who we want Him to be! We have changed the Name of our Savior, along with the dates of His birth, death and resurrection, and come up with our own "holy days" (Christmas, Easter, and the Sunday Sabbath for example), while ignoring His commanded *mo'edim* (dates and times) - all of which foreshadow the Mashiyach!

We haven't even bothered to obey the command to eat only "clean" animals which was so important to YHWH that even Noah knew of it well before Moses recorded the rules of clean and unclean! According to Christianity, the death of Jesus somehow abolished the necessity to follow

YHWH's command to eat only "kosher foods." What does "kosher" mean? It's very simple, really: The Book of Leviticus reveals that "unclean" animals are those that kill and eat other animals, or dine on "roadkill" or whatever comes into their path; and those water dwellers that eat dead carcasses off the bottom of rivers, lakes and oceans. For instance, if we eat a crow that just ate dead, mouldy or diseased "roadkill," or a lobster whose last meal consisted of dead fish and dung, chances are *we're* going to, one way or the other, ingest the remnants of their last meals, and maybe even get sick or die. It doesn't matter that we boiled or baked the crow or lobster; the fact is, we're deliberately putting something into our systems that YHWH considers "unclean" - an animal or crustacean that just finished dining on something "unclean". And part of the "uncleanness" that the above mentioned animals put into their system was blood, which is forbidden (Genesis 9:4, Deuteronomy 12:23, Leviticus 19:26).

The "unclean" includes the pig! Yes, your beloved ham, pork chops, and bacon are all unclean and forbidden by YHWH! Think about it…The pig eats all sorts of slop – anything, diseased or not. YHWH commanded us not to eat the pig, yet it is the staple of most restaurants today, world wide. I once had a pastor tell me, in his pathetic attempt to justify his willful disobedience that the "pig we have today is not the same pig as in the Biblical times…."

The bottom line is this: God said *not* to eat certain animals, and that command was never reversed! Yeshua never once, not one time, suggested that His death as our Final *SIN* Sacrifice, would somehow render unclean foods "clean" against His Father's will....

30

In short, *we must stay away from all forms of paganism, or else we are catering to Satan!* Paul warned us time and time again, as shown in the following example:

1 Corinthians 10: 15. I speak as to the wise; you judge what I say. 16. The cup of thanksgiving which we bless, is it not the fellowship of the blood of the Mashiyach? And the bread which we break, is it not the fellowship of the body of the Mashiyach? 17. As therefore that bread is one, so we are all one body; for we all take to ourselves from that one bread. 18. Behold the Israel who are in the flesh; are not they who eat the victims participators of the altar? 19. What then do I say? That an idol is anything? Or, that an idol's sacrifice is anything? No. 20. But that what the Gentiles sacrifice they sacrifice to demons, and not to Elohim. And I would not that you should be associates of demons. 21. You cannot drink the cup of our Master (Y'shua) and the cup of demons; and you cannot be partakers at the table of our Master, and at the table of demons. 22. Or, would we provoke our Master (Y'shua's) jealousy? Are we stronger than he?

Paul reveals in these scriptures that in later times (see 1 Corinthians 10:11) some will abandon the faith and follow deceiving spirits and things taught by demons....

Note also that where the AENT renders "Gentiles" in verse 20, many translations use "pagans". But the use of "pagans" (Aramaic: *aimmeh*) here is contrary to the original Aramaic *khanpa* in verse 20 which permits the interpretation to be "Gentiles" instead of "pagans" because Paul is addressing Gentiles who were under his guidance to learn Torah, rather than the pagan Gentile, who were not reachable since they were immersed in their anti-Torah practices.

For those who wish to argue (out of context, whether or not they're aware of it) that Paul is saying it is okay to eat of all foods, sacrificed to idols or not, I would remind you that Paul, like Yeshua, was completely Torah observant (see Acts 28:23-25). And he - contrary to popular belief - *never* spoke against the Torah, as you will see later in this study. Paul actually ***promoted*** the Torah:

Galatians 3: 21. Is the Torah we received against the promises of Elohim? Elohim forbid! For if Torah had been given, which was able to give life, then truly righteousness would have come as a result of Torah 22. But the Scripture has encircled all things and put them under sin, that the promise in the faith of Y'shua the Mashiyach might be given to those who believe. 23. But before faith came, Torah was guarding us while we were confined from the faith about to be revealed. 24. Torah was therefore a tutor for us, going towards the Mashiyach that we, by faith, might be made righteous. 25. But since faith came, we are no longer under tutors. (Torah is the only true tutor – which is being contrasted against false tutors, the Pharisees, who put their oral tradition above the written code of Moses and the Prophets. Today's pastors are guilty of doing the very same thing!) *For you are all the children of Elohim by faith in Y'shua the Mashiyach. 27. For those who have been immersed in Mashiyach have been clothed with Mashiyach for there is neither Jew nor Aramean, nor slave nor free, nor male nor female, but you are all one in Y'shua the Mashiyach. 29. And if you are of the Mashiyach then you are seeds of Awraham and inheritors by the promise.*

It is imperative to understand that Torah was very important in the Rabbinical Jewish world from which Rav Shaul (Paul) came. The point Shaul makes again and again is that while Torah is very important in our lives as our guide, the ***giver*** of Torah is even more important! YHWH gave Torah as an indicator of Faith in the Covenant (terms and conditions) between Him and His people, and we cannot disregard ***Him*** simply because we believe ourselves to be Torah experts; and we certainly have no right to erect

32

pedestals or traditions that become more important than YHWH and His Mashiyach. Many Christians seek the advice of a pastor (or anyone) they think smarter than themselves to question about God and the Bible without realizing they can go to YHWH Himself! Whether Jew or Gentile, faith in the Covenant demands that one seek an active relationship directly with YHWH and His Mashiyach Yeshua.

Continuing with Paul's writings:

Galatians 4: 1 But I say that for a period of time the heir is a child, no different from the servants, even though he is the Master over all of them; 2. However, he is under guardians and stewards of the house until the time which his Father has set. 3. Even so with us, when we were young, we acted as if subject to the elements of this world. 4. But when therefore the fullness of time had come, Elohim sent His Son who was born of a woman, and was subject to Torah, 5. To redeem those who are under Torah that we might receive adoption as sons.

Please note there is a difference between being "subject to Torah" and being "under Torah"! In many translations, the work "under " is used both times in verses 4-5, above, as well as "Torah" being replaced with "law". But the lack of discernment between these two words, "under" and "subject" has misled many into anti-Torah lifestyles. Torah is to be written upon the heart (Rom 10:80) by the *Ruach haKodesh* (Holy Spirit) by Grace and it is by willful obedience that one refrains from sin, as they become subject to the Word of YHWH. And by Grace one comes to know and accept the redemptive work of Yeshua; however, what some don't seem to realize is, the correct response to Yeshua's calling is to live a life subject to Torah, just as He did. You see, Torah observance, being "subject to" Torah, and having the desire for it on your heart is not just a "New Testament" or "Grace" thing, it is and always was a condition of the Covenant. See Isaiah 51:7 and Proverbs 3:1.

YHWH constantly extended His mercy to mankind, beginning in the Garden of Eden when He allowed Adam and Eve to live after they disobeyed His command to not eat the fruit from the Tree of the Knowledge of Good and Evil (Genesis 2:15-16). He extended His mercy to Noah and his family who were the only righteous people on earth (Genesis 6:5-8); and to Lot and his family (Genesis 19). YHWH's grace and mercy have always been around - but never was it more evident than the day He sent His own Son (see the Gospels), the "arm of YHWH" who possessed a divine Nature and was to become our Final Sin Sacrifice (Isaiah 53, Colossians 2:14).

Man, for the most part, has not bothered to keep YHWH's commands to be clean in body, deed and thought as outlined in the Books of Leviticus and Deuteronomy....So, after thousands of years of trying to reach us, it's no wonder His patience is finally coming to an end and the prophesied end times are upon us!

So, how do we know the "end times" are here?

Today, all the things YHWH ever considered "bad" are now considered "good" and vice-versa. We've watered down His Word to the point where it's completely unrecognizable, and pretend He likes it - because, after all, "we're under grace (as Christianity would have you believe) with nothing required of us except to 'believe' in Jesus!" This misconception (that we are under grace) is exactly why most today don't have a clue about God or the Bible, and why many of today's parents fail to teach their children proper morals or social etiquette; and it's why children exhibit little or no respect for their parents or teachers. It is also why we have so many teen pregnancies, divorces, cases of adultery, etc. Why, today, organizations such as the Episcopal Church are openly promoting gay men and lesbians into the church hierarchy citing "no prohibition in the Bible!"

No prohibition? No prohibition?!! What part of Leviticus 18:22, *"You are not to go to bed with a man as with a woman; it is an abomination"* is too hard to understand? And how about the following from the Episcopal Church's beloved New Testament-only theology – does it not speak clearly enough?

1 Corinthians 6: 9. Or don't you know, that the unrighteous will not inherit the Kingdom of Elohim? Make no mistake! Neither sexual sinners, nor idol-worshippers, nor adulterers, nor the corrupt, **nor men who lay down with other men,** *10. Nor the oppressors, nor thieves, nor drunkards, nor revilers, nor extortioners, will inherit the Kingdom of Elohim.*

Many, if not most, of today's "New Testament-only" advocates do not know YHWH; consequently, they also do not know Yeshua! They are at best "lukewarm" toward Him (Revelation 3:16). Plus, it seems many have too much time on their hands; they're "bored" and, as a result, they end up entertaining themselves - often, in unhealthy ways.

Back in pre-electricity days and pre-modern conveniences, no one had time to be bored. They were too busy eking out a living just to put food on the table. Entire families, children included, had to help work the fields and/or prepare the food, clean the house and wash and sew the family's clothing. There were no television-watching, video-playing "latch-key" kids getting into trouble due to boredom! This phenomenon didn't come about until after

35

the advent of electricity, when the lives of families everywhere were made easier via the invention of washers, dryers, microwaves, and supermarkets. Suddenly, mothers found themselves too "bored" to stay at home to nurture their children, and - coupled with the monster of greed that required them to help supplement household incomes so they could "keep up with the Joneses" - they began to enter the workforce and left their children home alone, or to be raised by strangers.

With parenting becoming more and more lax over the years, is it any wonder that today, rather than to teach our children abstinence and "being holy" and respecting our bodies when it comes to sex, we have reduced ourselves to letting "the world system" be our teacher. This system we're following because we're attempting to be "a friend" rather than a *parent* to our children, suggests abstinence is not the answer; that instead, children should be urged to "practice safe sex" via condoms and devices and birth control pills, and products such as Gardasil. Gardacil is the vaccine that protects against the cervical-cancer-causing human papillomavirus, which is caused by simple by genital contact - never mind that the product itself has actually *caused* deaths, according to a 2009 article by The Centers for Disease Control, entitled, "Reports of Health Concerns Following HPV Vaccination." All this, so our children can "express themselves" and have unholy sex outside of marriage.

It was the era of the me-centered "flower children" of the 1960's and their ilk that kicked off the "free love" movement, including the idea - thanks to the invention of the birth control pill - that mankind now had the freedom to do whatever he wanted with whomever he wanted. Nobody thought about the dangers of the pill's chemicals on a woman's body, or how this was a direct violation of

YHWH's command to "be fruitful and multiply" (Genesis 1:28)....let alone that this little pill would one day help to curb the numbers of believers in the God of Abraham, Isaac and Jacob and His Son, our Savior Yeshua!

What does this mean? Well, the three main religions in the world today are Judaism, Christianity, and Islam. When Western man (many of whom are believers in the God of Abraham, Isaac and Jacob) decided to control birth rates, he inadvertently allowed members of Islam (who do *not* practice birth control) to produce many more Muslims than Christians and Jews. Consequently, Islam with its approximately 1.2 billion adherents, is the fastest growing religion in the world today, having already overtaken Catholicism as the world's largest religion, according to L'Osservatore Romano, the Vatican newspaper, March 2008. In that article, Monsignor Vittorio Formenti observed: *"While Muslim families, as is well known, continue to make a lot of children, Christian ones on the contrary tend to have fewer and fewer."*

Meanwhile, Muslims who have been quietly infiltrating western countries while refusing to integrate into Western society, have done their best to impose their religion on their host countries. Geert Wilders, Chairman, Party for Freedom in The Netherlands, in his documentary movie "Fitna", suggests that Europe is undergoing the final stages of the Islamization - and that *"this not only is a clear and present danger to the future of Europe itself, it is a threat to America and the sheer survival of the West."* According to the website "Religious Tolerance": *At a level of 1.2 billion, they (Muslims) represent about 22% of the world's population...Islam is growing about 2.9% per year. This is faster than the total world population which increases about 2.3% annually. It is thus attracting a progressively larger percentage of the world's population."*

37

Soon, the political correctness and "me" centrism of Judaism and Christianity, will cause both societies to be so overwhelmed by Islam that they will fade into insignificance.

In the meantime, while Islam grows, Hollywood continues to bombard us with evermore explicit sex and violence on its "silver screen" glorifying all manner of decadence; thus anesthetizing their myopically-minded numb and dumbed-down viewers (including believers in YHWH) and causing them to yearn for more excitement in their own lives. And the Internet, while certainly an invaluable tool for today's information "surfer" also promotes its seedy downside, catering to pornographers, pedophiles and other sick and twisted individuals, leading more and more away from YHWH.

So, thanks, in part, to the advent of electricity and man's scientific mind which has taken us all the way to the outer planets, God's idea of "good" has become "bad" in the eyes of the world, because "good" undesirably limits our carnal desires. "Good" is boring. It hampers the demands for instant gratification in our pursuit of human desires in this fast-paced, "modern" world.

As you can draw from the above, man, in all his wisdom, has never gotten it right and his nature has never changed. Man does not want to obey YHWH. He is the only creature on earth who kills, just because he feels like it. He is the only creature on earth who makes war against his neighbor, just because he doesn't like his neighbor or his politics or his beliefs; or simply because he wants to take his neighbor's possessions. Man is evil because of our "fall from grace" in the Garden of Eden, and has been in continual tribulation ever since.

YHWH gave us the grace and mercy to do things HIS way...or Satan's. Unfortunately, most have chosen Satan's.

And There Was War in Heaven!
Surviving the End Times

Chapter 3

War and Rumors of War

2 Timothy 3: 1. But know this: That in the latter days hard times will come: 2. and men will be lovers of themselves and lovers of money, boasters, proud, revilers, unyielding towards their own people, deniers of grace, wicked, 3. unloving, addicted to irreconcilable malicious gossips, ferocious, haters of the good, 4. treacherous, rash, inflated, attached to pleasure more than to the love of Elohim, 5. having a form of respect for Elohim but wide from the power of Elohim. Them who are such, repel from you. 6. For of them are they who creep into this and that house and captivate the women who are plunged in sins and led away by divers lusts, 7. who are always learning, and can never come to the knowledge of the truth. 8. Now as Jannes and Jambres withstood Moshe,1 so also do these withstand the truth: men whose mind is corrupted and (are) reprobates from the faith. 9. But they will not make progress, for their infatuation will be understood by everyone, as theirs also was understood.

It was mentioned in the first chapter that **no one** has perfectly unlocked the mysteries of Daniel and Revelation.

---

1   "Jannes and Jambres" are never mentioned in the Tanakh and this is often used as a rationale to dismiss the writings of the B'rit Chadasha as false. According to a footnote about this in the AENT: "This is a very interesting reference by Rav Shaul as Jannes and Mambres are never directly named in any ancient version of the Tanakh as the magicians who tried to compete with Moshe. However, they are referred to in some Jewish targums and even in Roman sources such as Pliny the Elder's *Natural History*. Also the late Second century Church Father Origen made reference to "the Book of Jannes and Mambres" but no copies of it have come down to us intact. What this shows is that Rav Shaul is comfortable using both canonical and non-canonical sources to make his points with what he knows his audience is familiar with. While we may never know if Rav Shaul considered these names as authentic, it very much goes to acquitting other parts of the Renewed Covenant writings as spurious simply because they quoted from resources that we today don't give any authority to."

This particular study is meant to be "food for thought"; a comparison to other "end times" theories to allow you to make up your own mind as to what you choose to believe. This study is likely different from anything you have ever read before, because it is being presented from a Netzari/Messianic viewpoint which strives to restore the Scriptures back into their original context – and to put the blame concerning man's present predicament straight where it belongs: On mankind.

And so without further ado, let's begin discussing the points outlined in Chapter 1!

FIRST POINT: *Judging from the myriad earth-shattering natural and economic disasters around the world, we are not only in the "end times" as outlined in the Books of Daniel and Revelation, but we're in the proverbial "Twelfth Hour." And NOBODY gets "raptured out" before the bad times come!*

It would be hard to pinpoint a time in history which could compare to barrage of devastating events the world is experiencing today. There seems to be no relief in sight from the onslaught of natural disasters (fires, floods, earthquakes, hurricanes, and tornadoes); or from the vicious conflicts between the three major religions (Judaism, Christianity and Islam); or from the wars, threats of war and terrorist activities around the world (today, we even have "modern-day pirates" off the coast of Somalia and elsewhere!), not to mention the turmoil within the world's governmental systems and the personal problems of the people who lead those governments (corruption, adultery, pedophilia, homosexual activity, etc.).

For example, a famine ravaged North Korea in the mid- to late-1990's taking approximately 3 million lives – ten percent of North Korea's population. In 2004, a tsunami in the Indian Ocean was estimated to have released the energy of 23,000 Hiroshima-type atomic bombs and killed more than 150,000 people and displaced countless millions in 11 countries (including Sri Lanka, Indonesia, India, Thailand, Malaysia, Maldives and Myanmar and Somalia), making it perhaps the most destructive tsunami in the history of the world. In New Orleans on September 2005, Hurricane Katrina turned out to be one of the worst natural disasters in U.S. history, killing approximately 2,000 people - and it followed on the heels of then-President Bush's approval of, and involvement in, the "Gaza Disengagement." In 2007, raging wildfires in California caused the largest evacuation in California history - and various fires still continue to plague California even as this book is being written. A 2008 cyclone in Myanmar killed more than 22,500, while a magnitude 7.8 earthquake in China killed around 15,000 and left thousands homeless. In October, 2009, an 8.3-magnitude earthquake and the resulting tsunami killed 176 people in the Samoas and Tonga, near Australia....

And those are just the natural disasters!

Luke 21: 10. For nation will rise against nation and kingdom against kingdom. 11. And there will be severe earthquakes from place to place and famine and plagues. And there will be fears and terrors and great signs will be seen from Heaven. And the winters will be severe.

Revelation 6: 6. And I heard a voice in the midst of the four Creatures, saying: A quart of wheat for a denarius, and three measures of barley for a denarius; and hurt not the oil and the wine. 7. And when he had opened the fourth seal, I heard the fourth Creature say: Come, and see. 8. And I looked, and behold, a pale horse; and the name of him who sat on it was Death; and Gehenna followed after him. And there was given him authority over the fourth part of the earth, to slay with the sword, and by famine, and by death, and by the ravenous beast of the earth.

In the "plagues" department, the world has begun to experience all sorts of new diseases - among them the ongoing AIDS epidemic for which we've never found a cure; the Avian and Swine flu epidemics, "Mad Cow" and "Foot and Mouth" disease in cattle, and many more.

We are told that violence will increase and difficult times will come:

2 Timothy 3: 1. But know this: That in the latter days hard times will come: 2. and men will be lovers of themselves and lovers of money, boasters, proud, revilers, unyielding towards their own people, deniers of grace, wicked, 3. unloving, addicted to irreconcilable malicious gossips, ferocious, haters of the good, 4. treacherous, rash, inflated, attached to pleasure more than to the love of Elohim, 5. having a form of respect for Elohim but wide from the power of Elohim. Them who are such, repel from you. 6. For of them are they who creep into this and that house and captivate the women who are plunged in sins and led away by divers lusts, 7. who are always learning, and can never come to the knowledge of the truth.

One needs only look at today's television programming to find all of the behaviors described in 2 Timothy! Men (meaning mankind as a whole) are completely into themselves. Not only do many try to "keep up with the Joneses" when it comes to their cell phones, automobiles and residences, but we are also urged as a nation by the Hollywood "elite" (and countless advertisers), to "be beautiful" people who have to defy nature by getting surgery and injections to keep ourselves slim and trim and younger looking, even if it means we have to go thousands of dollars into debt to accomplish it. Billions of dollars are spent every year on appearance alone, on cosmetics promising ultra-white teeth, unblemished skin, and beautiful hair - not to mention, Botox injections designed to remove frown lines and wrinkles, and surgeries to alter our appearance altogether - breast implants, facelifts, "nose jobs," tummy tucks and liposuction. You need not go any further than your local gym to see in various stages of undress, people staring adoringly at their "buff" bodies in wall-length mirrors, clearly idolizing themselves....

Man's stupidity and arrogance knows no bounds. Today, one can even buy "designer babies" through genetic engineering. For instance, a New York clinic specializes in offering blue-eyed, blonde Scandinavian babies, while a California-based fertility company offers a selection of celebrity look-alike sperm donors to those who wish to turn their prospective children into the image of their favorite idols (Google: "Genetic Engineering") - and apparently, many are spending big bucks to participate in this abomination! These particular prospective parents obviously do not realize or care that they are on dangerous grounds on several levels - one being, that this goes against YHWH's plans for mankind; and another, that genetic engineering has not yet been perfected and, therefore, no one can accurately choose what a child will look like.

Furthermore, donor screening has often been lacking, which has resulted in the donor's genetic/inherited birth defects and/or diseases being passed on (built-in) to the "designed" children....Not to mention, the dangers involved in allowing the "sins of the fathers" from total strangers to infiltrate their own families (Exodus 34:7, Exodus 20:5)! Studies show that man cannot completely control genetics, which means these "designed" babies may NOT look like their chosen idols at all (and let's not forget that many movie stars have surgically altered their appearance and that surgical alteration is NOT in their genes!). It's mind-boggling to witness these events demonstrating that man actually thinks he can play God!

Moving on, gossip and evil speech have become the norm - just take a look at today's "reality shows" where "judges" demean and debase participants and each other. Some of these ungodly, carnal shows serve as "match makers" designed to help bachelors or bachelorettes find and marry their "soulmates." In these shows, the bachelor must meet and "date" and even cuddle with dozens of strangers dressed in "arousing" outfits leaving nothing to the imagination, all clamoring to become his (or her) spouse at the end of the show. Throughout, the contestants often fight with, curse at and belittle each other and generally behave like spoiled children when things don't go their way. In the end, the bachelor (or bachelorette) eliminates the contestants, one by one, to ultimately choose the one who managed to win his (or her) "heart" according to his (or her) "tastes"....

YHWH distinctly warns us about this type of behavior, yet hardly anyone is listening! (See Exodus 20:14; Job 31:1; Proverbs 2:16, 5:16-17, 6:25; Acts 15:20; 1 Corinthians 6:13-19; Revelation 14:4; etc.)

Today, our schools and universities demand no real intellect. Teaching has been "dumbed down" to the point where some students can hardly read or write upon graduation, let alone think critically or properly articulate ideas! We have ignored our own history, and no longer teach our founding ideology. Our mortgage industries and banking systems are on the verge of collapse due to bad loans, and major industries are failing due to greed and poor management. The societal norm is to encourage debt over fiscal responsibility. Millions of citizens are going bankrupt because of severe credit card and housing debt, in an economy that runs on credit and incessantly encourages its citizens to go *deeper into* debt!

Our system has failed, in part, because banks have been handing out credit cards to those who aren't qualified, much less, able to handle the responsibilities that come with credit. And yet, instead of allowing these mismanaged banks and other businesses to fail, President Barak Hussein Obama, early in his administration, spent billions in taxpayer dollars to "bail out" those who, frankly, were too dense or too greedy to operate their businesses properly with any sense of fiscal responsibility. The President's plan rewarded failure and stupidity, while punishing those of us who have frugally managed money with common sense! Instead of realizing that our credit-ridden system was a lesson in failure requiring some serious overhauling, the President suggested we STAY in debt by encouraging people to participate in his "Cash for Clunkers" promotion....(Yes, quickly - *run* to your local automobile dealers and apply for a $25,000 loan for a new car, so you can get a credit of up to $4,500! Good news *temporarily* for the car dealers - but now YOU, Mr. and Mrs. Broke-and-in-debt American, get stuck with a huge car payment every month which, oh-by-the-way, you can't afford! Of course, you always have the option of filing bankruptcy and forcing the rest of us to pay YOUR debts, once you wake up and realize you couldn't afford a new car, in the first place....)

The aforementioned doesn't require references; you can Google on any of these items and see for yourself the state of our economy, schools and governments, which seem to be stuck in a sickening downward spiral.

YHWH, via His Torah, provided the foundation for moral, holy living. He even gave us the basics of financial management:

Exodus 22: 25 *"If you loan money to one of my people who is poor, you are not to deal with him as would a creditor; and you are not to charge him interest. 26 If you take your neighbor's coat as collateral, you are to restore it to him by sundown, 27 because it is his only garment - he needs it to wrap his body; what else does he have in which to sleep? Moreover, if he cries out to me, I will listen; because I am compassionate.*

Leviticus 25: 14 *"If you sell anything to your neighbor or buy anything from him, neither of you is to exploit the other."*

Leviticus 25: 23 *"'The land is not to be sold in perpetuity, because the land belongs to me -you are only foreigners and temporary residents with me. 24 Therefore, when you sell your property, you must include the right of redemption. 25 That is, if one of you becomes poor and sells some of his property, his next-of-kin can come and buy back what his relative sold. 26 If the seller has no one to redeem it but becomes rich enough to redeem it himself, 27 he will calculate the number of years the land was sold for, refund the excess to its buyer, and return to his property. 28 If he hasn't sufficient means to get it back himself, then what he sold will remain in the hands of the buyer until the year of yovel (jubilee); in the yovel the buyer will vacate it and the seller return to his property. 29 "'If someone sells a dwelling in a walled city, he has one year after the date of sale in which to redeem it. For a full year he will have the right of redemption; 30 but if he has not redeemed the dwelling in the walled city within the year, then title in perpetuity passes to the buyer through all his generations; it will not revert in the yovel. 31 However, houses in villages not surrounded by walls are to be dealt with like the fields in the countryside - they may be redeemed [before the yovel], and they revert in the yovel. 32 "'Concerning the cities of the L'vi'im and the houses in the cities they possess, the L'vi'im are to have a permanent right of redemption. 33*

If someone purchases a house from one of the L'vi'im, then the house he sold in the city where he owns property will still revert to him in the yovel; because the houses in the cities of the L'vi'im are their tribe's possession among the people of Isra'el. 34 The fields in the open land around their cities may not be sold, because that is their permanent possession. 35 '"If a member of your people has become poor, so that he can't support himself among you, you are to assist him as you would a foreigner or a temporary resident, so that he can continue living with you. 36 Do not charge him interest or otherwise profit from him, but fear your God, so that your brother can continue living with you. 37 Do not take interest when you loan him money or take a profit when you sell him food. 38 I am ADONAI your God, who brought you out of the land of Egypt in order to give you the land of Kena'an and be your God.

Deuteronomy 23: *19 "You are not to lend at interest to your brother, no matter whether the loan is of money, food or anything else that can earn interest. 20 To an outsider you may lend at interest, but to your brother you are not to lend at interest, so that ADONAI your God will prosper you in everything you set out to do in the land you are entering in order to take possession of it.*

Common sense instructions, yes - straight from our Creator. But are we paying attention? "Naah...that old stuff was just for the Jews...Wasn't it?"

The Book of Revelation talks about children doing evil against their own parents in the end times; about widespread violence and chaos everywhere. We need only to listen to the news to hear about the latest school shooting, "road rage", etc. - things we never used to hear about in days gone by. Just take a look at what happened after Hurricane Katrina destroyed New Orleans: **Rescuers** were **shot at** by the very people they were trying to save! (And let's not forget that these same people who were warned to evacuate the area instead deliberately chose to

49

stay, and then complained bitterly when "the government" didn't come to their immediate, *individual* rescue....) Human violence - not just terrorism perpetrated by Islamic extremists - has become a world-wide epidemic, with many people attempting to take the law into their own hands.

Speaking of terrorism, we are not only encountering plenty of "wars and rumors of wars" (i.e., terrorism and threats not only from the radical Muslim world but also from nations like North Korea whose leader, Kim Jong Il who, as of this writing, keeps pounding his chest and kicking sand into the eyes of the world in hopes to provoke a fight). But we are personally witnessing the escalation in the Middle East of the ongoing "jealousy" between Yitz'chak (Isaac) with whom God made His covenant of circumcision, and his half-brother, Yishmael (Ishmael), who birthed the Arab population.

Let's discuss this further in the next chapter....

Chapter 4

Gnashing of Teeth

The history of Middle East problems have their roots in Genesis 16 when YHWH made His Covenant with Abraham's son Isaac, and in essence, sent the half-brother Ishmael on his merry way albeit to become "a great nation." (The present day Arabs, most of whom are Muslim, are the descendants of Ishmael).

In Genesis 16 we discover the beginning of that conflict, which began basically because the aging parents, Abraham and Sarah, failed to trust YHWH's promise for a son; so Sarah insisted Abraham impregnate her servant, Hagar, to produce an heir. The result was a bitter hatred between Sarah and Hagar, which ended in Hagar's escape into the desert where "the angel of ADONAI" paid her a visit to show that YHWH knew about and had mercy on her misery, and to describe the child in her womb thusly:

Genesis 16: 10 The angel of ADONAI said to her, "I will greatly increase your descendants; there will be so many that it will be impossible to count them." 11 The angel of ADONAI said to her, "Look, you are pregnant, and you will give birth to a son. You are to call him Yishma'el [God pays attention] because ADONAI has paid attention to your misery. 12 He will be a wild donkey of a man, with his hand against everyone and everyone's hand against him, living his life at odds with all his kinsmen."

Later, we discover that Isaac, the son YHWH promised would come from the body of Abraham's aged wife, is the one with whom He establishes His next covenant - just as He said He would, in the first place! This causes a bitter

51

rivalry between the two half-brothers and continues today. Here is how it unfolded:

*Genesis 17: 15 God said to Avraham, "As for Sarai your wife, you are not to call her Sarai [mockery]; her name is to be Sarah [princess]. 16 I will bless her; moreover, I will give you a son by her. **Truly I will bless her: she will be a mother of nations; kings of peoples will come from her."** 17 At this Avraham fell on his face and laughed - he thought to himself, "Will a child be born to a man a hundred years old? Will Sarah give birth at ninety?" 18 **Avraham said to God, "If only Yishma'el could live in your presence!"** 19 God answered, "No, but Sarah your wife will bear you a son, and you are to call him Yitz'chak [laughter]. I will establish my covenant with him as an everlasting covenant for his descendants after him. 20 But as for Yishma'el, I have heard you. I have blessed him. I will make him fruitful and give him many descendants. He will father twelve princes, and I will make him a great nation. 21 But I will establish my covenant with Yitz'chak, whom Sarah will bear to you at this time next year." 22 With that, God finished speaking with Avraham and went up from him.*

*Genesis 21: 1 ADONAI remembered Sarah as he had said, and ADONAI did for Sarah what he had promised. 2 **Sarah conceived and bore Avraham a son in his old age, at the very time God had said to him.** 3 Avraham called his son, born to him, whom Sarah bore to him, Yitz'chak. 4 Avraham circumcised his son Yitz'chak when he was eight days old, as God had ordered him to do. 5 Avraham was one hundred years old when his son Yitz'chak [laughter] was born to him. 6 Sarah said, "God has given me good reason to laugh; now everyone who hears about it will laugh with me." 7 And she said, "Who would have said to Avraham that Sarah would nurse children? Nevertheless, I have borne him a son in his old age!" 8 **The child grew and was weaned, and Avraham gave a great banquet on the day that Yitz'chak was weaned.** 9 But Sarah saw the son of Hagar the Egyptian, whom Hagar had borne to Avraham, making fun of Yitz'chak; 10 so Sarah said to Avraham, "Throw this slave-girl out! And her son! I will not have this slave-*

girl's son as your heir along with my son Yitz'chak!" 11 Avraham became very distressed over this matter of his son. 12 But God said to Avraham, "Don't be distressed because of the boy and your slave-girl. Listen to everything Sarah says to you, because it is your descendants through Yitz'chak who will be counted. 13 But I will also make a nation from the son of the slave-girl, since he is descended from you."

Genesis 21: 14 Avraham got up early in the morning, took bread and a skin of water and gave it to Hagar, putting it on her shoulder, and the child; then he sent her away. After leaving, she wandered in the desert around Be'er-Sheva. 15 When the water in the skin was gone, she left the child under a bush, 16 and went and sat down, looking the other way, about a bow-shot's distance from him; because she said, "I can't bear to watch my child die." So she sat there, looking the other way, crying out and weeping. 17 God heard the boy's voice, and the angel of God called to Hagar from heaven and said to her, "What's wrong with you, Hagar? Don't be afraid, because God has heard the voice of the boy in his present situation. 18 Get up, lift the boy up, and hold him tightly in your hand, because I am going to make him a great nation." 19 Then God opened her eyes, and she saw a well of water. So she went, filled the skin with water and gave the boy water to drink. 20 God was with the boy, and he grew. He lived in the desert and became an archer. 21 He lived in the Pa'ran Desert, and his mother chose a wife for him from the land of Egypt.

Galatians 4 tells us that Ishmael had been "born according to the flesh" (not God-ordained), while Isaac had been "born according to the promise". Thus, Isaac replaced Ishmael as the favored son and heir. This, of course, made Ishmael jealous and bitter. As a result, he mocked and disdained his half-brother. Eventually the situation became so intolerable that Abraham's wife Sarah demanded that Ishmael and his Egyptian mother, Hagar, be expelled permanently from Abraham's family.

Ishmael ultimately ended up in the wilderness region of Hejaz in what became known as the Arabian Peninsula. He indeed had twelve patriarchal sons, just as YHWH had promised, who became associated with the peoples known as Midianites, Edomites, Egyptians and Assyrians. The Bible and Islamic tradition both agree that Ishmael became the leader of all the great desert peoples of the Middle East.

YHWH provided many opportunities in this story for redemption of bad situations created mostly out of disobedience and lack of faith. He kept His promise and provided Ishmael a great kingdom of his own "to the east of his brother," but as we can see in the Middle East today, many Arabs hate their Jewish brothers and want them dead; not just out of Israel, but **completely annihilated**. Ishmael's descendants have always been jealous that Isaac's descendants were able to claim the full inheritance of Abraham. Once, during an email discussion with a very adamant Muslim, I was told: *"Your Bible lies! God made His covenant with Ishmael, not Isaac. Those Jewish and Christian accounts are wrong! Mohammed was God's last prophet, not Jesus, and Allah sent him to set the record straight."* (For those who don't know the history of Islam, it was started by an illiterate Arab man named Mohammed nearly 600 years after the death of Messiah Yeshua. It is nothing short of blasphemy to be told by some Muslim that YHWH would send a mere Arab human to come and "set the record straight" thousands of years *after* YHWH's covenant with Abraham which ultimately offered His **Divine Messiah** to the world!)

Be that as it may, this jealousy and resentment created a hatred that sparked wars and atrocities for thousands of years - and that is why the land of Israel, which YHWH promised to **Abraham's lineage through Isaac**, has been the major source of friction between the Jews and the Arabs, ever since.

And that is why it is very important to keep our eyes on Israel and events in the Middle East, because Israel is center stage in the end times scenario!

Numbers 33: 50 ADONAI spoke to Moshe in the plains of Mo'av by the Yarden, across from Yericho. He said 51 to tell the people of Isra'el, "When you cross the Yarden into the land of Kena'an, 52 you are to expel all the people living in the land from in front of you. Destroy all their stone figures, destroy all their metal statues and demolish all their high places. 53 Drive out the inhabitants of the land, and live in it, for I have given the land to you to possess. 54 You will inherit the land by lot according to your families. You are to give more land to the larger families and less to the smaller ones. Wherever the lot falls to any particular person, that will be his property. You will inherit according to the tribes of your ancestors. 55 But if you don't drive out the inhabitants of the land from in front of you, then those you allow to remain will become like thorns in your eyes and stings in your sides - they will harass you in the land where you are living. 56 And in this event, I will do to you what I intended to do to them."

What strong statements! Here we can now see that Israel is suffering today BECAUSE they allowed the Arabs and other settlers to remain in THEIR Land back in 1948 when Israel was returned to them! The Jews are being harassed and killed still today because they didn't obey YHWH to force ALL foreigners out of Israel and remain true to THEIR God, the one and only TRUE Creator....

Numbers 34: 1 ADONAI told Moshe 2 to give this order to the people of Isra'el: "When you enter the land of Kena'an, it will become your land to pass on as an inheritance, the land of Kena'an as defined by these borders. 3 "Your southern portion will extend from the Tzin Desert close to the border of Edom. The eastern terminus of your southern border is at the end of the Dead Sea. 4 From there your border turns, goes south of the 'Akrabbim Ascent and passes on to Tzin. From there it goes south of Kadesh-Barnea, on to Hatzar-Adar, and on to 'Atzmon. 5 Then the border turns and goes from 'Atzmon to the Vadi of Egypt and along it to the Sea. 6 "Your western border will be the Great Sea. 7 "Your northern border will be as follows: from the Great Sea mark a line to Mount Hor, 8 and from Mount Hor mark a line to the entrance of Hamat. The border goes out to Tz'dad. 9 Then the border goes to Zifron and finally to Hatzar-'Einan; this is your northern border. 10 "For the eastern border mark your line from Hatzar-'Enan to Sh'fam. 11 Then the border goes down from Sh'fam to Rivlah, on the east side of 'Ayin, then down until it hits the slope east of Lake Kinneret. 12 From there it goes down the Yarden River till it flows into the Dead Sea. These will be the borders of your land." 13 Moshe gave this order to the people of Isra'el: "This is the land in which you will receive inheritances by lot, which ADONAI has ordered to give to the nine tribes and the half-tribe. 14 The tribe of the descendants of Re'uven have already received their land for inheritance according to their clans, and so have the descendants of Gad and the half-tribe of M'nasheh. 15 These two-and-a-half tribes have received their inheritance on this side of the Yarden, across from Yericho and eastward, toward the sunrise."

It couldn't be any more clear....

Speaking of 1948 and the return of Israel to the Jews, when viewed through Spiritual eyes, one can see that *two* of YHWH's major end times prophecies were fulfilled in that one day, exactly as the Prophet Isaiah declared when he said that Israel would be "born" in one day and the Jews would become a nation once more. In other words, YHWH used for good what Hitler meant for evil, because Israel was returned to the Jews immediately after the Holocaust, when "the world" briefly felt sorry for them - thus fulfilling Isaiah's prophecy:

Isaiah 66: 5 Hear the word of ADONAI, you who tremble at his word: "Your brothers, who hate you and reject you because of my name, have said: 'Let ADONAI be glorified, so we can see your joy.' But they will be put to shame." 6 That uproar in the city, that sound from the temple, is the sound of ADONAI repaying his foes what they deserve. 7 Before going into labor, she gave birth; before her pains came, she delivered a male child. 8 Who ever heard of such a thing? Who has ever seen such things? Is a country born in one day? Is a nation brought forth all at once? For as soon as Tziyon went into labor, she brought forth her children. 9 "Would I let the baby break through and not be born?" asks ADONAI. "Would I, who cause the birth, shut the womb?" asks your God. 10 Rejoice with Yerushalayim! Be glad with her, all you who love her! Rejoice, rejoice with her, all of you who mourned for her; 11 so that you nurse and are satisfied by her comforting breast, drinking deeply and delighting in the overflow of her glory. 12 For ADONAI says, "I will spread shalom over her like a river, and the wealth of nations like a flooding stream; you will nurse and be carried in her arm and cuddled in her lap. 13 Like someone comforted by his mother, I will comfort you; in Yerushalayim you will be comforted." 14 Your heart will rejoice at the sight, your bodies will flourish like newly sprouted grass. It will be known that the hand of ADONAI is with his servants; but with his enemies, his fury.

History reveals that the above accurately describes the events of May 14, 1948, when the Jews declared independence for Israel as a sovereign nation for the first time in nearly three thousand years. Until then, Israel was a desolate and undesirable place where the Arabs exiled convicts. Once Jews regained Israel, they did not remove the Arab squatters from their land but, instead allowed them to remain and even treated them as brothers.

Please note that Isaiah said the birth would take place *before* the labor pains. An interesting article at George and Ray Konig's "AboutBibleProphecy.com" (see also The Refiner's Fire's article (www.therefinersfire.org): "Isaiah foretold the re-birth of Israel....") reveals that a movement called Zionism, which began in the 1800s to encourage Jews to return to Israel (which at that time was called Palestine) was instrumental in establishing and reaffirming Israel's status as a sovereign nation during the course of a single day. Israel's declaration of independence, according to the Konigs, was not the result of a war but, rather, the cause of one. Within hours of the declaration of independence in 1948, Israel was attacked by the surrounding countries of Egypt, Jordan, Syria, Lebanon, Iraq and Saudi Arabia. The Israelites, however, held their own, as they did later in the Six-Day War of June 5-10, 1967, when attacked by several neighboring countries (see "Six-Day War" at Wikipedia).

The Bible teaches that YHWH promised the land to the Jewish people as an "everlasting possession" (Genesis 15:18); He also promised that he would never again remove them from the land (Amos 9:15). According to an August 22, 2009 Arutz Sheva (Israel National News.com) article, archaeologists have confirmed Israel's settlement in this land in Biblical times. It states, in part:

> Jacques Gauthier, a non-Jewish Canadian lawyer who spent 20 years researching the legal status of Jerusalem, has concluded: Jerusalem belongs to the Jews, by international law.

Gauthier, according to the article, wrote a 1,300 page doctoral dissertation on the topic of Jerusalem and its legal history, based on international treaties and resolutions of the past 90 years, which he presented to a world-famous Jewish historian and two leading international lawyers.

The central issue is this: In Genesis 15:18-19, God *gave* the Land to Abraham and his descendants. Abraham *bought* a large burial site at Hebron (Genesis 23:1-20); David *bought* the Temple Mount (1 Chronicles 21:25). And *"the Jews" never sold the Land to anyone*! Arabs began settling it after the Jews were scattered into the nations, and have simply "squatted" there, ever since.

Nobody has ever been able to take the land from the Jews since 1948 – although the world, including the United States of America, is trying its best to divide it and hand it over to the Arabs! So, unless the Muslims are willing to *buy* the Land (which, as it happens, is *not* for sale!) then *NOBODY* has a right to it except for "the Jews" – the covenanted descendants of Abraham!

To the atheist, the Middle East situation is simply another "human" battle, with "the Jews" being the "bad guys" who supposedly took land away from the Palestinians and refuse to give it back. But those who know the Bible can clearly see the conflict between Isaac and Ishmael is Biblical, not human, and *we know that YHWH gave the Land to His Chosen People*.

Genesis 15: 18 That day ADONAI made a covenant with Avram: "I have given this land to your descendants - from the Vadi of Egypt to the great river, the Euphrates River - 19 the territory of the Keni, the K'nizi, the Kadmoni, 20 the Hitti, the P'rizi, the Refa'im, 21 the Emori, the Kena'ani, the Girgashi and the Y'vusi."

He even commanded that the land *never* be sold!

Leviticus 25: 23 *"The land is not to be sold in perpetuity, because the land belongs to me -you are only foreigners and temporary residents with me.*

As foretold (see Isaiah 60:15; Joel 3:2; Ezekiel 36:8-10; Matthew 24:9), most of the world is siding ***not*** with YHWHs people, but with the Muslims. Arabs and Jews have been fighting for thousands of years (long before they were even called Arabs and Jews!) over that tiny plot of holy land called "Israel". What neither side seems to realize is that the battle is not one of flesh and blood, but of principalities/spiritual things between Yeshua and His enemy, *haSatan*. The Bible states that the last great battle (Armageddon) will not only pit Israel against the Middle East and its allies, but against the ***whole world***, in general (Ezekiel 38:1-23).

In the meantime, a lot of hateful rhetoric has been, and will continue to be aimed at "the Jews" - simply because they are "God's Chosen People." Even many Christians are under the mistaken impression that God has turned His back on the Jews and replaced them with the Gentiles. But what did the Apostle Paul say?

Romans 11: 11. *But I say: Have they so stumbled as to fall entirely? May it never be! Rather, by their stumbling, life has come to the Gentiles for (awakening) their jealousy. 12. And if their stumbling was riches to the world, and their condemnation riches to the Gentiles; how much more is their perfection?*

If it hadn't been for God's ***Chosen*** being scattered into the nations (Ezekiel 36:19) who were ultimately referred to as "Jews," YHWH and Yeshua would have remained the best-kept secret of tiny, little Israel, and the rest of the world would still be writhing in paganism! One cannot condemn those Jews who reject Messiah, because YHWH hasn't yet "opened their spiritual eyes." You can be sure they are not about to believe in the Torah-less Christian "Jesus" - especially since YHWH, throughout the Torah continuously warns them against any kind of paganism or idolatry, and the entire Tanach contains story after story about the consequences of disobedience to YHWH.

Furthermore, one cannot blame traditional Jews for refusing the idea of a human "god" for several very strong reasons: *(1)* **God** cannot be born or die. *(2)* "Jesus" couldn't be God because (as mentioned previously) YHWH never demanded human sacrifices. *(3)* His death, according to Christianity, abolished YHWH's Torah (something which could never be!), without which we would have NO blueprint for moral, holy living. *(4)* His death somehow abolished the commanded Seventh Day Sabbath and all seven *mo'edim* (Feasts/appointed times) which Christianity blatantly ignores replacing them instead with the man-made "holy days" of Christmas and Easter.

Harsh words? Yes, but we are living in the end times as outlined in the Bible, and time is short. Jew-bashing is simply **NOT** the way to please God! The Bible tells us that anyone who goes up against His Chosen in any way will suffer His wrath:

Genesis 12: 1 Now ADONAI said to Avram, "Get yourself out of your country, away from your kinsmen and away from your father's house, and go to the land that I will show you. 2 I will make of you a great nation, I will bless you, and I will make your name great; and you are to be a blessing. 3 I will bless those who bless you, but I will curse anyone who curses you; and by you all the families of the earth will be blessed."

There are myriad websites on the World Wide Web which try to debunk this fact and make Jews out to be "bad guys"

- from the likes of the KKK and other "white supremacist" hate groups, to Christians who support the idea of "replacement theology" which insists that, with the "New Covenant" God turned His back on the Jews and transferred His promises to Gentile Christians. The question remains: Since God never had an *old* covenant with the Gentiles, how could He possibly have a *new* covenant with them? His New Covenant was made with the Torah observant Houses of Israel and Judah, not with Gentiles (see Jeremiah 31:32). It is imperative that we do not mistake this important fact!

Jeremiah 31: 35 This is what ADONAI says, who gives the sun as light for the day, who ordained the laws for the moon and stars to provide light for the night, who stirs up the sea until its waves roar -- ADONAI-Tzva'ot is his name: 36 "If these laws leave my presence," says ADONAI, "then the offspring of Isra'el will stop being a nation in my presence forever." 37 This is what ADONAI says: "If the sky above can be measured and the foundations of the earth be fathomed, then I will reject all the offspring of Isra'el for all that they have done," says ADONAI.

Romans 11: 25. (For I want you to know this) mystery, that blindness of heart has in some measure befallen Israel until the fullness of the Gentiles will come in: 26. And then will all Israel live. As it is written: A deliverer will come from Tsiyon and will turn away iniquity from Ya'akov. 27. And then will they have the covenant that proceed from me when I will have forgiven their sins."

In Romans 11:26 "all Israel" refers to those who turn to YHWH and welcome the Spirit of Mashiyach. Paul is not saying or implying that every Jew or Israelite will enter into the Kingdom of Elohim (refer to Matthew 22:2-14; 25:1-12).

Those who hate "the Jews" for whatever reason, are catering into and participating in YHWH's end times plan. Take a look at ancient prophecies unfolding *right now* as the whole world seems to be against Israel and the Jews:

Zechariah 14: "*For I will gather all the nations against Yerushalayim for war. The city will be taken, the houses will be rifled, the women will be raped, and half the city will go into exile; but the rest of the people will not be cut off from the city.*"

Ezekiel 38: *12 I will seize the spoil and take the plunder." You will attack the former ruins that are now inhabited and come against the people gathered from the nations, who have acquired livestock and other wealth and are living in the central parts of the land. 13 Sh'va, D'dan and all the leading merchants of Tarshish will ask you, 'Have you come to seize spoil? Have you assembled your hordes to loot; to carry off silver, gold, livestock and other wealth; to take much plunder?'" 14 "Therefore, human being, prophesy! Tell Gog that Adonai ELOHIM says this: 'Won't you be aware of it when my people Isra'el are living in security? 15 You will choose just that time to come from your place in the far reaches of the north, you and many peoples with you, all of them on horseback, a huge horde, a mighty army; 16 and you will invade my people Isra'el like a cloud covering the land. This will be in the acharit-hayamim; and I will bring you against my land, so that the Goyim will know me when, before their eyes, I am set apart as holy through you, Gog.'*

No tribe or race in history has remained a distinct people group outside of a national homeland for thousands of years as have the Jewish people. No people on earth have ever been repatriated after dozens of generations had forgotten their distinct language. No people, that is, except for YHWH's people.

Yes, there are plenty of Jew-hating Gentiles, but it seems Arabs are still their biggest enemies. The dimensions of the

Isaac-Ishmael conflict exploded when Mohammed started the religion of Islam in 622 AD. Islam now boasts approximately two billion followers. Tensions mounted over the years for various reasons, especially in 1967 when then-Israeli Minister of Defense Moshe Dayan handed administrative control over the Temple Mount to Jordan's Islamic Waqf.

It remains to be seen once things unfold, but when the Scriptures are examined in context, we can see that Islam may very well be "the beast" referred to in the Book of Revelation - which happens to lead us right into our....

SECOND POINT: *The "Mark of the Beast" (Revelation 13:17; 14:9-11; 16:2; 19:20) is nothing man-made, such as a microchip implant, etc. It is something much more complicated than that....*

Some have suggested that this "mark of the beast" is a tattoo of some sort or perhaps some kind of a credit card, national health card or bar code. Others are guessing it is the Radio Frequency Identification (RFID) microchip implant, which could be used by the government to spy on us round the clock.

But, let's get realistic: Since when does YHWH need **man's inventions**? Why can't the "mark" be an action; something that isn't necessarily visible to the naked eye – for instance, why can't the actual "mark" be our willingness to depart from YHWH and His teachings to follow Satan? Why can't it be the refusal to keep Torah? After all, the Bible isn't clear as to whether it's visible or invisible; but it does amply warn us that the "antichrist" does many things including that he seeks to alter the seasons and the law.

Daniel 7: 25 He will speak words against the Most High and try to exhaust the holy ones of the Most High. (The "holy ones" are those who obey His Torah!) *He will attempt to alter the seasons and the law; and [the holy ones] will be handed over to him for a time, times and half a time.*

The "seasons" include YHWH's Seventh Day Sabbath and the Feasts! And this is why I am making the following statement which will ring true once you have a chance to think about it:

> Every single religion in the world outside of Judaism has attempted, in one way or another, to change YHWH's seasons and His laws - including Christianity....

Of course, there are Christian preachers who teach about the true Sabbath and discuss the Feasts at the appropriate times, but rarely do we find any **church** that actually **keeps** the Feasts! This is why it is imperative to open our eyes during these last days, to make sure we are following YHWH to the best of our abilities. The time has come to stop being arrogant in our "Bible knowledge" and begin to see the Scriptures for what they say - and then *live* it.

To understand the "Mark of the Beast" we must first understand that there is a "Mark of YHWH", as well. God put "marks" on people throughout the Old Covenant:

- *Genesis 4: 15 ADONAI answered him, "Therefore, whoever kills Kayin will receive vengeance sevenfold," and ADONAI put a sign on Kayin, so that no one who found him would kill him.*

- *Ezekiel 9: 4 ADONAI said to him, "Go throughout the city, through all Yerushalayim, and put a mark on the foreheads of the men who are sighing and crying over all the disgusting practices that are being committed in it."*

- **Ezekiel 9:** *6 Kill old men, young men, girls, little children, women - slaughter them all! But don't go near anyone with the mark. Begin at my sanctuary." They began with the leaders in front of the house.*

The B'rit Chadasha (New Testament) refers to "seals" instead of a "mark":

- **John 6:** *27. Do not labor for food that perishes, rather for food that endures to life that is everlasting, that which the Son of man will give to you, for this man Elohim the Father has sealed.*

- **2 Corinthians 1:** *21. Now it is Elohim who establishes us, with you, in the Mashiyach, and has anointed us, 22. And has sealed us, and has given the earnest of his Spirit in our hearts.*

- **Ephesians 1:** *13. In whom you also have heard the Word of Truth which is the Good News of your life, and have believed in him; and have been sealed with the Ruach haKodesh who was promised; 14. Who is the earnest of our inheritance until the redemption of them that are alive and for the praise of his glory.*

- **Ephesians 4:** *30. And do not grieve the Ruach haKodesh of Elohim, whereby you are sealed for the day of redemption.*

- **2 Timothy 2:** *19. But the firm foundation of Elohim stands and it has this seal; Master YHWH knows them who are His: and, Let everyone who invokes the name of our Master (Y'shua) stand aloof from iniquity.*

From these scriptures we can see that YHWH uses "marks" and "seals" to separate the Godly from the ungodly. If you've read the Bible in its entirety, you know that the "Godly" are not only those who believe in Yeshua Mashiyach, but those who follow the teachings and instructions contained in Torah, as Yeshua did.

YHWH gave strict instructions to Moshe (Moses) who told the Israelites:

*Deuteronomy 6: 1 "Now this is the mitzvah, the laws and rulings which ADONAI your God ordered me to teach you for you to obey in the land you are crossing over to possess, 2 so that you will fear ADONAI your God and observe all his regulations and mitzvot that I am giving you - you, your child and your grandchild - as long as you live, and so that you will have long life. 3 **Therefore listen, Isra'el, and take care to obey, so that things will go well with you, and so that you will increase greatly,** as ADONAI, the God of your ancestors, promised you by giving you a land flowing with milk and honey.*

4 "Sh'ma, Yisra'el! ADONAI Eloheinu, ADONAI echad [Hear, Isra'el! ADONAI our God, ADONAI is one]; 5 and you are to love ADONAI your God with all your heart, all your being and all your resources. 6 These words, which I am ordering you today, are to be on your heart; 7 and you are to teach them carefully to your children. You are to talk about them when you sit at home, when you are traveling on the road, when you lie down and when you get up. 8 Tie them on your hand as a sign, put them at the front of a headband around your forehead, 9 and write them on the doorframes of your house and on your gates.

In other words, this scripture orders the Israelites (which includes *anyone* who believes in YHWH and does His will) to keep His commandments within their hearts and minds - which ultimately translates into the thought processes **behind our foreheads**, and the resulting **deeds performed with our hands**. Whoever belongs to YHWH with all his heart, mind, and soul, will do his best to keep his mind and hands from sinning....

Disciples of YHWH are sealed with His Torah, indicating this is a symbolic seal, not a literal one.

Exodus 31: 13 '"Tell the people of Isra'el, 'You are to observe my Shabbats; for this is a sign between me and you through all your generations; so that you will know that I am ADONAI, who sets you apart for me.

Exodus 31: 16 The people of Isra'el are to keep the Shabbat, to observe Shabbat through all their generations as a perpetual covenant. 17 It is a sign between me and the people of Isra'el forever; for in six days ADONAI made heaven and earth, but on the seventh day he stopped working and rested.'"

Many Christians today insist that since we have God's Word "written on our hearts" (2 Cor. 3:3) they are exempt from being Torah-observant. They insist we are "are under grace and that the only commandments are to love the Lord with all your heart and love your neighbor as yourself" (Matthew 22:37-39). However, this is not true, as Yeshua Himself said that He came not to abolish Torah, but to fulfill (Matthew 5:17-20). This has been misinterpreted to mean "ended" or "done away with." YHWH gave us a Renewed Covenant via Yeshua who was our final SIN Sacrifice - which did *not* automatically replace Torah. Even the final book of the Bible, Revelation, tells us that YHWH's people are those who bear witness to Yeshua *AND* obey His commands (Rev. 12:17; Rev. 14:12). Those Scriptures don't say "or"; they both say *"and"*.

So...those who have the "Mark of God" are the ones who not only have the testimony of our Messiah, but those who are Torah-observant. That, in itself, will be a very visible "mark" which will drive the YHWH-hating Antichrist insane enough to want to kill us all!

And that brings us back to the "Mark of the Beast":

Revelation 13: 11. And I saw another beast of prey which came out of the earth; and he had two horns like those of a lamb, and he spoke like the dragon.

I believe this particular "beast of prey" refers to the Antichrist and the ungodly system of beliefs he institutes, including the use of Islam. The first "beast" (Islam) suffered a terrible blow when the Ottoman era came to a close at the end of World War I and when the Caliphate (first form of government inspired by Islam) was abolished in 1924 (see Wikipedia).

Revelation 13: 12. And before him he exercised all the authority of the first beast of prey whose deadly wound was healed. (Wound was healed because Islam is now on the rise again!) *13. And he brought about great signs, even so as to make fire come down from heaven upon the earth, before men. 14. And he seduced them that dwell on the earth to erect an image to the beast of prey who had the wound from a sword and recovered. 15. And it was given him to put life into the image of the beast of prey; and to cause that all they who would not worship the image of the beast of prey, should be slain* (certainly sounds like Islam whose adherents threaten to behead anyone who refuses to bow down to Allah!): *16. and to cause that all, great and small, rich and poor, bond and free, should receive a mark on their right hands, or upon their foreheads; 17. so that no one might be able to buy or to sell, except those who had the mark of the name of the beast of prey, or the number of his name. 18. Here is wisdom: let him that has intelligence compute the number of the beast of prey; for it is the number of a man: and its number is six hundred and sixty and six.*

As an aside, referring to the number 666 in verse 18, the AENT explains:

In terms of the number of the Beast, the name 'Nero Caesar" adds up to a Gematria of 666 in Hebrew and Aramaic. However, this never works in Greek or Latin, as Origen found out to his dismay in the late Second Century. While this book of Revelation is written outside of specific "time" as we know it, the examples and instances of the past and present, ultimately repeat themselves while racing towards their final fulfillment. Although 666 is haSatan's identifying number, the Anti-Mashiyach types also wear this number. Anti-Mashiyach can relate to humans under haSatan's control, those who use positions of power and authority to wreak havoc. Rav Shaul teaches he is the "man of lawlessness" but still a man; 1 Thessalonians reveals that the man has false divine aspirations. Human manifestations of haSatan are men like Nero, who is a shadow of what is to come. Rome has long been the focal point of evil, so how much more would the Emperor reflect that, especially when he murdered both Rav Shaul and Keefa (Peter)!

Revelation 14: 9. And another, a third Messenger followed them, saying with a loud voice: If any man will worship the beast of prey and its image, and will receive its mark upon his forehead or on his hand, 10. he also will drink of the wine of the wrath of Elohim, which is poured undiluted into the cup of his indignation and will be tormented with fire and sulfur, before the Set Apart Messengers, and before the throne. 11. And the smoke of their torment ascends up for ever and ever; and there is no rest, by day or by night, to those that worship the beast of prey and its image.

Revelation 15: 2. And I saw as it were, a sea of glass mixed with fire: and they, who had been innocent over the beast of prey and over its image, and over the number of its name, were standing on the sea of glass; and they had the harps of Elohim.

Revelation 16: 2. And the first went and poured his cup upon the earth; and there was a malignant and painful sore upon those men who had the mark of the beast of prey, and who worshipped its image.

Revelation 19: 20. And the beast of prey was captured, and the false prophet that was with him, who did those prodigies before him, whereby he seduced them who had received the mark of the beast of prey and who worshipped his image. And they were both cast alive into the lake of fire which burns with sulfur.

So - what exactly is the "Mark of the Beast"? *No one* except YHWH knows for sure, but I tend to believe that Islam is the beast; the Antichrist will be a Muslim; and the "mark" will be the observance of Islam by those who claim to be believers in Messiah, simply because they fear death at the hands of Muslims. Thousands, probably millions, would readily cower and deny "Jesus" if threatened to "convert or die."

The religion of Islam isn't completely "anti-Christ"; Isa (their name for Yeshua), will supposedly return to restore peace and tranquility to the Arab lands, get married, have children, and then die 19 years after his arrival (www.everymuslim.com).

The goal of radical Islam - as evidenced by a history of violence that includes "9/11" and other atrocities - is to force the world into bowing down to Allah (Arabic title, "God"). Their "mark" is NOT visible, but you *know* a Muslim when you see him or her by their actions and dress, especially women in headscarves or *burkhas*! Google "Islam" – You'll see, they pray five times a day while facing Mecca (not Jerusalem – although they claim the Temple Mount is one of their holy places). They pray in mosques and they lead an antiquated way of life that includes keeping their women subdued and clothed from head to foot. Nothing they do or believe in any way resembles YHWH's Divine Instruction. They have taken Torah Scripture and twisted it to argue, for instance, that God made His covenant with Ishmael instead of Isaac (Genesis 16). When confronted about this lie, Muslims insist that their "final prophet" Mohammed was sent to correct all the things man has misinterpreted (never mind that Mohammed, unlike Yeshua, was just a mere man whose eleven wives included a nine year old girl – see Wikipedia, "Mohammad's Wives")....

The other reason Islam is likely to be "the beast" is that the Book of Revelation tells us that many believers in Messiah will be beheaded (not shot or stabbed or hanged, but beheaded):

Revelation 20: *4. And I saw thrones, and (persons) sat on them, and judgment was given to them, and to the **souls that were beheaded for the testimony of Y'shua and for the Word of Elohim:** and these are they who had not worshipped the beast of prey nor its image; neither had they received the mark upon their forehead or on their hand; and they lived and reigned with their Mashiyach those thousand years.*

Here's the thing: Islam is the only entity in the world today still employing the practice of beheading! Our generation has witnessed several Muslim beheadings including the February 2002 decapitation of Wall Street Journal reporter Daniel Pearl, and later Nicholas Berg, Jack Hensley, Eugene Armstrong, Paul Johnson, Dutch filmmaker Theo Van Gogh and scores of others whom the Muslim radicals have labeled "infidels." You might also remember that Muslims slaughtered an Egyptian Coptic family in New Jersey after the father had angered Islamists with Internet chat room criticisms of Islam. Radical Muslims have, in various ways, held the modern world hostage for nearly forty years and are the very reason for the long and tedious lines at the airports where travelers are forced to undergo searches of everything short of body cavity checks....

The Bible also tells us that, in the end times, those who refuse the "mark of the beast" won't be able to "buy or sell" (Revelation 13:16-18)....Several years ago, there was a radio program out of Atlanta, Ga., which featured the president of the Bank of Islam (which in 2005, in conjunction with its Atlanta subsidiary, Crescent Capital, took on the new, joint name of Arcapita - Google them and check out their world-wide investments). The Muslim president of the bank said that Arcapita had started buying up U.S. enterprises such as Church's Chicken (which was subsequently sold) and the Caribou Coffee chain, to name just a couple - and he emphasized his bank would NOT be doing business with anyone who didn't conform to Sha'ria Law (Muslim religious beliefs according to the Koran)....

Today, with many U.S. businesses failing and folding due to the fact that the entire economy runs on credit, our system is playing right into the hands of Muslim entities such as Arcapita Bank. What better time for Muslim bankers and investors to capitalize on the utter stupidity and greed of "upper management" types who ran their businesses into the ground! **All this should serve to make**

Bible literate people realize that if Muslims control the major businesses of the world and require the employees of those businesses to bow down to Allah - then those who refuse will lose their jobs and, consequently, they will not be able to "buy or sell"....

It doesn't take a rocket scientist to observe that although Muslims are taught to be kind and just, they are also committed (not to mention, *commanded* under certain conditions by the Koran) to eradicate all the "unbelievers" of the world perceived as acting aggressively against them. This, apparently, includes anyone who doesn't believe in Allah or follow Sharia Law. Events have unfolded exactly as the prophet Zechariah predicted 2,500 years ago (Zechariah 12:3) when he prophesied that Jerusalem would become a burdensome stone for all the peoples, and that all nations of the earth (not just the Arab countries) will be gathered for war because of it.

We are eyewitnesses to this end times calamity taking place right now, and that is why we know that Yeshua's soon return is imminent:

*Matthew 24: 27. For as the sunshine comes out from the East and is seen even in the West, thus will be the coming of the Son of man. 28. Wherever the carcass is, there will the eagles gather. 29. And immediately after the suffering of those days, the sun will be darkened and the moon will not shine its light. And the stars will fall from heaven, and the powers of heaven will be shaken. 30. And then will be seen the sign of the Son of man in heaven, and then all the tribes of the land mourn, when they will see the Son of man who comes upon the clouds of heaven with great power and glory. 31. And he will send his Messengers with a large trumpet, **and they will gather his chosen ones from the four winds from one end of heaven to the other.** 32. Now from the fig tree learn a parable. As soon as its branches become tender and bring forth its leaves, you know that* *summer has arrived. 33. Thus also when you have seen all these things, know that it has arrived at the door. 34. Truly I say to you, that this tribe will not pass until all these things happen. 35. Heaven and earth may pass, but my word will not pass. 36. About the day and about the hour no man knows, not even the Messengers of heaven, but the Father alone.*

Please note that these words are very important because they reveal that Yeshua did NOT in any way negate, usurp or abolish His Father's Word or authority. Yeshua, during the time He walked the Earth, wasn't privy to the "day or the hour" yet many people view Him as someone who came to do away with everything the Father ever commanded and basically replace YHWH as God.

*Matthew 24: 37. And as in the days of Nukh (Noah), thus will be the coming of the Son of man. 38. For as they were before the deluge, eating and drinking and taking women and giving them in marriage to men up to the day that Nukh entered into the ark. 39. And they did not know until the deluge came and took them all, thus will be the coming of the Son of man. 40. Then two men will be in the field, one will be taken and one will be left. 41. And two women will be grinding at the mill. One will be taken and one will be left. 42. Therefore be alert, because you do not know in what hour your Master will come. 43. And know this, that if the master of the house had known, he would not have allowed his house to be plundered. 44. Because of this also, you should be prepared, because in an hour that you do not expect, the Son of man will come. 45. Then who is the faithful and wise servant whom his master has appointed over his household to give them food in due time. 46. That servant is blessed when his master comes and finds him doing thus. 47. I say truly to you, that he will appoint him over all that he owns. 48. But if a servant being evil in his heart says that "My master will be delayed in coming." 49. And begins to beat his fellow-servants and to eat and drink with drunkards. 50. The master of that servant will come in a day that he does not expect, **and in an*** *hour that he does not know. 51. And he will cut him in two and give him his lot among the hypocrites, and there will be weeping and gnashing of teeth.*

Chapter 5

Caught Up in the Air

In the days of Noah, man was so evil, decadent and ungodly, that YHWH decided to wipe mankind from the face of the Earth. Thanks to *one single* righteous and obedient man and his family upon whom God showed mercy, mankind was spared annihilation and the Earth was eventually re-populated.

Genesis 6: 5 ADONAI saw that the people on earth were very wicked, that all the imaginings of their hearts were always of evil only. 6 ADONAI regretted that he had made humankind on the earth; it grieved his heart. 7 ADONAI said, "I will wipe out humankind, whom I have created, from the whole earth; and not only human beings, but animals, creeping things and birds in the air; for I regret that I ever made them." 8 But Noach found grace in the sight of ADONAI.

Genesis 6: 11 The earth was corrupt before God, the earth was filled with violence. 12 God saw the earth, and, yes, it was corrupt; for all living beings had corrupted their ways on the earth. 13 God said to Noach, "The end of all living beings has come before me, for because of them the earth is filled with violence. I will destroy them along with the earth.

The events of Genesis go on to describe the flood, destruction and recovery. But, by the time we reach Genesis 19 we discover that man, now centuries after the flood, had not learned his lesson or become any wiser because, as we see in the story of Lot, he was confronted by certain men in his town demanding to have sex with the two messengers (angels) from YHWH.

Genesis 19: *4 But before they could go to bed, the men of the city surrounded the house - young and old, everyone from every neighborhood of S'dom. 5 They called Lot and said to him, "Where are the men who came to stay with you tonight? Bring them out to us! We want to have sex with them!" 6 Lot went out to them and stood in the doorway, closing the door behind him, 7 and said, "Please, my brothers, don't do such a wicked thing. 8 Look here, I have two daughters who are virgins. Please, let me bring them out to you, and you can do with them what seems good to you; but don't do anything to these men, since they are guests in my house."2 9 "Stand back!" they replied. "This guy came to live here, and now he's decided to play judge. For that we'll deal worse with you than with them! Then they crowded in on Lot, in order to get close enough to break down the door. 10 But the men inside reached out their hands, brought Lot into the house to them and shut the door. 11 Then they struck the men at the door of the house with blindness, both small and great, so that they couldn't find the doorway.*

Since the day he was kicked out of the Garden of Eden, man has been killing, going to war with his fellow man, stealing, raping, lying, hating, cheating and making idols for himself. These idols are not just "other gods"; rather, they include money, possessions or status. We have even deified our fellow humans - people such as Marilyn Monroe, Elvis Presley, Princess Diana and Michael Jackson

---

2   Many argue here that Lot was an evil man for his willingness to give up his virgin daughters to the crowd. However, Lot was desperate to keep YHWH's messengers safe from harm! After all, these men, the messengers, were holy! It is interesting to note that many today are under the impression that angels are female, but there is no mention in the Scriptures of any females among the angel population. Whenever gender is addressed in the Scriptures regarding angels, they are always male (Genesis 19:10-12; Revelation 7:2; 8:3; 10:7). Matthew 22:30 provides evidence that angels are without gender, i.e. "sexless": *For in the resurrection of the dead, men do not marry women, nor are women given to husbands. Rather, they are as the Messengers of Elohim in Heaven.* Angels do not procreate, so there is really no requirement for gender.

who were ultimately nothing more than pawns in a game of greed.

In other words, we've generally exhibited willful disobedience against YHWH since the day Adam and Eve ignored His command to stay away from the Tree of the Knowledge of Good and Evil (Genesis 2:17). Throughout the Bible we are warned about giving in to our sinful natures, but most simply aren't paying attention....and the results have been devastating. This is evidenced today where we are witness to a steep and steady decline of morality and a rise in decadence, aggressive behavior and violence. We saw this sharp downturn beginning in the late 1950s/early 1960s - or, about the time when atheists began to be verbal about their unbelief, and Christians gave in to their demands - such as eliminating school prayer and removing the Ten Commandments from public and government buildings. More recently, Christians have begun appeasing atheists in their quest to be free from encountering Nativity scenes at Christmas time, or seeing or hearing the words, "Merry Christmas." Oddly, at the same time atheists, humanists, Satanists and others who cry out against Nativity Scenes, can be seen Christmas shopping....

When you really think about it, it is no wonder that Christmas and Easter are being attacked by unbelievers, as both of these "holy days" are man-made and have no real spiritual value. Amazingly, atheists have never attempted to attack the YHWH-commanded "Jewish" holidays - the seven *mo'edim* (Feast times) of Passover/Pesach; Unleavened Bread/Hag HaMatzot; Firstfruits/Yom HaBikkurim; Feast of Weeks/Shavuot; Jewish Civil New Year/Feast of Trumpets/Rosh Hashanah; Day of Atonement/Yom Kippur; and the Feast of

Tabernacles/Sukkot. (For more on the Feasts, please see Appendix 3.)

These Biblical holy days have not been attacked, probably because atheists know next to nothing about YHWH's Appointed Times, and therefore, His Feasts don't pose much of a threat. Thanks, in part, to the media which doesn't normally report on, or even acknowledge them, the true Appointed Times remain a "best-kept secret" of obedient followers of YHWH.

Basically, the only "Jewish holiday" ever mentioned in the media is Hanukkah, because it falls in the same timeframe as Christmas; yet Hanukkah isn't a commanded Feast at all. It's a tradition to commemorate the victory of a small band of Jews over the occupying army of Syrian king Antiochus Epiphanes who desecrated the Jewish Temple and forbade the Jews to practice their faith. This small group of rebels, known as the Maccabees, later initiated a revolt against the Syrian army and, fighting with little more than sticks and farm tools, won victory after victory over the Syrian army and took back the Temple.

The first thing they did was to light the golden menorah, which was supposed to burn continuously, but at the time there was only enough oil enough to keep it burning for 24 hours. Somehow, as they worked fervently day after day to clean and repair the Temple, the oil in the Menorah never ran out. It burned for eight days, long enough for new oil to be made. And thus, Hanukkah is an eight-day celebration.

In today's "modern" world, the things that YHWH considers "bad" are now considered "good" by society-at-large. Case in point, homosexuality is still a sin (YHWH and Yeshua's Apostles call it "an abomination" and something to be shunned - see Leviticus 18: 22, Deuteronomy 22:5, Romans 1:22-32, 1 Timothy 1:9-11); yet today, we are being forced by all manner of media, the film industry and the world's governments to be "tolerant" and accepting. In fact, if you do not accept homosexuality, YOU are damned!

In our Torah-less world, most have decided there is no God and we can do whatever we please. It's all about "me" and never mind the consequences! Even many Christians have become so lethargic about God, they've chosen to turn a blind eye to all kinds of sin because they erroneously feel they cannot "judge" others because they are commanded to "love and forgive." While it is true we are to love and forgive, most don't seem to realize that the scriptures about "judging" our neighbors are not suggesting we turn a blind eye to our neighbor's sins or keep mum about them; but rather, we are to weigh against the **Torah** the things we see our neighbors doing, and then "rebuke them sharply" (Titus 1:13, Leviticus 19:17) if they have veered from God's Path.

James 4: 10. Humble yourselves before Master YHWH and He will exalt you. 11. Speak not against each other, my Brothers; for he that speaks against his brother, or judges his brother speaks against Torah and judges Torah. And if you judge Torah, you are not a doer of Torah, but its judge.

The scripture above means, if you **add your own** judgments to those already established in the Torah of YHWH, then you have judged Torah as insufficient, and are not allowing *it* to be your judge....

Many examples could be cited about the present state of our world, but the bottom line is this: Today "tolerance" has become the norm. "Political correctness" is in. So is stupidity, and ignorance and arrogance and brazen selfishness. *"Jesus abolished the Law at the cross! Heck, we're no longer bound by those ol' rules!"* The question is, **where** did YHWH ever suggest that His Torah would be abolished the moment His Son died? How does it even make sense that Torah - which is our ONLY blueprint for moral, holy living - would be abolished? If we don't have Torah, how else are we going to determine what sin is? (See 1 John 3:4.)

*1 Peter 4: 18. **For the Mashiyach also once died for our sins**, the righteous for sinners; that he might bring you to Elohim. And he died in body but lived in spirit. 19. And he preached to those souls which were detained in Sheol (Hades) 20. which were formerly disobedient **in the days of Noah when the long suffering of Elohim commanded an ark to be made, in hope of their repentance;** and eight souls only entered into it and were kept alive in the waters.* (i.e., *Mikveh*, the complete immersion [baptism] into living waters after one has repented of sin and begun to walk in the newness of life (the Kingdom) as provided through Mashiyach.)

Those believers who are old enough to remember, are witnesses to the fact that our nation's moral decline began around the same time that organized prayer in public schools was banned, along with the removal of the Ten Commandments in public buildings. Divorce rates, teen pregnancy, violent crime, and drug use have all increased since then, as revealed in a wonderful DVD by WallBuilders (wallbuilders.com) entitled, "America's Godly Heritage". This DVD reveals that the current concept of "separation of church and state" was never intended by our Founders and examines the parallel between the Supreme Court's 1962 redefinition of the phrase and the beginning of America's moral decline in the Sixties. (Wallbuilders is "an organization dedicated to presenting America's forgotten history and heroes, with an emphasis on the moral, religious, and constitutional foundation on which America was built.")

By the way, the concept of the "separation of church and state" is *not* in the US Constitution. What the Constitution actually says is this: "Congress shall make no law respecting an establishment of religion, or prohibiting the free exercise thereof." This means no particular religion will be forced on you! Your free exercise however, guaranteed by the Constitution, has been trampled upon over and over.

But the church will be raptured before Jesus returns, won't it?

In a word: No. "The church" won't be raptured, because, when it comes right down to it, there is no such thing as "the church" in YHWH's eyes. The reality is, there never was such thing as the "church" in the days of the original, Torah observant, Seventh Day Sabbath and Feast-keeping Apostles; only a renewed Israel which Gentiles were welcome to join!

Jeremiah 31: 31 "Here, the days are coming," says ADONAI, "when I will make a new covenant with the house of Isra'el and with the house of Y'hudah.

Please note exactly who the recipients of the Renewed Covenant were: The Houses of Israel and Judah – both of whom were Torah observant! That scripture says nothing about Gentiles, Catholics, Christians, Buddhists or anyone else. "Church" is a man-made term denoting that only believing Christians will go to heaven - those who "believe" in a Torah-less entity they call "Jesus"....

The truth is, **no one** who teaches lawlessness and anti-Torah doctrine based on the misinterpreted writings of Paul (upon which Catholicism and Christianity are based) will enter the Kingdom! Yeshua teaches in Matthew 5:19, that they who break the least of the Commandments will also be least in the Kingdom of Heaven. True *Kedoshim* (Set Apart) people in Mashiyach keep YHWH's commandments, including the Seventh Day Sabbath and His Biblical Feasts; and they do not dine on swine, or any other unclean animals according to Leviticus 11 and Deuteronomy 14. The Renewed Covenant, in Jeremiah 31, writes Torah upon the heart, meaning once we have studied and understood YHWH's "forever" commandments as outlined in the Torah, we tend to remember and obey them. You cannot have something "written on your heart" that you've never before seen or practiced! Man isn't born with YHWH's commands "written on his heart." If he was, then would never engage in sin of any kind.

Also, Yeshua even said He came NOT to abolish His Father's original divine teaching/instruction, yet Christians keep insisting He did. Let's check out exactly what He said:

Matthew 5: *17. Do not think that I have come to loosen Torah or the prophets, I have not come to loosen but to fulfill. 18. For truly I say to you that until heaven and earth pass away not one Yodh or one stroke will pass from Torah until everything happens. 19. All who loosen, therefore, from one (of) these small commandments and teach thus to the sons of man, will be called little in the Kingdom of Heaven, but all who do and teach this will be called great in the Kingdom of Heaven. 20. For I say to you that unless your righteousness exceeds more than that of the scribes and the Pharisees, you will not enter the Kingdom of Heaven.*

Let's briefly discuss verse 17 which uses the terms "loosen" Torah and "fulfill". Some Bibles use the term "abolish" rather than the term "loosen" which is from the original Aramaic. In the interest of understanding the original meaning (see Deuteronomy 4:2; 13:1) we must understand that Yeshua at no time in His ministry "loosened" ("abolished") either Torah or the Prophets! The Word YHWH revealed to His prophets cannot be abolished, and neither can the Torah of YHWH. The Word of YHWH is both Torah (instruction and grounding in righteousness) and Prophecy declaring, foretelling and divulging the will of YHWH to all through eternity.

"Fulfill" expressed by Yeshua means to "carry out" not as sometimes translated as "to complete". Here it means to bring to realization, perform or do, as a duty; or to satisfy the Commandments by obeying them: *Isaiah 42: ADONAI was pleased, for his righteousness' sake, to make the Torah great and glorious.* Isaiah 42 prophecies the work of the Mashiyach. We have the full assurance that Mashiyach would never abrogate Torah; rather, he would magnify Torah and write Torah upon the willing hearts of his people. Yeshua carried out (fulfilled) the prophecies of the Mashiyach. He lived Torah, taught Torah, and was Torah, which was His duty and promise as Mashiyach; otherwise He would not have qualified to be Mashiyach ben Yoseph.

The point is, Yeshua did not come to abolish but to fulfill, and YHWH will allow *individuals* (not groups, such as "the church") to enter His heaven - those who believe in Yeshua as their Final SIN Sacrifice, and have allowed themselves to be changed from the inside out, doing YHWH's will as "new creatures" (2 Corinthians 5:17) who sought to obey and grow ever closer to Him. Only YHWH has the power to determine who is or isn't going to be "caught up in the air" to meet Yeshua during the "rapture", and those who will be allowed into Heaven at the end of the Millennium on Judgment Day. (As a matter of fact, it is no inconceivable that He may even leave some believers behind here on Earth so they can witness to unbelievers - only time will tell). YHWH alone has the power. It's His call.

This brings us to our....

THIRD POINT: *Although the word "rapture" is found nowhere in the Scriptures, we are told there will be a "catching up" of **believers only** upon Yeshua's Second Coming (1 Corinthians 6:14; 1 Thessalonians 4:13-17); **not of the unbelievers** who will only be called up before God on Judgment Day at the end of the Millennium. This "catching up" will be when Yeshua returns to Earth; not before. It will occur at the end of that seven year period which begins when the Antichrist makes a seven year peace treaty with Israel.*

Yeshua Himself explains what will happen upon His return to Earth:

*Luke 17: 20 The P'rushim asked Yeshua when the Kingdom of God would come. "The Kingdom of God," he answered, "does not come with visible signs; 21 nor will people be able to say, 'Look! Here it is!' or, 'Over there!' Because, you see, the Kingdom of God is among you." 22 Then he said to his talmidim, "The time is coming when you will long to see even one of the days of the Son of Man, but you will not see it. 23 People will say to you, 'Look! Right here!' or, 'See! Over there!' Don't run off, don't follow them, 24 because **the Son of Man in his day will be like lightning that flashes and lights up the sky from one horizon to the other**. 25 But first he must endure horrible suffering and be rejected by this generation. 26 "Also, at the time of the Son of Man, it will be just as it was at the time of Noach. 27 People ate and drank, and men and women married, right up until the day Noach entered the ark; then the flood came and destroyed them all. 28 Likewise, as it was in the time of Lot -*

people ate and drank, bought and sold, planted and built; 29 but the day Lot left S'dom, fire and sulfur rained down from heaven and destroyed them all. 30 That is how it will be on the day the Son of Man is revealed. 31 On that day, if someone is on the roof with his belongings in his house, he must not go down to take them away. Similarly, if someone is in the field, he must not turn back - 32 remember Lot's wife! 33 Whoever aims at preserving his own life will lose it, but whoever loses his life will stay alive. 34 I tell you, on that night there will be two people in one bed - one will be taken and the other left behind. 35 There will be two women grinding grain together - one will be taken and the other left behind." 36 (Some manuscripts have verse 36: Two men will be in a field -- one will be taken and the other left behind.")

Matthew 24: 21. For then will be great suffering such as has not been from the beginning of the world until the present, nor will ever be again. 22. And if those days were not shortened, not any flesh would live, but because of the chosen, those days will be shortened.

Who are the "chosen" (or "elect" in some versions)? The Bible tells us. Following is an example; please read it very carefully:

*1 Peter: 1. PETER, a Shaliach of Y'shua the Mashiyach, to the elect and sojourners who are dispersed in Pontus and in Galatia and in Cappadocia and in Asia and in Bithynia, 2. **to them who have been chosen, by the foreknowledge of Elohim the Father through sanctification of the Spirit, to the obedience** and the sprinkling of the blood of Y'shua the Mashiyach: May grace and peace abound towards you.*

The "elect" are those who are considered righteous; those who have the testimony of Yeshua **AND** keep YHWH's commandments:

*Revelation 12: 17. And the dragon was enraged against the woman; and he went to make war upon the remnant of her seed who keep the Commandments of Elohim **and** have the testimony of Y'shua.*

*Revelation 14: 12. Here is the patience of the Set Apart believers who keep the commandments of Elohim, **and** the faith of Y'shua.*

> **NOTE:** Two very distinct groups; one willfully breaks the Commandments of Elohim and causes others to do the same, but the other group keeps the Commandments of Elohim and observes Torah. It is important to note, the above scriptures don't mention just the "Ten Commandments". They simply refer to "the Commands" or "the Commandments", depending on which Bible version you use....God warns us in Proverbs 4:2 - *"For I have given you a good teaching, do not forsake my Torah."* (Stone Edition of the Tanach). With the advent of Catholicism and Christianity, the entire "Old Testament", along with God's original teaching and instruction, basically became null and void. Therefore, when "the rapture" finally happens, many will be very surprised to discover they were left behind....

Being "elect" or "chosen" is *entirely* dependent upon whether or not one chooses and maintains obedience to YHWH. The "elect" are **NOT** comprised of those who disobeyed YHWH's "forever" Torah commands (such as keeping the Seventh Day Sabbath, which is a sign between YHWH and His people, see Ezekiel 20:11-12).

Rav Shaul (Rabbi/Apostle Paul) says in several places - namely Romans 3:31, Romans 11, Ephesians 2:11-16, that believers are grafted into Israel, but they don't replace Israel. ***Rather, they are subject to Israel's laws.*** That is why he quotes Torah in the first place! As we saw earlier, in Numbers 15:13-16 YHWH reiterates four times that anyone who chooses to accept Him as their God is *to do exactly as the Torah observant Houses of Israel and Judah do* (with whom He made His New Covenant - Jeremiah 31:32).

Unfortunately, the "church" has decided the above was negated once "Jesus" died, and that all one has to do to "be saved" is to "believe in Jesus" - an erroneous doctrine that Christians have been holding over the heads of "the Jews" for the last two thousand years. Referencing verses such as Ephesians 5:25-27, they suggest that only "the church" will be "raptured" and that everyone who doesn't "believe in Jesus" will go to hell:

Ephesians 5: 25. Husbands, love your wives, even as the Mashiyach loved his assembly and delivered himself up for it; 26. That he might sanctify it and cleanse it by the washing of water and by the Word; 27. And might constitute it a glorious assembly for himself, in which is no stain and no wrinkle and nothing like them; but that it might be Set Apart and without blemish.

Remember, the word "rapture" does not appear in the Scriptures, and what's more, it is *not* a gentle "floating into the clouds" as some scholars would have you believe; but rather, a quick "translation" from physical to spiritual flesh while alive - happening on a massive scale *for the righteous* at a specific moment in time when we suddenly cease to be here on Earth, and immediately find ourselves in the Presence of Yeshua "in a flash, in the twinkling of an eye" (1 Cor. 15:52). Evidence of this "translation" comes from several sources including 1 Thessalonians 4:13-18 which tells us there will be a "catching up" of Believers, and 1 Corinthians 15:49-58 which tells us that *all* believers who have ever lived and died will "rise" and be "changed" instantaneously:

*1 Corinthians 15: 35. But some one of you may say: How will the dead arise and with what body will they come forth? 36. Foolish man! **The seed which you sow, is not resurrected unless it dies.** 37. And that which you sow, you do not sow the body that is to be, but the naked kernel of wheat or barley, or of the other grains: 38. And Elohim gives it a body, according to His will; and to each of the grains its natural body. 39. And every body is not alike; for the body of a man is one thing, and that of a beast is another, and that of a bird is another, and that of a fish is another. 40. And there are bodies celestial, and bodies terrestrial; but the glory of the celestial (bodies) is one, and that of the terrestrial is another. 41. And the glory of the sun is one thing, and the glory of the moon is another, and the glory of the stars is another; and one star exceeds another star in glory. 42. So (it is) also with the resurrection of the dead. They are sown in corruption, they arise without corruption: 43. They are sown in dishonor, they arise in glory: they are sown in weakness, they arise in power. 44. is sown an animal body, it arises a spiritual body. For there is a body of the animal life, and there is a body of the spirit. 45. So also is it written: "Adam, the first man, became a living soul;" the second Adam (became) a resurrecting spirit. 46. And the spiritual was not first; but the animal, and then the spiritual. 47. The first man was of dust from the earth; the second man was Master YHWH from heaven. 48. As he was of the dust, so also those who are of the dust; and as was he who was from heaven, so also are the heavenly. 49. And as we have worn the likeness of him from the dust, so will we wear the likeness of him from heaven. 50. But this I say, my Brothers that flesh and blood cannot inherit the Kingdom of Heaven: neither does corruption inherit incorruption. 51. **Behold, I tell you a mystery; we will not all sleep, but we will all be changed, 52. Suddenly, as in the twinkling of an eye, at the last shofar, when it will sound; and the dead will arise, without corruption; and we will be changed.** 53. For this which is corruptible, is to put on incorruption; and that which dies, will put on immortality. 54. And when that which is corruptible,* *will put on incorruption, and that which dies, immortality; then will take place the Word that is written, "Death is absorbed in victory." 55. Where is thy sting, O death? And where is thy victory, O Sheol? 56. Now the sting of death is sin; and the strength of sin is Torah. 57. But thanks be to Elohim that gives us the victory, through our Master Yshua the Mashiyach. 58. Wherefore, my Brothers and my beloved, be steadfast, and not weak willed; but be at all times generous in the work of Master YHWH; seeing you know that your labor is not in vain in Master YHWH.*

Please note in verse 56 it says, *"the strength of sin is Torah"* This means, when Torah is weakened, knowledge of sin is correspondingly diminished; when Torah is reinforced, knowledge of sin is heightened. The strength of sin is Torah because it is Torah which identifies just what sin is. Without Torah, only man's feeble "law" determines consequences of behavior and sin is no longer defined.

1 Thessalonians 4: 13. And I wish you to know, my Brothers, that you should not mourn over them who have fallen asleep, like other people who have no hope. 14 For if we believe that Yshua died and rose again, even so them who sleep, will Elohim, by Yshua, bring with him. 15. And this we say to you by the word of our Master (Yshua), that we who may survive and be alive at the coming of our Master (Yshua), will not precede them who have slept. 16. Because our Master (Yshua) will himself descend from heaven with the mandate and with the voice of the chief Messenger and with the Qarna (trumpet/shofar) of Elohim; and the dead who are in the Mashiyach will first arise; 17. and then we who survive and are alive will be caught up together with them to the clouds to meet our Master (Yshua) in the air; and so will we be ever with our Master.

Please note, 1 Thessalonians 4:17 refers ONLY to the believers, both dead and alive, who will meet Yeshua in the air; *not* the unbelievers! Unbelievers don't rise until the end of the millennium when we will ALL will stand before YHWH on Judgment Day (Revelation 20:11-15).

Ironically, these same scriptures also show beyond a shadow of a doubt, that the so-called "Pre-tribulation rapture" (which suggests "the church" will be zapped out of here before "the tribulation" comes, is a complete myth! *No one* is going to be "caught up" away from the Earth *UNTIL* Yeshua's Second Coming!

John 6: 39. And this is His will, that of Him who sent me, that all that He has given to me I do not lose even one. 40. For this is the will of my Father, that all who see the Son and believe in Him, will have life that is eternal. And I will raise him up on the last day.

John 6: 44. No man is able to come to me unless the Father who sent me draws him. **And I will raise him up in the last day.** *45. For it is written in the prophets that all of them will be taught of Elohim. Everyone who hears therefore and learns from the Father comes to me. 46. It is not that man can see the Father, rather he who is from Elohim is he who sees the Father. 47. Amen, amen I say to you that whoever believes in me has life that is eternal.*

Here, Y'shua reiterates that eternal life begins after the resurrection, otherwise known as the "First Resurrection" (Revelation 20:5-6) or the "Resurrection of the Righteous" (Daniel 12:1-2; Luke 4:14; Acts 24:15), *not at the time of a person's death*. This event will occur for believers (dead and alive) at Yeshua's return, and again within a time span known as the *acharit hayamim* (the End of Days), which is at the *end* of the Millennium (allowing those who became believers AFTER Yeshua returned to Earth to be resurrected to eternal life).

Theories abound on "the rapture" but, while no one really knows precisely how things will unfold or the exact timing of the "catching up," the Scriptures do provide many clues. Unfortunately, these clues have fallen victim to man's religiosity - the various ideas, thoughts and opinions spawned from the minds of the bottomless pool of Bible teachers and pastors from a plethora of Christian denominations who, with their limited human mindsets, have managed to twist much of YHWH's Truth.

This is what we do know, however - and here you will gain some insights that probably differ from what you've heard before - which lead us right into our Fourth Point....

Chapter 6

Two Resurrections

FOURTH POINT: *Yeshua will rule and reign for a thousand years, at which time there will be the resurrection of ALL (those who became believers during the Millennium, and all the DEAD unbelievers since the beginning of time who had heretofore remained in their graves). (See Isaiah 13:6,9; Jeremiah 46:10; Joel 1:15; 2:11; Amos 5:18; Obadiah 1:15, Revelation 20:1-15 and Acts 24:15). This will happen at what is described as* **Jacob's Trouble** *(Jeremiah 30:7; 2 Peter 3:10-12).*

What exactly is "Jacob's Trouble?" According to Aramaic scholar Andrew Gabriel Roth:

> It's a time of terrible chaos and confusion. "Jacob" is an allegory of all souls who have not passed from death to life in Mashiyach; in other words, they are not 'born again.' The war is waged within the spiritual worlds, good triumphs against evil and the Bride of Mashiyach is Israel who has wrestled out the blessings, endured to the end and won the victory over darkness."

(Please remember that "Israel" includes anyone and everyone who is grafted in to the Olive Tree through the atoning blood of Messiah Yeshua - Romans 11:16-24.)

The difficult thing to grasp is how Mashiyach will reclaim the earth for YHWH, which is obviously not a big job for Him, but a totally impossible mission for us. The physically and morally polluted earth is a consequence of sin; therefore, when sin is exposed and eradicated, the earth will return to Eden, but we His people will participate in the reconstruction during the Millennium where there is rest and completion of YHWH-ordained directives.

The following sequence is outlined in the Bible:

- Yeshua is crucified.

- His *Ruach* (Holy Spirit) administers to some souls in *Sheol* (hell), presumably to the righteous like Samuel who were sleeping. (This may be related to the small righteous resurrection at the end of Matthew.)

- He resurrects three days later with *ruach* (spirit) and *nefesh* (soul) in a restored physical body.

- Yeshua ascends to heaven (twice), the last time just prior to *Shavuot* (Feast of Weeks/Pentecost, which is celebrated during the May/June timeframe on the Gregorian calendar), and becomes "the Word of YHWH" once more.

- Emerges after the "catching up" as the Word of YHWH but in physical form (Revelation 19:13), and we "resurrected" Believers rule and reign with Him for a thousand years on Earth. After that Yeshua's bodily state is unclear: Revelation 19: 13. *And he was clothed with a vesture sprinkled with blood; and his name is called, The Word of Elohim.*

Believers will identify the following events:

- Our *nefesh* (soul) dies (Ezekiel 18:20 and Romans 6:23) and our *ruach* (spirit) returns to YHWH who gave it (Ecclesiastes 9).

- Those who died *pre-Yeshua*, excepting Enoch (Genesis 5:23-25) and Elijah (2 Kings 2) and "many of" the Set Apart believers mentioned in Matthew 27:51-53, are still in the grave awaiting judgment. (**Note:** Being "Set Apart" unto YHWH, means to be led by the *Ruach haKodesh* to keep the Commandments of YHWH. Belief in the Mashiyach alone does not make one Set Apart; even the demons "believe" [James 2:19]).

- In Matthew 24 we begin to see that some believers will be *translated* (i.e., cease to exist here on Earth to suddenly find themselves in the Presence of Yeshua). No clear Scriptural criteria is given (other than being righteous) as to who among the believers are taken up and who are left behind upon Yeshua's Second Coming. It seems that, just because you are left behind, doesn't mean you are *not* righteous. You may have simply been chosen to minister to others left in the wake of the "rapture".....

- Those who have died *since* Yeshua became our Final Sin Sacrifice are still in the grave awaiting judgment.

- At judgment, "the day of YHWH" - a time of awe, judgment and gathering (see Isaiah 13:6,9; Jeremiah 46:10; Joel 1:15; 2:11; Amos 5:18; Obadiah 1:15) which happens after Yeshua's thousand year reign on Earth (Revelation 20:1-15), there is a resurrection of the righteous *and* of the wicked (Acts 24:15). The righteous go to eternal life; the wicked, to eternal destruction. Yeshua specifically says to fear his Father in heaven *who can destroy both body and soul in Gehenna (hell) (Luke 12:5).*

Jude 1: *11. Woe to them; for they have gone in the way of Cain; and after the error of Balaam, they have lusted for gain; and in the rebellion of Korah, they have perished. 12. These are they who, in their feastings, riot while polluting themselves, feeding themselves without fear; clouds without rain, moved about by the winds; trees whose fruit has failed, and they are without fruit, twice dead, and uplifted from their root; 13. raging waves of the sea which, by their foam, manifest their confusion; shooting stars for which is reserved the blackness of darkness forever. 14. And of them also prophesied Enoch who was the seventh from Adam when he said:* **Behold, Master YHWH comes with myriads of his Set Apart believers; 15 to execute judgment upon all and to convict all the wicked because of all the deeds they have wickedly committed; and because of all the hard speeches which they, sinners without Elohim, have uttered.** *16. These are they who argue and complain of everything while they walk according to their lusts; and their mouth speaks shocking things; and they flatter people for the sake of gain. 17. But do you, my beloved, remember the words which were spoken before by the Shlichim of our Master Yshua the Mashiyach; 18. because they told you that in the end of the times there would be scoffers going after wickedness according to their lusts. 19. These are they that separate (themselves), sensual persons, not having the Spirit. 20. But, my beloved, you be newly strengthened in your Set Apart faith through the Ruach haKodesh, while you pray. 21. And let us keep ourselves in the love of Elohim while we wait for the mercy of our Master Yshua the Mashiyach to our eternal life.*

2 Peter 2: *9. Master YHWH knows how to rescue from afflictions those who fear him,* **and he will reserve the wicked for the day of judgment to be tormented,** *10. and especially them who go after the flesh in the lusts of pollution, and despise government. Daring and boasting without cause they do not quake with awe while they* *blaspheme; 11. as opposed to the Messengers, greater than they in might and valor, do not bring against them a reproachful judgment. 12. But these, like nasty beasts that by nature are for slaughter and corruption, while engaging in evil speech regarding things they don't know, will perish in their own corruption; 13. they being persons with whom iniquity is the reward of iniquity, and by them rioting in the daytime is accounted delightful; defiled and full of blemishes (are they), indulging themselves at their ease while they give themselves up to pleasure; 14. having eyes that are full of adultery and sins that never end; seducing unstable souls; and having a heart exercised in greed; children of cursing: 15. And, having left the correct path, they have wandered and gone in the way of Balaam the son of Beor who loved the wages of iniquity, 16. and who had for the corrector of his transgression a mute mule which, speaking with the speech of men, rebuked the madness of the prophet. 17. **These are wells without water, clouds driven by a storm, persons for whom is reserved the blackness of darkness.** 18. For, while they utter astonishing vanity, they seduce with obscene lusts of the flesh, them who have almost abandoned these that walk in error. 19. And they promise them liberty while they themselves are the slaves of corruption: for, by whatever thing a man is vanquished, to that is he enslaved. 20. For if, when they have escaped the pollutions of the world by the knowledge of our Master and Redeemer Yshua the Mashiyach, they become again involved in the same and are vanquished, their latter state is worse than the former. 21. **For it would have been better for them not to have known the way of righteousness, than after having known (it), to turn back from the Set Apart Commandment that was delivered to them.**

- It is important to note that the "rapture" is not something linked only to the end times, because it happened to Enoch and Elijah who, we are told,

were taken BODILY up to heaven without dying
(Genesis 5:24, 2 Kings 2:11). Once in heaven, we can
only make guesses as to what happened to their
physical bodies because, as 1 Corinthians 15 has
shown, YHWH gives us a new spiritual body.

Again, this doesn't mean our physical bodies, upon
Yeshua's return, will float up into the air - but this is
something we will only know for sure when that time
comes. From 1 Corinthians 15:51-52 we find it will be "in
the twinkling of an eye," and Matthew 24:40 reveals that
this "translation" from physical to spiritual bodies will be
sudden:

*Matthew 24: 40. Then two men will be in the field, one will be
taken and one will be left. 41. And two women will be grinding at
the mill. One will be taken and one will be left. 42. Therefore be
alert, because you do not know in what hour your Master will come.*

Now, please pay close attention here: John 5 tells us that
everyone will ultimately be "translated" - some to eternal
life and some to judgment:

*John 5: 28. Do not marvel at this for the hour is coming when all
those who are in the grave will hear his voice! 29. And those who
have done good things will go forth to the resurrection of life, and
those who have done evil things to the resurrection of judgment.*

**"Wait! I thought you said only believers would be
raptured!"**

Yes...they will be "raptured" first. But we see in the
Scriptures that there are *two resurrection events* separated
by a thousand years! The "resurrection of life" is the first
resurrection, which happens just prior to Yeshua's Second
Coming; and the "resurrection of judgment" does not occur

until a thousand years later at the end of Messiah's millennial reign, when everyone who has ever lived will stand before YHWH on Judgment Day. These events are outlined in the following scriptures:

Daniel 12: 1 "When that time comes, Mikha'el, the great prince who champions your people, will stand up; and there will be a time of distress unparalleled between the time they became a nation and that moment. At that time, your people will be delivered, everyone whose name is found written in the book. 2 Many of those sleeping in the dust of the earth will awaken, some to everlasting life and some to everlasting shame and abhorrence. 3 But those who can discern will shine like the brightness of heaven's dome, and those who turn many to righteousness like the stars forever and ever.

Acts 24: 15. And I have a hope in Elohim, which they also themselves expect, that there is to be a resurrection of the dead, both of the righteous and the wicked.

Luke 14: 14. And you will be blessed because they have nothing to repay you. For your repayment will be in the resurrection of the righteous.

While we're on this particular subject, and before we continue, let's discuss the "eternal life" promise....

"Eternal life" according to the Bible, doesn't necessarily mean "living forever" as we understand it; there is more to it than that. John 17:2-3 tells us exactly what it is, as Yeshua explains:

John 17: 2. Just as you have given him authority over all flesh that whomever You have given him, he will give to him life that is eternal. 3. Now this is life that is eternal, that they might know You, that You are the Elohim of Truth, and he alone whom You have sent, the Mashiyach Y'shua.

In Yeshua's own words He is saying that eternal life is not just "believing" or "trusting" but, rather, it is *knowing YHWH and Yeshua*!

Just how do we do get to "know" YHWH and Yeshua? We get a clear clue in 1 John 2:3-6:

1 John 2: 3. And by this we will be sensible that we know him, if we keep his Commandments. 4. For he that says I know him, and does not keep his Commandments, is a liar and the truth is not in him. 5. But he that keeps his Word, in him is the Love of Elohim truly completed: for by this we know that we are in him. 6. He that says I am in him, is bound to walk according to his halacha (walking).

According to the Scriptures, man, whom YHWH created, is mortal, with life ending in eternal death for those who choose to ignore Him (Romans 6:23). Simple as that. Had YHWH *not* been full of grace and mercy all along, He would have killed Adam and Eve instead of simply removing them from the Garden of Eden after they chose to disobey Him. But, through His grace and mercy, He decided to allow man to continue to live because He had an ultimate plan - and that plan included rules for His creation to follow, and these rules are contained within His Torah. Torah is illustrated in the scriptures which follow, representing just a tiny percentage of the number of times YHWH warned Israel to obey Him:

Deuteronomy 10:13 - to obey, for your own good, the mitzvot and regulations of ADONAI which I am giving you today.

Deuteronomy 11:1 - "Therefore, you are to love ADONAI your God and always obey his commission, regulations, rulings and mitzvot.

Deuteronomy 11:8 - *Therefore, you are to keep every mitzvah I am giving you today; so that you will be strong enough to go in and take possession of the land you are crossing over to conquer;*

Deuteronomy 11:22 - *"For if you will take care to obey all these mitzvot I am giving you, to do them, to love ADONAI your God, to follow all his ways and to cling to him,*

Deuteronomy 11:27 - *the blessing, if you listen to the mitzvot of ADONAI your God that I am giving you today;*

Deuteronomy 11:28 - *and the curse, if you don't listen to the mitzvot of ADONAI your God, but turn aside from the way I am ordering you today and follow other gods that you have not known.*

Deuteronomy 12:1 - *Here are the laws and rulings you are to observe and obey in the land ADONAI, the God of your ancestors, has given you to possess as long as you live on earth.*

Deuteronomy 12:28 - *Obey and pay attention to everything I am ordering you to do, so that things will go well with you and with your descendants after you forever, as you do what ADONAI sees as good and right.*

Ignoring those rules, as seen throughout the entire Tanach, can have dire consequences as illustrated in the near end of mankind by the flood:

Genesis 3: 22 ADONAI, God, said, "See, the man has become like one of us, knowing good and evil. Now, to prevent his putting out his hand and taking also from the tree of life, eating, and living forever -" 23 therefore ADONAI, God, sent him out of the garden of Eden to cultivate the ground from which he was taken.

Genesis 6: *5 ADONAI saw that the people on earth were very wicked, that all the imaginings of their hearts were always of evil only.*

Genesis 6: *17 "Then I myself will bring the flood of water over the earth to destroy from under heaven every living thing that breathes; everything on earth will be destroyed.*

Genesis 7: *6 Noach was 600 years old when the water flooded the earth. 7 Noach went into the ark with his sons, his wife and his sons' wives, because of the floodwaters.*

Genesis 7: *11 On the seventeenth day of the second month of the 600th year of Noach's life all the fountains of the great deep were broken up, and the windows of the sky were opened. 12 It rained on the earth forty days and forty nights.*

Genesis 7: *24 The water held power over the earth for 150 days.*

Revelation 19: *11. And I saw heaven opened: and lo, a white horse; and he that sat on it is called Faithful and True: and in righteousness he judges, and makes war. 12. His eyes (were) like a flame of fire, and on his head (were) many diadems; and he had names inscribed; and the name which was written on him, no one knew, except himself. 13. And he was clothed with a vesture sprinkled with blood; and his name is called, The Word of Elohim. 14. And the army of heaven followed him on white horses, clad in garments of fine linen, pure (and) white. 15. And from his mouth issued a sharp two-edged sword, that with it he could strike the nations; and he will rule the nations with a rod of iron; and he will tread the wine-press of the wrath of Elohim Almighty. 16. And he has upon his vesture and upon his thigh the words written: King of Kings, and Master of Masters.*

As you can see, YHWH is not kidding around. **He demands we obey His Torah!** And yet, rather than to dive head-first into "God's swimming pool," most people continue to sit at the side with their feet dangling in the water, singing *Kumbaya*, and deluding themselves that God doesn't mind the paganism they've mixed into their worship....

There is so much to learn about our God and His Word! Did you know that the scriptures tell us that even our souls are mortal?

Ezekiel 18: 20 The person (or soul, Hebrew nephesh; something that is human and temporal) who sins is the one that will die....

The Gospels record Yeshua's assertion that the *Ruach* (Spirit) of YHWH was within him (see also Isaiah 11:1-2 and Zechariah 12:10). He taught that while his *nefesh* (soul) would die, YHWH would reanimate both his *neshama* (human spirit/ruach) and *nefesh*. Yeshua never claimed his nefesh was anything other than human and that as such, it would die.

Are you beginning to see how awesome is the Grace of YHWH? Although man fell from grace, YHWH continued to reach out to us, and to offer believers the reward of eternal life - just because He loves us!

So what happens to the unbelievers?

Unbelievers and the "lukewarm" *will* stand before YHWH on Judgment Day, and they *will* give an account of their lives - after which they will realize their huge mistake in rejecting Him. It will then finally "hit home" that their reward consists of the punishment of eternal death *and* eternal separation from God.

Those who reject Him will be cast off into nothingness forever. It will be as though they never existed, while believers will live forever with YHWH throughout eternity. Although the wicked will end up in hell for a period, they will suffer consciously for their individual sins so that they may know and ponder what they have brought upon themselves: The eternal death of soul and body; the eternal loss of immortality.

*Revelation 20: 12. And I saw the dead, great and small, standing before the throne; and the books were opened; and another book was opened, which is (the book) of life. And the dead were judged from the things written in the books, according to their deeds. 13. And the sea gave up the dead in it; and **death and Sheol** gave up the dead in them. And they were judged, each one according to his deeds. 14. And death and Sheol were cast into the lake of fire. This is the second death, (namely,) this lake of fire. 15. **And if any one was not found enrolled in the book of life, he was cast into this lake of fire.***

Revelation 21: 5. And He who sat on the throne, said: Behold, I make all things new. And he said: Write; because these are the faithful and true Words of Elohim. 6. And he said to me: I am Alap and the Taw, the Beginning and the Completion: to him who thirsts, will I give of the fountain of living water, freely. 7. He that overcomes will inherit these things; and I will be his Elohim, and he will be my son. 8. But to the timid and the unbelieving, and to the sinful and polluted, and to manslayers and whoremongers, and sorcerers, and idolaters, and to all false persons, their portion will be in the lake that burns with fire and sulfur, which is the second death.

Speaking of "Sheol" – what exactly is it?

Sheol is hell. The Bible makes many references to Hell:

- It is an abyss, a place of physical agony, mental suffering, loneliness and emotional sorrow where there is weeping and gnashing of teeth. (Jude 6; Matthew 8:12, 13:42 and 50, and 25:30; Revelation 20:1)

- It is a pit of darkness; totally devoid of light, a place of instability, a lake of fire, a place where every moment is lived in uncertainty. (Matthew 5:21-23; 2 Peter 2:3-5; Revelation 20:15)

- It is a place of dissatisfaction, a fire, a fiery furnace where there is an overwhelming yearning for God and all He stands for, and for a life that will never be. (Matthew 13:42; 18:8-9; 25:41; Mark 9:43-48)

- It is a place of eternal separation from YHWH and a place where your body and soul will be destroyed. (Matthew 10:27-29)

Where is Sheol?

The truth is, no one can really say. Most likely it is in another dimension (as is heaven), but it could be in the depths of our own Earth. Here are some examples:

Matthew 11: 23. *And you Capurnakhum which has been raised to heaven will be brought down to Sheol (grave, or pit)....*

Luke 16: 23. *And while he was tormented in Sheol, he lifted up his eyes and gazed from afar upon Awraham and upon Lazar at his bosom....*

Numbers 16: 31 *The moment he finished speaking, the ground under them split apart - 32 the earth opened its mouth and swallowed them up with their households, all the people who had sided with Korach and everything they owned. 33 So they and everything they*

107

owned went down alive into Sh'ol, the earth closed over them and their existence in the community ceased.

The bottom line is: Hell is a real place, and all those who do not regard Yeshua as the Final SIN Sacrifice sent by YHWH (Yahweh) will end up there:

Matthew 13: 41. The Son of man will send his Messengers out, and they will pluck from His Kingdom all stumbling blocks and all workers of iniquity. 42. And they will cast them into the furnace of fire, and there will be weeping and gnashing of teeth.

Matthew 25: 41. Then he will also say to those that are on his left, "You cursed! Go away from me to the everlasting fire that which is prepared for the adversary and his Messengers.

Luke 13: 3. I say no to you, but that all of you if you do not repent also, you will likewise be destroyed.

At this point the following must be mentioned: Yeshua said both body AND soul (*nefesh*) are destroyed. (*Nefesh* means "personality" or "memory" - in other words, the characteristics making us human). Hell is place of eternal punish**MENT** not eternal punish**ING.** The *nefesh* is DESTROYED like the proverbial tree Yochanan (John the Immerser) compares it to. **Only Satan and the false prophet are tormented "day and night forever."**

Revelation 19: 20 But the beast was taken captive, and with it the false prophet who, in its presence, had done the miracles which he had used to deceive those who had received the mark of the beast and those who had worshipped his image. The beast and the false prophet were both thrown alive into the lake of fire that burns with sulfur.

Revelation 20: The Adversary who had deceived them was hurled into the lake of fire and sulfur, where the beast and the false prophet were; and they will be tormented day and night forever and ever.

Yeshua always contrasted hell with LIFE and, therefore, existence. To go to "hell" is to *lose your life* and **consciousness** and **perish**. Although many will have a problem with that, the fact is that only the fire itself is eternal.

By the way, YHWH doesn't "send" anyone to hell. It was created for Satan and his demons. We send ourselves to hell when we choose to ignore and/or refuse YHWH and His gracious offer of salvation and eternal life through our belief in His Son:

John 3: 16. Thus, for Elohim loved the world so as he would give His Only-Begotten Son, that whoever would believe in him would not perish, but would have life that is eternal. 17. For Elohim did not send His Son into the world to condemn the world, but to give life to the world through him. 18. He who does not believe in him is judged, and he who does not believe is already judged because he does not believe in his name, that of the Only-Begotten, the Son of Elohim.

One might ask why ANYONE in their right minds would wish to be part of the *eternal death*! Unfortunately, that is exactly what most of the world is doing by rejecting our Creator. Nearly 400 Bible prophecies have already come true, and there are just a few more to go - and you can be sure they *will* happen exactly as YHWH planned!

YHWH has given us ample opportunity to "get ourselves right with Him," yet most remain lukewarm at best. Please read the following scriptures wherein our Savior attempts to explain how man tends to reject God and lean on his own intelligence and understanding, and ask the *Ruach* (Holy Spirit) to help you understand this **in context**:

Luke 16: *14. But when the Pharisees heard these things, because they loved money, they were mocking at him. 15. And Y'shua said to them, You are those who justify themselves before the sons of men. But Elohim knows your hearts. Because the thing that is esteemed among men is abominable before Elohim! 16. Torah and the prophets were until Yochanan. Since then, the Kingdom of Elohim is preached, and all press into it to enter. 17. **And it is easier for heaven and earth to pass away than for one letter of Torah to pass away.** .... 20. And there was a certain poor man whose name was Lazar. And he would lay at the gate of that rich man, while being afflicted with sores. 21. And he was longing to fill his stomach from the crumbs that fell from the table of that rich man. Even the dogs would come and lick his sores. 22. **Then it happened that this poor man died and the Messengers carried him to the bosom of Awraham, and also that the rich man died and was buried. 23. And while he was tormented in Sheol, he lifted up his eyes and gazed from afar upon Awraham and upon Lazar at his bosom. 24. And he cried out in a loud voice and said, "My father Awraham, have compassion on me and send Lazar that he may dip the tip of his finger in water and to moisten my tongue for me. For behold I am tormented in these flames." 25. Awraham said to him, "My son, remember that you received your good things during your life, and Lazar his bad things. And now behold he is comfortable here and you are tormented. 26. Besides all these things, a great chasm is placed between you and us so that those who desire to pass over from here to you are not able. And neither are those from there able to pass over to us." 27. He said to him, "If so, I beseech you my father that you send him to my father's house. 28. For I have five brothers. Let him go and witness to them that they will not also come to this place of torment." 29. Awraham said to him, "They have Moshe and the prophets, let them hear them." 30. But he said to him, "No my father Awraham, but if a man from the dead should go to them, they will repent." 31. Awraham said to him, "If they do not listen to*

Moshe and the prophets, they would also not listen and believe him if a man from the dead should rise they would not believe him."

2 Peter 2: 9. Master YHWH knows how to rescue from afflictions those who fear him, and he will reserve the wicked for the day of judgment to be tormented, 10. and especially them who go after the flesh in the lusts of pollution, and despise government. Daring and boasting without cause they do not quake with awe while they blaspheme; 11. as opposed to the Messengers, greater than they in might and valor, do not bring against them a reproachful judgment. 12. But these, like nasty beasts that by nature are for slaughter and corruption, while engaging in evil speech regarding things they don't know, will perish in their own corruption; 13. they being persons with whom iniquity is the reward of iniquity, and by them rioting in the daytime is accounted delightful; defiled and full of blemishes (are they), indulging themselves at their ease while they give themselves up to pleasure; 14. having eyes that are full of adultery and sins that never end; seducing unstable souls; and having a heart exercised in greed; children of cursing: 15. And, having left the correct path, they have wandered and gone in the way of Balaam the son of Beor who loved the wages of iniquity, 16. and who had for the corrector of his transgression a mute mule which, speaking with the speech of men, rebuked the madness of the prophet. 17. These are wells without water, clouds driven by a storm, persons for whom is reserved the blackness of darkness. 18. For, while they utter astonishing vanity, they seduce with obscene lusts of the flesh, them who have almost abandoned these that walk in error. 19. And they promise them liberty while they themselves are the slaves of corruption: for, by whatever thing a man is vanquished, to that is he enslaved. 20. For if, when they have escaped the pollutions of the world by the knowledge of our Master and Redeemer Y'shua the Mashiyach, they become again involved in the same and are vanquished, their latter state is worse than the former. 21. For it would have been better for them not to have known the way of righteousness, than after having known (it), to turn back from the Set Apart Commandment that was delivered to them. 22. But the true proverb has happened to them: the dog returns to his vomit and the pig that was washed, to her wallowing in the mire.

*2 Peter 3: 1. This second letter, my beloved, I now write to you; in (both of) which I stir up your honest mind by admonition: 2. **that you may be mindful of the words which were formerly spoken by the Set Apart prophets, and of the commandment of our Master and Redeemer by the hand of the Shlichim: 3. knowing this previously, that there will come in the last days scoffers who will scoff, walking according to their own lusts 4. and saying, Where is the promise of his coming? for, since our fathers fell asleep, everything remains just as from the beginning of the creation. 5. For this they** willingly forget, that the heavens were of old; and the earth rose up from the waters, and by means of water, by the Word of Elohim. 6. (And), by means of these (waters), the world which then was, (being submerged) again perished in the waters. 7. And the heavens that now are, **and the earth, are by His Word stored up, being reserved for the fire at the day of judgment and the perdition of wicked men.** 8. And of this one thing, my beloved, be not forgetful: That one day to Master YHWH, is as a thousand years; and a thousand years, as one day. 9. **Master YHWH does not delay His promises as some estimate delay; but He is long suffering for your sakes, being not willing that any should perish, but that everyone should come to repentance. 10. And the day of Master YHWH will come like a thief; in which the heavens will suddenly pass away; and the elements, being ignited, will be dissolved; and the earth and the works in it will not be found. 11. As therefore all these things are to be dissolved, what persons should you be, in Set Apart conduct and in the Fear of Elohim,** 12. expecting and desiring the coming of the day of Elohim in which the heavens being tried by fire will be dissolved and the elements being ignited will melt? 13. But we, according to his promise, expect new heavens and a new earth in which righteousness dwells. 14. **Therefore, my beloved, as you expect these things, strive that you may be found by him in peace, without spot and without blemish.***

Mankind has been given chance after chance, but the majority pay no real attention. Judgment Day is around the proverbial corner, and hardly anyone realizes what lies ahead in these end times.

The following are but a few scriptures (all from the Aramaic English New Testament/AENT complete with footnotes) which amply illustrate that *no one* is exempt from Judgment Day. They also reveal, however, that YHWH willingly gives eternal life to those who believe in Him, and attempt to do their best to please Him while on Earth:

Matthew 19: 29. And anyone who has left houses or brothers or sisters or father or mother or wife or children or fields for the sake of my name, will receive one hundredfold and will inherit eternal life. (In other words, those who followed Him willingly....)

Matthew 25: 46. And these will depart to everlasting torment, but the righteous to everlasting life.

> **NOTE:** Please note this is eternal torment, not eternal tormenting! The second death Daniel 12:1-2, Luke 14:14 and John 11:24-25) is eternal; it is complete separation from YHWH into nothingness.

John 4: 14. But everyone who drinks from the waters that I give to him will not thirst forever. But those waters that I give to him will become in him a spring of water that will spring up into life that is eternal.

John 5: 24. Amen, amen: I say to you that whoever hears my word and believes in Him who sent me has life that is eternal, and does not come into judgment but has passed from death into life.

John 5: 39. Search the Scriptures, because in them you think you have that life that is eternal, and they testify concerning me.

John 6: 27. Do not labor for food that perishes, rather for food that endures to life that is everlasting, that which the Son of man will give to you, for this man Elohim the Father has sealed.

John 6: 40. For this is the will of my Father, that all who see the Son and believe in Him, will have life that is eternal. And I will raise him up on the last day.

> **Note from the AENT:** Y'shua reiterates that eternal life begins after the resurrection, otherwise known as the "First Resurrection" (Revelation 20:5-6) or the "Resurrection of the Righteous" (Daniel 12:1-2; Luke 4:14; Acts 24:15), not at the time of a person's death. This event will occur within a time span known as the *acharit hayamim* (the End of Days), which is just prior to Mashiyach's return (compare Revelation 20 and 22).

John 6: 54. And he who eats from my body and drinks from my blood has life that is everlasting, and I will raise him up on the last day. 55. For truly my body is food and truly my blood is drink. 56. He who eats my body and drinks my blood abides in me and I in him. 57. As the Living Father has sent me, and I live because of the Father, and whoever eats of me he also will live because of me. 58. This is the Bread that has descended from Heaven. It is not as manna your forefathers ate and died. He who eats this Bread will live forever!

John 10: 28. And I give to them life that is eternal and they will not perish and no man will ever snatch them from my hands.

John 12: 25. Whoever loves his soul will destroy it, and whoever hates his soul in this world will keep it to life eternal.

John 12: 50. And I know that His commands are eternal life. Therefore, these things that I speak just as my Father told me, thus I speak.

John 17: 2. Just as you have given him authority over all flesh that whomever You have given him, he will give to him life that is eternal. 3. Now this is life that is eternal, that they might know You, that You are the Elohim of Truth, and he alone whom You have sent, the Mashiyach Y'shua.

Acts 13: 48. And while the Gentiles were hearing, they were rejoicing and were glorifying Elohim. And those who believed were ordained to life that is everlasting.

Romans 2: 7. To them who, by perseverance in good works, seek for glory and honor and immortality, to them he will give life eternal. 8. But to them who are obstinate and obey not the truth, but obey iniquity, to them he will return with wrath and fire.

Romans 5: 21. So that, as sin had reigned in death, so grace might reign in righteousness to life eternal, by means of our Master Y'shua the Mashiyach.

Romans 6: 22. And now, as you have been emancipated from sin and have become servants to Elohim, your fruits are Set Apart; and the result thereof is life everlasting. 23. For the wages of sin is death; but the free gift of Elohim is life eternal, through our Master Y'shua the Mashiyach.

Galatians 6: 8. That which is from the flesh, sowed from the flesh, reaps corruption. But for those who are sown in the Spirit, from the Spirit eternal life is given.

Titus 1: 2. *concerning the hope of eternal life which the Ever-truthful Elohim promised before the times of the world; 3. and in due time He has manifested His Word by means of our announcement which was confided to me by the command of Elohim our Life-Giver;*

1 John 2: 25. *And this is the promise which he has promised us: (even) life eternal.*

1 John 5: 11. **And this is the testimony that Elohim has given to us life eternal, and this life is in his Son. 12. Everyone that takes hold of the Son takes hold of life; and everyone that takes not hold of the Son, has not life. 13. These things have I written to you that you may know that you have life eternal, you who believe in the name of the Son of Elohim.** 14. *And this is the confidence that we have towards him, that whatever we ask of him, agreeably to his will, he hears us. 15. And if we are persuaded that he hears us respecting what we ask of him, we are confident of receiving presently the petitions which we asked of him. 16 If anyone will see his brother sin a sin which doth not deserve death, he will ask, and life will be given him, to them (I say) who sin not as to death. For there is a sin of death; and I do not say of this that a man should pray for it. 17. For all unrighteousness is sin; and there is a sin which is not of death. 18. And we know that everyone who is born of Elohim sins not: for he that is born of Elohim keeps himself, and the evil one touches him not. 19. We know that we are of Elohim; and all the world is reposing on the evil one. 20.* **And we know that the Son of Elohim has come and has given us knowledge that we might know the True One; and that we might be in the True One, in his Son Yshua the Mashiyach. He is the true Elohim, and the life eternal. 21. My children, keep yourselves from idolatry.**

Please pay special attention to what follows as it shows that, to receive eternal life, one must have **obeyed YHWH's Torah** - and this is the exact reason why "the church" cannot be the "chosen" or the "elect" who will be caught up in the air to meet Yeshua in the clouds:

Romans 2: 7. To them who, by perseverance in good works, seek for glory and honor and immortality, to them he will give life eternal. 8. But to them who are obstinate and obey not the truth, but obey iniquity, to them he will return with wrath and fire. 9. And tribulation and anguish (will be) to every man that does evil; to the Jews first, and also to the Arameans. 10. But glory and honor and peace to every one that does good; to the Jews first, and also to the Arameans. 11. For there is no respect of persons with Elohim. 12. For those without Torah, who sin, will also perish without Torah; and those under Torah, who sin, will be judged by Torah. 13. For not the hearers of Torah are righteous before Elohim; but the doers of Torah are being made righteous. 14. For if Gentiles who have not Torah will, by their nature, do the things of Torah; they, while without Torah, become a Torah to themselves. 15. Additionally, they show the work of Torah as it is inscribed on their hearts; and their conscience bears testimony to them, their own reflections rebuking or vindicating one another.

Please read and reread if necessary, verses 9-15 to understand that the Christian insistence that "all we need to do is love God and each other" is in serious error. Note the word "Arameans" in verse 9 as opposed to "Gentiles" who have no ancestral claim to Israel. Paul is very careful to make proper distinction between these two, although the point of his message is clear that YHWH makes no distinction of persons (verse 11). Also notice how those "under Torah" (verse 12) and those "doers of Torah" (verse 13) are in contraposition; therefore, both cannot simultaneously be in error. This is made clear with the phrase "for doers of Torah will be made righteous." So, if **Torah-doers are made righteous, it stands to reason Torah itself does not pass away!** Paul does not suggest that Gentiles somehow spontaneously master Torah. Rather, the point is, they should learn Torah without distraction from Pharisaic traditions which deviate significantly from the plain instruction of Torah.

Gentiles were not given Torah; but, as YHWH outlined in Numbers 15:13-16, if they choose to accept Him as their God, and wish to become righteous before Him, they must do *exactly* as His "natural children" do.

"The same Torah and standard of judgment will apply to both you and the foreigner living with you" (Numbers 15:16). This was not a suggestion, but a command for it to be a *"permanent regulation through all your generations"* (Numbers 15: 14 and 15)! The "foreigner" in Moses' time, consisted of those who followed the Hebrews out of Egypt and chose to accept YHWH. Today, the "foreigner" consists of any non-Jew who chooses to believe in YHWH (the God of Abraham, Isaac and Jacob who commanded His People to obey Torah) and is grafted in through the atoning blood of Messiah.

For the Gentile who worships YHWH and believes in His Messiah, it's a simple matter of loving Him enough to *want* to please this awesome God who has offered them eternal life. And that God said the same rules would apply to *ALL*!

This is also what is meant by having "Torah written on your heart." Yeshua said in Matthew 22: 36-40 that the greatest Torah commandments are to love God, and to love your neighbor as yourself – and He continued with: *"On these two commandments hang Torah and the prophets.* He never said, "Forget about the rest and just do those two." Why? Because, to truly understand what it means to "love God" and "love your neighbor as yourself," you first have to have a working knowledge of the "bigger picture"....There is no way around it! [See also Appendix 2, page 237-238].

There is a popular expression among Christians who wear a bracelets inscribed with the letters "WWJD?" ("What Would Jesus Do?"). *Yeshua* would be obedient to the Torah of YHWH! If He did it, what makes us think we don't have to?

And There Was War in Heaven!
Surviving the End Times

Chapter 7

Eternal Life

Okay, so when does this "eternal life" begin?

(As a reminder, the thousand year period is not "heaven," but a time of Mashiyach reclaiming what belongs to his Father YHWH.)

For believers in YHWH, both past and present, "eternity" actually begins the day Yeshua returns to Earth to defeat the Antichrist. This is when the "saved" receive their "new, eternal bodies during the "rapture" so they can rule and reign with Yeshua. Our earthly bodies, as you know, are neither eternal nor holy, as we have corrupted them at some point during our lifetimes with all sorts of "unclean" foods, unclean lips, cigarettes, drugs, alcohol, illicit sexual acts, etc., and so we cannot stand before YHWH on Judgment Day in our "filthy rags"....If you'll remember, Yeshua Himself appeared to His own apostles in a form they didn't even recognize:

Luke 24: 14. And they were talking with one another about all these things that had transpired. 15. And while they were speaking and questioning with one another, Y'shua came and met up with them and was walking with them. And their eyes were so that they did not recognize him.

Regardless, we *will* be resurrected to become "new creatures"....

2 Corinthians 5: 17. Whoever therefore is in the Mashiyach, is a new creature: old things have passed away; 18. And all things are made new, by Elohim; who has reconciled us to himself by the Mashiyach, and has given to us the ministry of reconciliation.

1 Corinthians 6: 14. And Elohim has raised up our Master; and he will raise us up, by his power.

1 Corinthians 4: 14. Knowing that He, who resurrected our Master Yshua, will also resurrect us by Yshua, and will receive us, with you, to himself.

Raising "us" in 1 Corinthians 6:14 refers to **believers in Yeshua and doers of His will**. Remember, this refers only to believers; unbelievers have NOT yet been raised. Unbelievers will be raised *at the end* of the Millennium to stand briefly before YHWH before He casts them into the Lake of Fire to be eternally separated from Him (Revelation 20:15).

Okay, but wait a second! How do we know Yeshua is actually returning to Earth?

Because the Scriptures directly tell us! Yeshua Himself declares he will return, and this was seconded by angels and prophets alike.

*John 14: 1. Do not let your heart be troubled. Believe in Elohim and believe in me. 2. There are many rooms in my Father's House, and if not I would have told you so. For I go to prepare a place for you. 3. And if I go and prepare a place for you, **I will come again for you and take you with me, that where I am, you may be also.***

*Acts 1: 10. And while they were staring into heaven as he was departing, two men were found standing near them clothed in white. 11. And they said to them, Galilean men, why are you standing and staring into heaven? **This Yshua who was taken up*** *from you to heaven, likewise he will come just as you have seen him who ascended into heaven.*

Titus 2: 11. For the all-resurrecting grace of Elohim is revealed to all men; 12. and it teaches us to deny that which is without Elohim and worldly lusts, and to live in this world in sobriety and in uprightness and in the Fear of Elohim, 13. looking for the blessed hope and the manifestation of the glory of the great Elohim and our Life-giver, Y'shua the Mashiyach 14. who gave himself for us that he might recover us from all iniquity and purify for himself a new people who are zealous in good works.

1 Timothy 6: 13. I charge you before Elohim who resurrects all, and (before) Y'shua the Mashiyach who attested a good testimony before Pontius Pilate, 14. that you keep the injunction, without stain and without blemish, until the manifestation of our Master Y'shua the Mashiyach; 15 which Elohim will, in due time make visible; Almighty Elohim, King of Kings and Master of Masters 16. who only is incorruptible and dwells in light to which no one can approach; and whom no man has seen, or even can see: to him be glory and dominion forever and ever. Amen.

Revelation 17: 14. They will make war upon the Lamb; and the Lamb will vanquish them; because he is Master of Masters and King of Kings, and these with him (are) called and chosen and faithful.

Revelation 19: 11. And I saw heaven opened: and lo, a white horse; and he that sat on it is called Faithful and True: and in righteousness he judges, and makes war. 12. His eyes (were) like a flame of fire, and on his head (were) many diadems; and he had names inscribed; and the name which was written on him, no one knew, except himself. 13. And he was clothed with a vesture sprinkled with blood; and his name is called, The Word of Elohim. 14. And the army of heaven followed him on white horses, clad in garments of fine linen, pure (and) white. 15. And from his mouth issued a sharp two-edged sword, that with it he could strike the nations; and he will rule the nations with a rod of iron; and he will tread the wine-press of the wrath of Elohim Almighty. 16. And he has upon his vesture and upon his thigh the words written: King of Kings, and Master of Masters.

A quick note about Revelation 19:11-16 above. To understand its proper context, it is imperative to realize that Jews and Gentiles view God and the Bible from entirely different perspectives - this is the "Greek" vs. "Hebrew" point of view. What does this mean? Here is an explanation from my book, "Should Christians be Torah Observant?" (Netzari Press 2007, 2008):

> What is meant by "Hebrew mindset" vs. "Greek mindset"? It refers to the idea that there is a discrepancy between the Jewish and Christian concepts about life, God and Truth; in other words, they were "set" in their respective ways of thinking about these issues. In the mindset of the Hebrews, YHWH was the Creator. Period. Greeks, on the other hand, were Gentiles prone to be atheistic, agnostic, or into pagan gods - and that's why the Apostle Paul used different methods when he spoke to the Hebrew and Greek cultures.

> **Example:** The "Greek" mindset visualizes a tattoo (or something similar) on the thigh of Jesus when he returns as "King of Kings, and Lord of Lords" (Revelation 19:11-13, 16), while the Hebrew mindset sees something deeper, more realistic, more Torah-based. The Hebrew mindset visualizes Yeshua, the Torah observant Jewish Messiah wrapped in a tallit (prayer shawl) as He sits atop a white horse, headed back to Earth with the *tzit-tzits* (braids, knots, tassels) that fall across

His thighs spelling out the Name of YHWH. (Each letter of the Hebrew alphabet has a numerical value and, consequently, the number of knots on the tzit-tzits on the four corners of a tallit, tied properly, spell out the name of YHWH. No tattoo required!)

Another example of a Hebrew as opposed to Greek mindset can be seen in the respective calendars/timelines. YHWH's timelines are amply evidenced throughout the Bible, whereas our Gregorian calendars are speckled with the names of pagan deities representing the days and months. According to YHWH, a "day" is not from midnight to midnight, but from "sunset to sunset" (Genesis 1:5). He called the days of the week the "first day," "second day," etc., whereas "the world" has named its days and months after pagan gods and goddesses.

Even though we're used to these names, we must search our hearts and be very honest with ourselves when posing the question: Since YHWH adamantly warned people about paganism and even put people to death for inserting anything unusual into our worship of Him (i.e., as in the case of Aaron's sons), why would He be happy about it *today*?

Anyway, the end result of these two different mindsets was devastating because, due to their misinterpretation, mistranslation, misunderstanding and misapplication of the Scriptures, Gentile church leaders managed to twist the Word of God and insert their own opinions into the equation. And their followers, of course, blindly accepted their "truth" as gospel. Down through the ages, rather than to examine the Bible and Messiah Yeshua's teachings for themselves, people continued to adhere to the teachings of the "Church fathers" without question, thus helping to perpetuate the "law is a curse" myth.

During the time Yeshua walked on Earth, both the Jews and the Greeks were "set" in their thinking about what and how they believed. This is why Rav Shaul (the Apostle Paul) used different approaches when he spoke or wrote to the Hebrew and Greek cultures. While addressing Hebrews, he could preach the Gospel directly because they already believed in YHWH and in creation. But in his dealings with the Greeks, he first had to present Messiah Yeshua as an "arm" of YHWH before actually giving them the Gospel.

Continuing with the "eternal life" issue, we once again find a perfect explanation in the Aramaic English New Testament, in an appendix entitled "Rapture", page 928:

> Mashiyach says, *"Blessed are they who are meek because they will inherit the earth."* (Matt. 5:5; Psalm 37:11; 149:4). Isaiah wrote: *"And one cried unto another, and said, Kadosh, Kadosh, Kadosh, is YHWH of hosts: the whole earth is full of his glory"* (Isaiah 6:3), which was echoed by Rav Shaul: *"For the earth is MASTER YHWH's, in its fullness."* (1 Cor. 10:26). Certainly the Earth is headed towards catastrophe of unimaginable proportion; but regardless of what man does to destroy it, it is YHWH's property and He clearly intends to redeem every molecule of it.

"For in six days YHWH made heaven and earth, the sea, and all that is in them, and rested the seventh day: wherefore YHWH blessed the Shabbat day, and hallowed it." (Exodus 20:11). YHWH calls *tov* (good) all that He created; therefore, fallen man's plans to destroy the Earth will come to an end long before the Earth does - which is why Mashiyach says, *"For then will be great suffering such as has not been from the beginning of the world until the present, nor will ever be again. And if those days were not shortened, not any flesh would live, but because of the chosen, those days will be shortened."* (Matthew 24:21, 22).

The goal then is not Rapture (or religion) but Spiritual Regeneration, because the time of Ya'akov's trouble is coming for the benefit of "the church." Ya'akov had his name changed to Israel; Ya'akov represents Christians who are deceived and cheating themselves and others by not entering into the protection of the Kingdom of Elohim. Mashiyach Y'shua was put to death on the merits of religious tradition, but so is religion (false Christianity) putting Y'shua to "death" by turning their backs on Torah, which is Mashiyach preincarnate. The post-apostolic Western Church (inspired by haSatan) has always been at war with the true followers of Mashiyach but: *"Judgment begins in the house of YHWH"* (1 Peter 4:17, 18), so as the One World Government continues to rape and pillage the Earth of righteousness, one can expect even more false prophets to advertise cheap religious travel packages into the clouds.

Matthew 24 reveals in great detail what we can expect:

Matthew 24: 1. And Y'shua went out of the temple to depart, and his disciples drew near and were showing him the construction of the temple. 2. But he said to them, Behold, don't you see all these things? Truly I say to you, nothing will be spared. Not one stone here will be left upon another, which will not be torn down. 3. And while Y'shua was sitting on the Mount of Olives, his disciples drew near and were saying among themselves and to him, "Tell us when these things will be and what is the sign of your coming and the end of the world."

Matthew 24: 4. Y'shua answered and said to them, Beware, let no man deceive you. 5. For many will come in my name and will say that "I am the Mashiyach." And many they will deceive. 6. For you are bound to hear of revolutions and rumor of wars. Watch out and do not be disturbed, for it is necessary that all these things happen, but it is not yet the end. 7. For nation will rise against nation, and kingdom against kingdom. And there will be famines and plagues and earthquakes in different places. 8. But all these things are only the beginning of sorrows. 9. Then they will deliver to afflictions and they will kill you and you will be hated by all nations because of my name. 10. Then many will stumble and will hate one another and will betray one another.

*Matthew 24: 11. And many false prophets will arise and deceive many. 12. And because of the growth of iniquity, the love of many will grow cold. 13. But whoever has patience until the end, he will have life. 14. And this Good News of the Kingdom will be preached in all the world as a testimony to all the nations, and then the end will come, 15. **And when you see the sign of uncleanness and desolation, that was spoken of by Daniel the prophet, which will stand in the Set Apart place (Daniel 9:27; 11:31; 12:11). He that reads, let him understand.** 16. Then those who are in Yehuda, let them flee to the mountain.*

What is the "sign of uncleanness and desolation" identified above? Many believe the sign will occur when the Antichrist claims the Third Temple for his own, and begins to abolish the reinstated animal sacrifices to force the world to return to paganistic rituals of the "beast" system, whatever that may entail. (**Please see Appendix 5** which discusses the Third Temple.)

Who will flee to the mountains? Apparently, the believers living in the hills of Judea (the modern "West Bank") who will be severely persecuted once the Antichrist takes control of the Temple and begins to force people to do his will. Continuing with Matthew 24:

Matthew 24: 17. And he who is on the roof, let him not come down to take that which is in his house. 18. And he who is in the field, let him not turn back to take back his clothes. 19. And woe to the pregnant and to those who are nursing in those days. 20. And pray that your flight will not be in winter, nor on the Shabbat. 21. For then will be great suffering such as has not been from the beginning of the world until the present, nor will ever be again. 22. And if those days were not shortened, not any flesh would live, but because of the chosen, those days will be shortened. 23. If anyone should say to you then, behold the Messiah is here or there, do not believe it. 24. For false Messiahs and lying prophets will arise and they will produce signs and great wonders in order to deceive if possible even the chosen. 25. Behold, I have told you beforehand. 26. Therefore, if they say to you, "Behold, he is in the wilderness," do not go out. Or, "Behold, he is in the inner chamber," do not believe it. 27. For as the sunshine comes out from the East and is seen even in the West, thus will be the coming of the Son of man. 28. Wherever the carcass is, there will the eagles gather.

In other words, Torah observant believers in YHWH and His Messiah won't have to go out to look for Yeshua; they will be "raptured" upon His return. This will be near some future *Rosh Hashana* (Feast of Trumpets, when YHWH calls His people together); and after the "marriage supper of the Lamb" they will return with Him to defeat the Anti-Messiah and his minions and then help Him rule and reign for one thousand years. This is also right around *Sukkot* (Feast of Tabernacles)….

Matthew 24: 29. And immediately after the suffering of those days, the sun will be darkened and the moon will not shine its light. And the stars will fall from heaven, and the powers of heaven will be shaken. 30. And then will be seen the sign of the Son of man in heaven, and then all the tribes of the land mourn, when they will see the Son of man who comes upon the clouds of heaven with great power and glory. 31. And he will send his Messengers with a large trumpet, and they will gather his chosen ones from the four winds from one end of heaven to the other.

It cannot be emphasized enough that we are *in* the end times now because of our failure to obey YHWH! Yeshua Himself obeyed YHWH's Torah, and yet, many insist that He came to basically replace His Father and do away with the "Old Testament" commands. But that totally contradicts what Yeshua personally stated:

*Matthew 5: 17. Do not think that I have come to loosen Torah or the prophets, I have not come to loosen but to fulfill. 18. For truly I say to you **that until heaven and earth pass away not one Yodh or one stroke will pass from Torah until everything happens.** (Isaiah 40:12-25; 2 Samuel 23:1-5; Deuteronomy 30:11-20) 19. All who loosen, therefore, from one (of) these small commandments and teach thus to the sons of man, will be called little in the Kingdom of Heaven, but all who do and teach this will be called great in the Kingdom of Heaven.*

Has "everything happened" yet? Have Heaven and Earth passed away? Since they haven't, it's safe to assume that Torah still stands!

So, to follow Mashiyach Yeshua means to walk as He did in order to gain our goal of eternal life:

1 John 2: 3. And by this we will be sensible that we know him, if we keep his Commandments. 4. For he that says I know him, and does not keep his Commandments, is a liar and the truth is not in him. 5. But he that keeps his Word, in him is the Love of Elohim truly completed: for by this we know that we are in him. 6. He that says I am in him, is bound to walk according to his halacha. ("Walk according to his walking.") 7. My beloved, I write no new commandment to you, but the old Commandment which you had from the beginning; and the old Commandment is the Word which you have heard.

1 John 2: 16. For all that is in the world is the lust of the body and the lust of the eyes and the pride of the world, which are not from the Father but from the world itself. 17. And the world is passing away, (both) it and the lust thereof; but he that does the pleasure of Elohim abides for ever. 18. My children, it is the latter time; and as you have heard that a false Messiah was to arise, so there are now many false Messiahs; and from this we know that it is the latter time. 19. From us they went out, but they were not of us; for if they had been of us they would have continued with us: but they went out from us that so it might be known that they were not of us. 20. But you have an anointing from the Set Apart (One); and you discriminate every person. 21. I have not written to you because you don't know the truth, but because you know it and because no falsehood is of the truth. 22. Who is false but he that denies that Y'shua is the Mashiyach? And that person is a false Messiah. He that denies the Father denies also the Son. 23. And he that denies the Son also does not believe the Father. He that confesses the Son confesses also the Father. 24. And what you heard from the first, let that remain with you. For if that which you heard from the first remains with you, you also will remain in the Father and in the Son. 25. And this is the promise which he has promised us: (even) life eternal. 26. And these things I have written to you on account of those who seduce you. 27. And you also, if the anointing which you have received from him remains in you, you need not that any one should teach you; but as that anointing is from Elohim, it teaches you all things; and it is true, and no falsehood is in it. And as it has taught you, remain you in Him.

"He that says I am in him, is bound to walk according to his halacha" (1 John 2:6) means surrendering to Yeshua and living the way He did, in righteousness and equality, not as lords over others. It means renouncing the abominations of baal worship, paganism and idols. It means renouncing the abomination to drink any kind of blood (including the blood found in "rare" steaks oozing with the animal's blood), especially human blood (Leviticus 17:11) or consuming human flesh (as did the Donner Party, the California-bound American emigrants caught up in the "westering fever" of the 1840s, who resorted to cannibalism after becoming snowbound in the Sierra Nevada in the winter of 1846–1847: See Wikipedia). It means not to become self-absorbed with flattering titles, getting caught up in the web of purchasing only expensive name-brand clothing or items, or employing all manner of "stuff" - including lofty religious accoutrements (as is amply evident in not only the Catholic Church but also in "mega-churches" with their extravagant layouts, sound systems and video feeds...and some even boast Automatic Teller machines so you can be sure to obtain plenty of cash to throw into their passed plates; see 1 Peter 5).

Chapter 8

About the "Antichrist"

At this time it would be appropriate to discuss the....

FIFTH POINT: *The "Antichrist" is not necessarily one man, but a system or body of men animated by one spirit. There have been many "anti-christs" (anyone who is against Messiah Yeshua) in the world over the last two millennia, and so the dubious honor cannot go to just one man.*

Think about this for a minute. Men through the ages have qualified as "anti-Christ" including the "Church Fathers" who were instrumental in shaping the Catholic Church...Notables such as Ignatius(35-107 CE), Marcion (110-160 AD) and Tertullian (155-230 CE) come to mind. Tertullian coined the word "trinity" and helped to make "Mary" the center of Catholicism. He and the others were instrumental in twisting Scripture and inserting their own opinions - which, of course, was swallowed by "the world" as "true Gospel" which sought to free the Church from "false Jewish doctrines". Let's briefly discuss these miscreants:

Ignatius: Ignatius was considered an "auditor" and "disciple" of John. He pioneered the Greek-based Christianity and was instrumental in the assimilation of paganism into the early Christian religion, "packaging" Christianity for a Greco-Roman Hellenic culture. Ignatius perceived Jewish followers of Y'shua as nothing more than legalists and Judaizers. He despised the observance of the Seventh Day Shabbat in favor of his Ishtar sunrise "Lord's day" Sun-Day teachings. It is scarcely possible to exaggerate the importance of Ignatian letters to modern

Christian institutions. He was a key player in the development of the modern Christo-Pagan church, promoting concepts of the "infallibility of the church" and the "universal church". If there ever was a hierarchy loving "Christian" with a Hellenistic autocratic mindset, it was Ignatius who gave himself the nickname Theophoros (the God-bearer) and taught that deacons, presbyters and bishops were a separate category of people, high and lifted up, and infused with a Jesus-like authority to be lords over people. Christians consider Ignatius as one of the all time biggest movers and shakers of the all-Gentile church. He strongly instructed that "without the bishop's supervision, no baptisms or love feasts are permitted." He also believed Mary to be the eternal virgin mother of God. Hardly anyone has questioned for nearly two thousand years how GOD could possibly have a mother!

Marcion: Every Christian who uses the term "Old" and "New" testament must take their hats off to Marcion as he was the one who coined these terms which perfectly reflect the Hellenistic mindset of the pagan world which is ignorant of Torah. Marcion taught that the Old and New Testaments could not be reconciled with each other, and this is what you still hear in Christian churches today.

Tertullian: One of Tertullian's better known "achievements" was to fall into a trance and then prophesy under the influence of the "Holy Spirit", insisting his utterances were the voice of the "Holy Spirit". Also, Tertullian, in his dealings with paganism and spiritism, picked up an "anointing" of the "Holy Ghost" and, as mentioned above, coined the word "Trinity", one of the most beloved doctrines of the church to this very day. The "persons of the trinity" doctrine flourishes in the hierarchy-based religion which sees itself as a three-sided pyramid structure. Tertullian's works abound with puns, wit,

134

sarcasm and a continual pounding of his opponents with invectives.

Then, of course, there were men like the mass murderer Hitler, who was one of the biggest "anti-Christs" in the world because he went directly against what YHWH commanded and Yeshua taught - not only by breaking the Sixth Commandment (Exodus 20:13, "You shall not murder"), but also by ignoring YHWH's warning that anyone who goes up against His Chosen, will suffer His wrath. Here are the very words YHWH said to Abram:

Genesis 12: 1 Now ADONAI said to Avram, "Get yourself out of your country, away from your kinsmen and away from your father's house, and go to the land that I will show you. 2 I will make of you a great nation, I will bless you, and I will make your name great; and you are to be a blessing. 3 I will bless those who bless you, but I will curse anyone who curses you; and by you all the families of the earth will be blessed."

Deuteronomy 7: 6 For you are a people set apart as holy for ADONAI your God. ADONAI your God has chosen you out of all the peoples on the face of the earth to be his own unique treasure. 7 ADONAI didn't set his heart on you or choose you because you numbered more than any other people - on the contrary, you were the fewest of all peoples. 8 Rather, it was because ADONAI loved you, and because he wanted to keep the oath which he had sworn to your ancestors, that ADONAI brought you out with a strong hand and redeemed you from a life of slavery under the hand of Pharaoh king of Egypt. 9 From this you can know that ADONAI your God is indeed God, the faithful God, who keeps his covenant and extends grace to those who love him and observe his mitzvot, to a thousand generations. 10 But he repays those who hate him to their face and destroys them. He will not be slow to deal with someone who hates him; he will repay him to his face. 11 Therefore, you are to keep the mitzvot, laws and rulings which I am giving you today, and obey them.

Romans 11: 25 For, brothers, I want you to understand this truth which God formerly concealed but has now revealed, so that you won't imagine you know more than you actually do. It is that stoniness, to a degree, has come upon Isra'el, until the Gentile world enters in its fullness; 26 and that it is in this way that all Isra'el will be saved. As the Tanakh says, "Out of Tziyon will come the Redeemer; he will turn away ungodliness from Ya'akov 27 and this will be my covenant with them, . . . when I take away their sins." 28 With respect to the Good News they are hated for your sake. But with respect to being chosen they are loved for the Patriarchs' sake, 29 for God's free gifts and his calling are irrevocable.

PLEASE NOTE: Many are under the false impression that "the Jews" are God's Chosen, but this is not exactly true. "The Jews" has simply become a blanket description for all Israelites - but in actuality, only someone born into the Tribe of Judah can claim they are Jews. The fact is, *there were no Jews* until after Jacob begat the Tribe of Yehudah (Judah - Genesis 29:35; Matthew 1:1-2). The Tanach ("OT") shows that His Chosen were called Hebrews (Genesis 14:13). (See the lives of Abraham, Isaac and Jacob in the Hebrew Tanach).

However, if we read the Scriptures in context, we can see that EVERYONE, beginning with Cain and Abel, was Torah observant - which negates the Christian claim that they don't have to obey God's divine instructions! It is indisputably clear that *anyone* who believes in the God of Abraham, Isaac and Jacob is to be Torah observant, a fact that YHWH Himself reiterated FOUR TIMES IN A ROW in Numbers 15:13-16! YHWH chose

Abraham because He wanted to (Deuteronomy 7:6-8) and He reinforced this fact in Jeremiah 31:32 by making His New Covenant with the Houses of Israel and Judah - both of whom were *Torah observant.*

The good news is, believing Gentiles who are grafted into the Olive Tree (Israel - Romans 11:16-24) automatically become part of Israel spiritually. That doesn't mean they become "Hebrews" or "Jews" or physical citizens of Israel or that they must "convert" to Judaism; it means they are in royal company and complete God's Family!

Although Hitler was supposedly raised Catholic, he made many, often contradictory public comments to suggest otherwise, and today, no one really knows for sure what he believed or practiced, if anything. According to Wikipedia:

"Hitler was raised by Roman Catholic parents, but after he left home, he never attended Mass or received the sacraments. [Rißmann, Michael, Hitlers Gott. Vorsehungsglaube und Sendungsbewußtsein des deutschen Diktators, Zürich München: Pendo, 2001, ISBN 3-85842-421-8]. However, after he had moved to Germany, where the Catholic and the Protestant church are largely financed through a church tax collected by the state, Hitler (like Goebbels) never 'actually left his church or refused to pay church taxes. In a nominal sense therefore,' the historian Steigmann-Gall states, Hitler 'can be classified as Catholic'. [Steigmann-Gall, Richard, The Holy Reich: Nazi Conceptions of Christianity, 1919–1945, Cambridge; New York: Cambridge University Press, 2003, ISBN 0521823714]. "

Among the things Hitler seemed to forget in his undeniable hatred of "the Jews" was that YHWH loved them. Rav Sha'ul (Paul) summed it up thusly:

Romans 11: 11. But I say: Have they so stumbled as to fall entirely? May it never be! Rather, by their stumbling, life has come to the Gentiles for (awakening) their jealousy. 12. And if their stumbling was riches to the world, and their condemnation riches to the Gentiles; how much more is their perfection?

As mentioned earlier, Hitler also didn't realize that, if it hadn't been for "the Jews" being scattered into the nations (Ezekiel 36:19), YHWH and Yeshua would have remained the best-kept secret of tiny, little Israel, and the rest of the world would still be writhing in Paganism!

Romans 11: 24. For if you were plucked from the wild olive-tree which was natural to you, and were grafted, contrary to your nature, into a good olive-tree; how much more may they be grafted into their natural olive-tree? 25. (For I want you to know this) mystery, that blindness of heart has in some measure befallen Israel until the fullness of the Gentiles will come in: 26. And then will all Israel live. As it is written: A deliverer will come from Tsiyon and will turn away iniquity from Ya'akov. 27. And then will they have the covenant that proceed from me when I will have forgiven their sins. 28. Now, in the Good News, they are enemies for your sake; but in the election, they are beloved for the fathers' sake. 29. For Elohim is not changeable in his free gift and in his calling.

So, the bottom line is, "anti-Christ" includes many, not just one central person - although it does seem there will be only one central person who will make the Seven Year peace treaty with Israel (Daniel 9:27) - which denotes that the Millennium, kicked off by Yeshua's return, will start exactly seven years later....

138

Who will this one central character be? Only time will tell, but you can be sure that believers who know the Scriptures will recognize him! In the meantime, please keep in mind this: The Bible provides ample description of this particular Anti-Messiah who is opposed to YHWH and Yeshua. Some of the key passages describing him are found in Daniel 7, 8, 11; Matthew 24; 2 Thessalonians 2; and Revelation 13, 17 and 18 - where Antichrist is referred to as a "beast," a "little horn," a "false Christ," that "wicked one," and "the man of sin."

Below are some examples depicting "the Antichrist" drawn from key scriptures:

Daniel 7: 15 "As for me, Dani'el, my spirit deep within me was troubled; the visions in my head frightened me. 16 I approached one of those standing by and asked him what all this really meant. He said that he would make me understand how to interpret these things. 17 'These four huge animals are four kingdoms that will arise on earth. 18 But the holy ones of the Most High will receive the kingdom and possess the kingdom forever, yes, forever and ever.' 19 'Then I wanted to know what the fourth beast meant, the one that was different from all the others, so very terrifying, with iron teeth and bronze nails, which devoured, crushed and stamped its feet on what was left; 20 and what the ten horns on its head meant; and the other horn which sprang up and before which three fell, the horn that had eyes and a mouth speaking arrogantly and seemed greater than the others. 21 I watched, and that horn made war with the holy ones and was winning, 22 until the Ancient One came, judgment was given in favor of the holy ones of the Most High, and the time came for the holy ones to take over the kingdom. 23 This is what he said: 'The fourth animal will be a fourth kingdom on earth. It will be different from the other kingdoms; it will devour the whole earth, trample it down and crush it. 24 As for the ten horns, out of this kingdom ten kings will arise; and yet another will arise after them (refer also to Revelation 17). *Now he will be*

*different from the earlier ones, and he will put down three kings. 25
He will speak words against the Most High and try to exhaust the
holy ones of the Most High. He will attempt to alter the seasons
and the law; and [the holy ones] will be handed over to him for a
time, times and half a time. 26 But when the court goes into session,
he will be stripped of his rulership, which will be consumed and
completely destroyed. 27 Then the kingdom, the rulership and the
greatness of the kingdoms under the whole heaven will be given to
the holy people of the Most High. Their kingdom is an everlasting
kingdom, and all rulers will serve and obey them.'" 28 This is the end
of the account. As for me, Dani'el, my thoughts frightened me so
much that I turned pale; but I kept the matter to myself.*

There have been many theories about what the "ten horns"
depict and which kingdoms they represent (including
"Satan," the "Holy Roman Empire" and/or the "European
Union"). But, realistically, we can ponder and guess all we
want, and the bottom line remains: **Nobody really knows
for sure**! We cannot predict with absolute certainty which
"kingdoms" or leaders are represented unless they are
mentioned in the scriptures (which some are), or until
these things actually begin to unfold.

What we can see, however, is that there will be great
power struggles, and that one man will end up exalting
himself to the point where he fools people into believing
he is God Almighty....

*Daniel 8: 15 After I, Dani'el, had seen the vision and was trying to
understand it, suddenly there stood in front of me someone who
appeared to be a man. 16 I heard a human voice calling from
between the banks of the Ulai, "Gavri'el (Gabriel), make this man
understand the vision!" 17 He came up to where I was standing,
and his approach so terrified me that I fell on my face. But he said
to me, "Human being! Understand that the vision refers to the time
of the end." 18 As he was speaking with me, I fell into a deep sleep,*

with my face toward the ground; but he touched me, set me on my feet, 19 and said, "I am going to explain to you what will happen at the end of the period of fury, because [the vision] has to do with the time at the end. 20 You saw a ram with two horns which are the kings of Media and Persia. 21 The shaggy male goat is the king of Greece, and the prominent horn between its eyes is the first king. 22 As for the horn that broke and the four which rose up in its place, four kingdoms will arise out of this nation, but not with the power the first king had. 23 In the latter part of their reign, when the evildoers have become as evil as possible, there will arise an arrogant king skilled in intrigue. 24 His power will be great, but not with the power the first king had. He will be amazingly destructive, he will succeed in whatever he does, and he will destroy the mighty and the holy ones. 25 He will succeed through craftiness and deceit, become swelled with pride, and destroy many people just when they feel the most secure. He will even challenge the prince of princes; but, without human intervention, he will be broken. 26 The vision of the evenings and mornings which has been told is true; but you are to keep the vision secret, because it is about days in the distant future."

Daniel 11: 21 "There will arise in his place a despicable man not entitled to inherit the majesty of the kingdom, but he will come without warning and gain the kingdom by intrigue. 22 Large armies will be broken and swept away before him, as well as the prince of the covenant. 23 Alliances will be made with him, but he will undermine them by deceit. Then, although he will have but a small following, he will emerge and become strong. 24 Without warning, he will assail the most powerful men in each province and do things his predecessors never did, either recently or in the distant past; he will reward them with plunder, spoil and wealth while devising plots against their strongholds, but only for a time.

25 "He will summon his power and courage against the king of the south with a great army, and the king of the south will fight back with a very large and powerful army; but he will not succeed, because of plots devised against him. 26 Yes, those who shared his food will destroy him; his army will be swept away; and many will fall in the slaughter. 27 These two kings, bent on mischief, will sit at the same table, speaking lies to each other; but none of this will succeed; because the appointed end will not have come yet. 28 Then the king of the north will return to his own land with great wealth; with his heart set against the holy covenant, he will take action and then return home. 29 "At the time designated, he will come back to the south. But this time, things will turn out differently than before; 30 because ships from Kittim will come against him, so that his courage will fail him. Then, in retreat, he will take furious action against the holy covenant, again showing favor to those who abandon the holy covenant.

31 Armed forces will come at his order and profane the sanctuary and fortress. They will abolish the daily burnt offering and set up the abomination that causes desolation. 32 Those who act wickedly against the covenant he will corrupt with his blandishments, but the people who know their God will stand firm and prevail. 33 Those among the people who have discernment will cause the rest of the people to understand what is happening; nevertheless, for a while they will fall victim to sword, fire, exile and pillage. 34 When they stumble, they will receive a little help, although many who join them will be insincere. 35 Even some of those with discernment will stumble, so that some of them will be refined, purified and cleansed for an end yet to come at the designated time.

36 "The king will do as he pleases. He will exalt himself and consider himself greater than any god, and he will utter monstrous blasphemies against the God of gods. He will prosper only until the period of wrath is over, for what has been determined must take place. 37 He will show no respect for the gods his ancestors worshipped, or for the god women worship - he won't show respect for any god, because he will consider himself greater than all of them. 38 But instead, he will honor the god of strongholds; with gold, silver, precious stones and other costly things he will honor a god unknown to his ancestors. 39 He will deal with the strongest fortresses with the help of a foreign god. He will confer honor on those he acknowledges, causing them to rule over many and distributing land as a reward.

40 "When the time for the end comes, the king of the south will push at him; while the king of the north will attack him like a whirlwind, with chariots, cavalry and a large navy. He will invade countries, overrun them and move on. 41 He will also enter the Land of Glory, and many [countries] will come to grief, but these will be saved from his power - Edom, Mo'av and the people of 'Amon. 42 He will reach out his hand to seize other countries too. The land of Egypt will not escape - 43 he will control the treasures of gold and silver, as well as everything else in Egypt of value. Put and Ethiopia will be subject to him. 44 However, news from the east and north will frighten him, so that he moves out in great fury to ruin and completely do away with many. 45 Finally, when he pitches the tents of his palace between the seas and the mountain of the holy Glory, he will come to his end, with no one to help him.

The above is echoed in 2 Thessalonians and other New Testament passages:

2 Thessalonians: 2. that you be not soon uprooted in your mind nor be troubled, neither by word nor by spirit nor by letter, as coming from us that behold, the day of our Master (Y'shua) is at hand. 3. Let no one deceive you in any way because (that day will not come) unless there previously come a defection and that man of sin be revealed; the son of perdition; 4. who is an opponent and who exalts himself above all that is called Elohim and praiseworthy; so that he also sits in the temple of Elohim as a deity and displays himself as if he were a deity.

Note in verse 3, the term "defection" (or "falling away" or "the Great Apostasy") refers to the fallen state of "religion" and "religiosity" as a whole. In the Christian Faith of the 1st Century (Christian originating as a Greek term which referred to Greek followers of Yeshua) believers were

Torah observant just as the Netzarim (Nazarene) Jewish followers of Yeshua. Yet, even in Paul's day, an all-Gentile church was emerging, which aimed to cast off Torah and "reinvent" the Mashiyach to be more in line with Hellenism, polytheism and paganism.

1 John 2: 18. My children, it is the latter time; and as you have heard that a false Messiah was to arise, so there are now many false Messiahs; and from this we know that it is the latter time.

1 John 2: 22. Who is false but he that denies that Y'shua is the Mashiyach? And that person is a false Messiah. He that denies the Father denies also the Son. 23. And he that denies the Son also does not believe the Father. He that confesses the Son confesses also the Father.

1 John 4: My beloved, do not believe all spirits; but discriminate among spirits whether they are of Elohim: for many false prophets have gone out into the world. 2. By this the Spirit of Elohim is known; every spirit that confesses that Y'shua the Mashiyach has come in the flesh is of Elohim. 3. And every spirit which does not confess that Y'shua the Mashiyach has come in the flesh is not of Elohim; but he is of the false Messiah of whom you have heard that he comes and now is he already in the world.

2 John: 7. Because many seducers have gone forth into the world who do not confess that Y'shua the Mashiyach has come in the flesh. This is a seducer and antiChristos.

Chapter 9

Give Me Tribulation!

And now to our....

SIXTH (and final) POINT: *The so-called "seven year tribulation" is a myth, as the Scriptures never suggest the* **tribulation** *lasts seven years. Man has endured "tribulation" since he was evicted from the Garden of Eden - including disease, wars, famine, pestilence, etc. (Yeshua, our Savior, personally endured a Tribulation that resulted in a horrendous death which included humiliation and torture at the hands of spiritually blinded people. What would one call that, if not "tribulation"?)*

A seven year period referred to in the Scriptures starts on the day the "prince yet to come" (referring to some well-known, well-loved, charismatic world leader at the time) makes a seven-year covenant/peace treaty with Israel (Daniel 9:26-27).

Daniel 9: 24 Seventy weeks have been decreed for your people and for your holy city for putting an end to the transgression, for making an end of sin, for forgiving iniquity, for bringing in everlasting justice, for setting the seal on vision and prophet, and for anointing the Especially Holy Place. 25 Know, therefore, and discern that seven weeks [of years] will elapse between the issuing of the decree to restore and rebuild Yerushalayim until an anointed prince comes. It will remain built for sixty-two weeks [of years], with open spaces and moats; but these will be troubled times. 26 Then, after the sixty-two weeks, Mashiach will be cut off and have nothing. The people of a prince yet to come will destroy the city and the sanctuary, but his end will come with a flood, and desolations are decreed until the war is over. 27 He will make a strong covenant with leaders for one week [of years]. For half of the week he will put a stop to the sacrifice and the grain offering. On the wing of detestable things the desolator will come and continue until the already decreed destruction is poured out on the desolator.

There are many opinions concerning the meaning of Daniel 9:24-27, and it cannot be explained in a mere few words or sentences but it seems clear that Messiah would be "cut off" (and He was, on the day He was nailed to the stake), and that Daniel pinned down the *precise timing* when this would happen.

This is when the "end times scenario" actually begins to unfold, with the horrendous events leading toward Armageddon (Revelation 16:12-20). Starting at the halfway mark (after three and a half years) of the covenant or treaty the "prince" begins to "back-pedal" on his promises to allow the Jews to worship according to Torah. (Daniel 9:27) This follows the events which have already happened; i.e., the Machiyach was "cut off", and the Temple destroyed. Now, here in Daniel 9:27, much time has elapsed and end time events begin with the covenant for the seven year period. (Remember, believers *will be here* through these events because, as the scriptures reveal, Yeshua does NOT return until the end of those seven years.)

Here, in Daniel, lies the problem with the "seven year tribulation" myth. Though the scriptures never say there is a "seven year tribulation" somewhere, somehow, the idea took root. It seems the argument is tied to Matthew 24:15-22 where Yeshua refers to Daniel:

Matthew 24: 15. And when you see the sign of uncleanness and desolation, that was spoken of by Daniel the prophet, which will stand in the Set Apart place. 16. Then those who are in Yehuda, let them flee to the mountain.

The time of "uncleanness and desolation" in Daniel is found in Chapter 9, verse 27, the same verse in which Daniel reveals that the "prince yet to come" has made a covenant with leaders for seven years. Yeshua goes on to say:

Matthew 24: *21. For then will be great suffering such as has not been from the beginning of the world until the present, nor will ever be again* (Joel 2:2; Daniel 12:1). *22. And if those days were not shortened...*

Tie Matthew 24:15, Matthew 24:21 and Daniel 9:27, and it's easy to see how one can conclude that: *(1)* there is a seven year covenant (Daniel 9:27); *(2)* Yeshua says that when "you see this" (Matthew 24:15-16) you need to flee; and *(3)* so we must have seven years of trouble (Daniel 9:27 combined with Matthew 24:21-22).

The problem is, this is a circular argument, complete with inaccuracies. Notice that the argument begins and ends with Daniel 9:27 – the scripture is used for both the seven year covenant, and the seven years of trouble.

Now, note that where Yeshua says *"when you see the sign of uncleanness and desolation"*... this is used to *imply* the entire period of the seven year covenant, even though there is no time reference. Thus, the implication is that the time to flee is at the *beginning* of the covenant; i.e., at the beginning of the "tribulation". This is the first error in the argument. There is nothing in Yeshua's words implying the period of uncleanness and desolation is seven years, or that the time to flee is at the beginning of the seven year period.

The second error in the argument is that the seven years of trouble implied by Daniel 9:27 and Matthew 24:21-22 simply has no foundation. Daniel 9:27 says only two things: First, the covenant is for seven years; second, the covenant is broken at the halfway point. Matthew 24:21 says there will be great suffering, and Matthew 24:22 says "if the time had not been shortened..." The myth of the seven year tribulation is apparently tied to this "shortening". If "shortened" and the scriptures talk about a seven year covenant, then "the time" of the tribulation must be the seven years of the covenant.

Whew! That's a lot to dissect a simple misinterpretation. First, the time of "uncleanness and desolation" in Daniel 9:27, is at the halfway point of the seven year covenant. Second when Yeshua says *"when you see the sign of uncleanness and desolation, that was spoken of by Daniel the prophet,* this is the same period; i.e., the halfway point of the covenant. Third, the time to flee (Matthew 24:16) is also after the sign of the uncleanness and desolation, and before Yeshua says, *"then will be great suffering such as has not been from the beginning of the world"* which means the "suffering" or the "tribulation" actually does not begin until the half way point of the covenant.

The Bible, it turns out, is entirely consistent in this matter: The "seven year tribulation" is a *myth*, not substantiated by scripture.

The key to understanding the prophecy of Daniel is, in part, comprehension of words such as "uncleanness" ("abomination" in some Bible versions) and "desolation." The word "abomination" according to the Merriam-Webster Dictionary means: *"Something abominable; extreme disgust and hatred: loathing."* This is the same meaning in this case as the Aramaic which translated as "uncleanness". The word "desolation" means: *"The action of desolating; grief, sadness, loneliness; devastation, ruin."*

148

"Abominations" (uncleanness) and "desolations" have always been around, since the day Adam and Eve chose to disobey YHWH in the Garden of Eden. Their act was an *abomination* in YHWH's eyes when He discovered that His beloved human creation had decided to ignore HIS word over Satan's – the evil entity whose only purpose in the universe is to destroy YHWH's creation in any way possible before "the end" comes! Therefore, to teach man the consequence of his grievous sin, He made the lives of Adam and Eve *desolate*.

Unfortunately, instead of learning a lesson from Adam and Eve, man has continued all along to disobey YHWH; thus making his life on earth "desolate" to this very day. Instead of adhering to the commands of YHWH's Torah which were designed to keep us safe and on HIS path **(see Appendix 4)**, mankind has instead been listening to the whisperings of the adversary. This has resulted in the steady insertion of false teachings into the Holy Word which ultimately served to breed myriad religions and theologies - *none* of which line up with Torah, YHWH's divine instructions to mankind.

But Daniel, and by reference Yeshua, is talking about a *change*. This "uncleaness and "desolation" is beyond what will be normal for the day. Yeshua decrees, in fact, in Matthew 24:15-22 that this change will be so sudden, so appalling, so much worse than has ever been seen before that when we see it begin, we should not even take time to prepare before we flee.

Matthew 24: 21. For then will be great suffering such as has not been from the beginning of the world until the present, nor will ever be again.

Yeshua and Daniel make it clear that only the righteous have any hope of surviving.

Mattew 24:13 But whoever has patience until the end, will have life.

Daniel 12: 1 "When that time comes, Mikha'el, the great prince who champions your people, will stand up; and there will be a time of distress unparalleled between the time they became a nation and that moment. At that time, your people will be delivered, everyone whose name is found written in the book. 2 Many of those sleeping in the dust of the earth will awaken, some to everlasting life and some to everlasting shame and abhorrence. 3 But those who can discern will shine like the brightness of heaven's dome, and those who turn many to righteousness like the stars forever and ever. 4 "But you, Dani'el, keep these words secret, and seal up the book until the time of the end. Many will rush here and there as knowledge increases."

> **NOTE:** "Knowledge increases" does not necessarily refer to man's knowledge or inventions such as the computer or mathematics, or of physics or astronomy (as amply evidenced by our school systems where knowledge is so lacking that some high school students graduate unable to read!). Rather, in the end times, proper TORAH knowledge will be restored to Israel (which includes believing Gentiles) so that they may serve YHWH perfectly again!

So, we see that Daniel's prophecy is complex; tied to both the first coming of the Mashiyach Yeshua, and to the second. Further, we see that Yeshua's reference to Daniel *in no way* prescribes that the tribulation is seven years.

The myth of the "seven year tribulation," and "tribulation" in general is much misunderstood and I've amply shown above that the seven year tribulation is a simple misinterpretation of scripture. But there is more to the story, which brings me to the last part of the sixth point, that *man has endured "tribulation" since he was evicted from the Garden of Eden.*

When Adam had to subsist by the sweat of his brow (Genesis 3:19), what was that if not "tribulation"? When Noach had to build an ark, and endure the flood (Genesis 6-8), what was that if not "tribulation"? When the people of Israel wandered the desert with Moshe for 40 years (Exodus), what was that if not "tribulation"? And when Yeshua suffered at the hands of the Pharisees, what was that if not "tribulation"?

Tribulation is not new. It is not an "as yet to be experienced" phenomenon. All of YHWH's people will face tribulation, but only the righteous will overcome death to enter the Kingdom. (Matthew 19:29, Mark 10:29-30, Luke 18:29, John 5:24).

The suffering referred to by Yeshua in Matthew 24:21 is decidedly during the second half of the seven year covenant of Daniel 9:27. It is in this context that the word "tribulation" or the phrase "Great Tribulation" should be used. And it is in this context that the followers of the Mashiyach Yeshua need to understand – they are as vulnerable as the unbeliever during the end times because they certainly CAN lose their life during the "tribulation". No "rapture" is certain to save them. The difference is, the believer will rise to eternal life, while the unbeliever will die again to be eternally separated from God.

Which brings us to the next chapter.

151

Chapter 10

Scheisters

In this study I have continuously expressed that believers will *not* be "raptured" before the "Tribulation" begins - a fact supported by 1 Corinthians 15:51-52 which talks about our "being changed" when the *"last shofar"* (trumpet) sounds. Many horrendous things will have occurred by the time that last shofar sounds, and the Book of Revelation - which we are about to discuss in detail – delivers just what we are in for.

But first, we must understand what makes the Book of Revelation so special. It was not written by some obscure person, or some "wannabe" prophet; rather, by Yochanan Bar Zawdi (John, son of Zebedee), one of the Twelve Apostles who was chosen by YHWH Himself to receive the visions. John (Yochanan Bar Zawdi), the brother of James, as you might remember, was referred to as Yeshua's "favorite" or "beloved" disciple.

According to some historians, John was the only Apostle to survive to old age (Yeshua even alluded to his longevity in John 21:20-23). He was witness to many of the important events in Yeshua's ministry and was the only apostle to stand at the foot of the cross/stake when Yeshua was crucified (John 19:26). Also, John was the one to whom Yeshua entrusted His widowed mother as He was being led away to be executed (John 19:27).

> NOTE: No one can say for sure what happened to all the Apostles after the death of Yeshua, although some historians point out that they were

all martyred. We do know, however, that Stephen is generally regarded as the first martyr (Acts chapters 6 and 7); that John The Baptist was beheaded by Herod (Matthew 14:1-12); and that James was "put to death with the sword" by King Herod (Acts 12:2). Regardless whether or not the rest were all martyred, Luke 22 shows that Yeshua planned to reward them in the afterlife for their faithful service to Him:

Luke 22: 28. And you are those who have continued with me during my trials. 29. And I promise to you as my Father has promised to me, a Kingdom, 30. That you may eat and drink at the table of my Kingdom. And sit upon thrones and judge the twelve tribes of Yisrael.

John wrote what became the Book of Revelation after receiving a disturbing vision while being held prisoner by the Romans on the Island Of Patmos some time after 90 A.D. His purpose was to share his vision with the Seven Messianic communities of Asia (Revelation 1:11). These communities are reminiscent of today's congregations where disobedience and "worldliness" reign.

Revelation 1: 1. The Revelation of Y'shua the Mashiyach, which Elohim gave to him to show to his servants the things that must shortly occur: and he signified (it) by sending, through his Messenger to his servant Yochanan; 2. who bore witness to the Word of Elohim, and to the testimony of Y'shua the Mashiyach, as to all that he saw. 3. Blessed is he that reads, and they who hear the words of this prophecy, and keep the things that are written in it; for the time is near.

In Revelation 1:8, we come to one of the most important revelations in the entire Bible, as it brings to light something that many people - especially "trinitarians" -

overlook when they read this particular passage, because it reveals YHWH's nature and His "oneness."

Revelation 1: 8. *I am Alap, also Taw, says the Master YHWH, Elohim; who is, and was, and is to come, the omnipotent.*

Please note our Creator did not say, "I am Master **Yeshua**." This was YHWH, **THE** Creator Himself speaking of Himself as the Alap-Tav – the "First and the Last" (sometimes seen as "Alpha and Omega" when translated into Greek). Please read the following explanation very carefully and do not go any further until you fully understand the explanation provided by Andrew Gabriel Roth concerning the nature of our God:

> *Alap-Taw* (Alpha-Omega) holds a universe of meaning; each Hebrew/Aramaic letter holds many specific values. *Aleph* speaks of the absolute Unity of YHWH; *Taw* is the Perfection of YHWH; this is a *remez* (hint) of the Urim and Thummin (Exodus 28:29-31, Leviticus 8:7-9, Numbers 27:20-22, 1 Samuel 14:41, Ezra 2:62-64, Nehemiah 7:64-66). This also reveals "YHWH is Salvation" as the First, Last, Beginning and the End.
>
> The Ten Commandments begin with the letter Aleph, "*Anochi* (I) am YHWH your Elohim who has brought you out of the land of Egypt..." (Exodus 20:2). The Father YHWH is *Ain Sof* (without end) He is infinite; therefore, "the Arm of YHWH" (Mashiyach Yeshua) spoke and appeared to Moshe. *Taw* reveals the Perfection of Mashiyach; *Taw* is the first letter of *Tefilin* (prayers), Torah, *Teshuva* (turning to YHWH) which speaks of the transformation of the natural man into a *Tzadiq*, spiritual man. *Alap-Taw* speaks

155

of *Alap*/Head (*Keter*) and *Taw*/Feet (*Malchut*) of the *sefirot* and both the government of Mashiyach and the harmony of all things; and there are countless other Hebraic connections.

These words and letters are important to reveal the nature of Mashiyach, which is why such a sober warning is given in Revelation 22:18-19 ("Do not add to or subtract from this Book..."). The Greek translators either did not realize the prophetic significance of each word and letter, or perhaps the revelation was far too controversial in the religio-political system of their day, and that is why it is so important for Bible students to consider the original language (Aramaic), and the application of the four basic levels of interpretation: *peshat* (simple), *remez* (hint), *drash* (allegory) and *sod* (hidden) as they study. *Alap-Taw* speaks of Truth (*emet*) which is the basis for the true Faith (*emunah*) "which was once delivered to the set-apart believers."

YHWH was never, ever a "trinity" or "three persons" as espoused, for instance, in Baptist theology. If there were "three persons," then how could the "person" of the Holy Spirit possibly get inside each of us? Yeshua was not part of any "trinity"; rather, He was an "arm" of YHWH (Isaiah 53:1); the Son sent to us by YHWH in human form, the *only* part of YHWH who can actually claim to be a "Person." Yeshua came to represent His Father and to proclaim the Kingdom of YHWH (Luke 4:43). He was not someone who came to replace YHWH or to usurp His power, but to personally show us how to please and obey YHWH - and then to offer Himself as our Final *SIN* Sacrifice. YHWH is a Spirit, as is the *Ruach* - the Holy Spirit; the Bible tells us this:

*2 Corinthians 3: 17. Now Master YHWH Himself is the Spirit. And where the Spirit of Master YHWH is, there is freedom. 18. And we all, with uncovered faces, behold as in a mirror the glory of Master YHWH; and are transformed into the same likeness, from glory to glory, **as by Master YHWH the Spirit.***

The Son, Yeshua, had a Divine Nature - *qnoma* as we are told in John 5 and elsewhere:

John 5: 26. For as to the Father, there is life in his Qnoma (underlying substance).

1 Thessalonians 4: 9. Now concerning love to the Brothers, you need not that I should write to you; for your own Qnoma taught you of Elohim (and) to love one another.

Qnoma, as explained in the AENT, literally means, "Underlying substance." As Roth goes on to suggest, this very important term has been greatly diluted and misunderstood over the centuries.

> Through an exceedingly complex linguistic chain of events this word, meaning "an occurrence of a nature," was morphed and perverted into "person" in Greek. As a result, the One Elohim (YHWH) is represented in a pagan manner in the Greek New Testament as a "person" distinct and equal with "Elohim the Son" and "Elohim the Ruach haKodesh." Instead, it is the oneness of YHWH that manifests in Mashiyach, not that Mashiyach's divinity is separate from his Father's.
>
> In this case we are talking about humanity and not YHWH, and both of them have "natures" that cannot be seen, and yet are a root part of their being. Or, to put it another way, a "nature" is like

a body hidden behind a curtain. For those in the audience, nothing of that nature can be seen. Then, all of a sudden, a hand and part of an arm appears through the veil. While we know there is a body attached to that limb, the limb is all we see. Furthermore, that arm moves with full force, will and agreement of the mind that controls the body. For the viewers, the arm appearing out of the curtain is the *qnoma* (occurrence) and the hidden mind behind that limb's movement is its *kyanna* (nature).

As the centuries moved along, the ancient meaning of *qnoma* as "occurrence of a nature" devolved by Aramaic assemblies who compromised with the Byzantine Empire. Gradually, "core substance" became the common definition; at first it closely paralleled its Greek counterpart, *hypostasis*. More time passed and Greek redactors changed the meaning of *hypostasi*, taking it further from the original definition of *qnoma*. *Qnoma/hypostasis* became equivalent to "person" to line up with Greek passages that used this meaning in the form of the word *prospon*. In Greek, "person" implies a physical presence as opposed to Aramaic where body metaphors like "I will set my face towards" are very common. The revision began at the beginning of the Third Century when these same "westernized" Aramaic Christians began to proffer up readings in their "Peshitt-o" versions of Acts 20:28 and Hebrews 2:9 that were meant to align with the Byzantine majority Greek. However, the original eastern "Peshitt-a" escaped these revisions as it was in the rival Persian Empire. Aramaic, as in this verse, retains the original meaning of *qnoma*. It is NOT the external "person" that teaches someone about Elohim, but the *Ruach* (Holy Spirit) working through their "inner being." The idea of "person" in Greek, unfortunately, does not address the *neshama* (spirit) of a person as the likeness or "image of Elohim."

Getting back to John's revelation on Patmos:

Revelation 1: 10. *I was in the Spirit on the day of our Master YHWH; and I heard behind me a great voice, as of a shofar, which said: 11. That which you see, write in a book, and send to the seven assemblies; to Ephesus, and to Smyrna, and to Pergamos, and to Thyratira, and to Sardis, and to Philadelphia, and to Laodicea. 12. And I turned myself to look at the voice that talked with me; and when I had turned, I saw seven menorahs of gold; 13. and, in the midst of the menorahs, one like the Son of man, clothed to the feet, and turned about in a robe reaching to his feet with a girdle of gold. 14. And his head and his hair were white, like white wool, like snow; and his eyes, like a flame of fire: 15. and his feet were like fine brass, flaming in a furnace: and his voice, like the sound of many waters. 16. And he had in his right hand seven stars; and from his mouth issued a fervent spirit; and his countenance was like the sun shining in its strength. 17. And when I saw him, I fell at his feet like one dead. And he laid his right hand upon me, and said, fear not: I am the First and the Last; 18. and who lives and was dead; and behold, I am alive for ever and ever. Amen. And I have the keys of death and of the unseen world. 19. Therefore, write what you have seen, and the things that are; and the things that are to be after this: 20. the mystery of these seven stars which you saw in my right hand, and the seven menorahs of gold. Those seven stars are the Messengers of the seven assemblies; and the seven menorahs are the seven assemblies.*

What a terrifying experience it must have been for John to see Yeshua in His resurrected Body with "hair...white, like white wool, like snow; and his eyes, like a flame of fire" - the "Lion of Judah" (Revelation 5:5)! Unlike today's so-called "prophets" who are arrogant enough to believe Yeshua would visit someone who has never bothered to keep the Seventh Day Sabbath and the commanded Feasts while insisting the original divine instructions to mankind are a "curse", the **Torah observant** Apostle John (who had personally known Yeshua) *fainted* at the sight of our Savior! He then went on to describe events (as you will soon see) that NO ONE could possibly have known or understood two thousand years ago!

Of today's "prophets" who claim they've received a "word from Jesus", *none* ever suggest they saw Him as described above - let alone, *fainted* at the sight of Him. Instead, they normally utter nonsense about their supposed angelic visitations and describe in the "first person" the things "Jesus" supposedly said; things like, "*I, the Lord God, say to you, my child, I love you and am coming for you very soon*". These types of "prophecies" are normally circulated on the Internet by those who have deluded themselves into thinking they have some special insight into the Kingdom of YHWH, even though what they "prophesied" is pure "fluff" which in *no way* lines up with the Scriptures! Examples include the following:

- Marvelous "signs" from certain religious lunatics who try to tell the world they've unlocked the mysteries of the "Bible codes" (in which they often see their own names and the name of the President of the United States, etc.). These signs supposedly tell us that God is angry and is about to return and retaliate. Nothing new at all and - not surprisingly - these "codes" never tell us to start *obeying* YHWH's Word! (As an aside, the only "codes" in the Bible would be only those embedded in the Torah in the original languages of Hebrew and/or Aramaic. There is no way these codes could possibly end up in Bible versions translated into any other language!)

- Christian pastors and Messianic rabbis/teachers who are guilty of date-setting or presenting "new words from God," designed to enlighten the world. Some of these same pastors and rabbis are usually very overbearing, becoming angry and even abusive with anyone who doesn't agree with them. Case in point, there are a couple of Messianic rabbis who have written books about "the words from YHWH" they have presumably received; among them that YHWH wants men to have multiple wives and that "sister wives" should get themselves male concubines if they cannot wait for their husbands to "get around" to them. The Bible, understood in context, reveals that YHWH never, ever suggested that man should have more than one wife. He did, however, provide rules for those who took multiple wives in order to ensure their fair treatment.

- Flying saucer cults such as the "Raelians" whose founder "Rael" (apparently he took his name from the last four letters of Israel) freely sprinkles Bible quotes throughout the "messages" he supposedly received from an all-knowing, all-seeing four-foot tall alien who supposedly created life on Earth (see rael.org). Rael quotes on his website: "In fact, we were created in their image as explained in the Bible."

- Those who believe themselves to have special insight into, and attempt to set exact dates and times for the "rapture." No one, including Yeshua

Himself, while walking on the earth, was privy to the exact date and time (Matthew 24:36, Mark 13:29-32, Acts 1:7). We are commanded to know when it's "near at the door," but not to speculate about the *exact* time, because YHWH wants us to concentrate *not* on worldly events but, rather, on our "getting spiritually right" with Him, which is the most important thing we could possibly do.

*Mark 13: 21. If at that time a man should say to you, "Behold, here is the Mashiyach!" or "Behold, there he is!" do not believe him. 22. **For false Messiahs and lying prophets will give signs and wonders and will deceive even the elect if it is possible.** 23. But you take heed! Behold, I have told you everything beforehand. 24. And in those days after that suffering, the sun will be darkened and the moon will not give its light. 25. And the stars will fall from heaven, and the powers of heaven will be shaken. 26. And then they will see the Son of man when he comes in the clouds with great power and with glory. 27. Then he will send his Messengers and assemble his chosen from the four winds - from the beginning of the earth and up to the beginning of heaven. 28. Now from the fig tree learn the parable that when its branches are tender and sprout its leaves, you know summer has arrived. 29. **Likewise, also when you see these things occur, know that it is near at the door.** 30. Truly I say to you, that this tribe will not pass until all these things occur. 31. **Heaven and earth will pass, but my words will not pass.** 32. **But concerning that day and concerning that hour, man does not know, not even the Messengers of heaven nor the Son, only the Father knows.** 33. Watch! Be alert and pray for you do not know when is the time.*

- I've known one Christian pastor for many years who has a "prophetic ministry"; and, instead of telling the people on his mailing list to get themselves *spiritually right* with God, he mainly concentrates on perpetuating anti-government "conspiracy theories" and urging people to move out of the cities, to buy as much gold as they can, and to hoard canned food and water, etc. I've asked him what good *gold* could possibly do when the entire world in those days will be trying to figure out how to survive from day to day, scrounging whatever food and water they are able to get....I guess he forgot about all the scriptures that tell us not to "store up treasures for ourselves" (Proverbs 23:4, Matthew 6:19, Matthew 19:21, Luke 12:21, Luke 18:22, 1 Timothy 6:9, 1 Timothy 6:10, Hebrews 13:5, James 5:2.)

- Christian "prophets" who proclaim to be speaking on behalf of YHWH, often in first person terms, providing vague generalities such as, *"I, the Lord your God, am judging the raging sins of America and the nations. I am about to destroy your religiosity and secular foundations."* If YHWH were truly to speak to someone, He wouldn't be repeating the obvious, or the "old news" which has been outlined in the Bible for several millennia. One of the first things He would do is to correct the behavior of the "prophets," telling them to start using His true Name instead of the simple title of "God," and to quit ignoring His commanded Seventh Day Sabbath and the Feasts. He would tell them to stop eating "unclean" foods and get their own houses in order before attempting to tell everyone else what to do. Unfortunately, many people fall for these so-called "prophets" and actually change their entire lives based on what these *scheisters* have said.

Romans 1: 22. And, while they thought within themselves

that they were wise, they became fools. 23. And they changed the glory of the incorruptible Elohim into a likeness to the image of a corruptible man, and into the likeness of birds and four-legged animals and reptiles on the earth. 24. For this cause, Elohim gave them up to the fill your lusts of their hearts, to dishonor their bodies with them. 25. And they changed the truth of Elohim into a lie; and worshipped and served the created things, much more than the Creator of them, to whom belong glory and blessing, forever and ever. Amen. 26. For this cause, Elohim gave them up to vile passions: for their females changed the use of their natures and employed that which is unnatural. 27. And so also their males set aside the use of females, which is natural, and burned with lust toward one another; and, male with male, they did what is shameful, and received in their core substance the just recompense of their error. 28. And as they did not determine with themselves to know Elohim, Elohim gave them over to a vain mind; that they might do what they should not. 29. Being full of all iniquity and lewdness, and bitterness and malice, and covetousness and envy, and slaughter and strife, and deceit and evil machinations 30. And backbiting and slander; and being haters of Elohim, scoffers, proud, vain-glorious, devisers of evil things, destitute of reason, disregardful of parents. 31. And to whom a covenant is nothing, neither affection, nor peace, and in whom is no compassion. 32. These, while they know the judgment of Elohim, that he condemns those to death who perpetrate such things, are not only doers of them, but the companions of such as do them.

- One can find off-the-mark teachings in every religion or denomination. Case in point: A female bishop of the Episcopal church had some "insight" that led her to believe she should begin referring to Yeshua as "Mother Jesus" (Miami Herald, Nov. 2, 2006). So much for the fact that **HE *was circumcised*** on the eighth day (Luke 2:21)! This same woman also made the comment, "God makes some people gay." Apparently, YHWH contradicts Himself? In Scripture (see Leviticus 18:22,1 Corinthians 6:9-10; Romans 1:22-32 and Revelation 22:14-15) He calls homosexuality an abomination and outlines His utter disgust over this issue....

- There are even "prophet schools" that claim to *teach* people how to become prophets. (So much for the idea that *YHWH* gives us various gifts that are not learned or taught by men - 1 Corinthians 12:9-11, 1 Corinthians 14:21-23, 2 Peter 1:19-21, 2 Peter 1:20-21, Romans 12 and Ephesians 4.)

The bottom line is this: Yeshua said in Mark 13:23: *"But you take heed! Behold, I have told you everything beforehand."* This means *there are no new* revelations from God; the Bible already contains everything we need to know...And it amply warns us to watch out for end times false teachers and prophets who insist they have received a "word from God" that goes beyond Scripture, or doesn't line up with what is written:

Matthew 7: 20. Therefore, by their fruits you will know them. 21. It will not be that just anyone who says to me "My master, my master" will enter the Kingdom of Heaven, but whoever does the will of my Father who is in heaven. 22. Many will say to me in that day, "My master, my master. By your name, have we not prophesied? And by your name have we cast out demons? And by your name have we done many miracles?" 23. And then I will profess to them that from everlasting, I have not known you. Depart from me, you workers of iniquity!

Matthew 24: 11. And many false prophets will arise and deceive many. 12. And because of the growth of iniquity, the love of many will grow cold. 13. But whoever has patience until the end, he will have life.

Matthew 24: 24. For false Messiahs and lying prophets will arise and they will produce signs and great wonders in order to deceive if possible even the chosen.

2 Timothy 4: 3. For the time will come when they will not give ear to sound teaching; but, according to their lusts, will multiply to themselves teachers in the itching of their hearing; 4. and will turn away their ears from the truth, and incline after fables.

2 Peter 2: 1. But in the world there have been also false prophets, as there will likewise be false teachers among you who will bring in destructive heresies denying Master YHWH that bought them; thus bringing on themselves swift destruction.

Chapter 11

The Covenant and Seal

Moving on, let's continue with the Book of Revelation which was written by a *true* prophet, Yochanan Bar Zawdi (John), who provided insights into the end times that no one of that time could possibly have foretold, much less understood:

Early in Revelation, we are told that those who draw close to YHWH and do His will, will be rewarded:

Revelation 2: 7. He that has ears, let him hear what the Spirit says to the assemblies. 8. To him who is victorious, will I give to eat of the tree of life which is in the paradise of my Elohim.

Revelation 2: 10. Be faithful to death, and I will give you the crown of life. 11. He that has ears, let him hear what the Spirit says to the assemblies. He that is victorious, will not be harmed by the second death.

What is the "second death"? We first encountered this term in Chapter 6 when discussing what happens to unbelievers. According to the Bible, the first resurrection is for the righteous; the second for the wicked who are destined for destruction. (See Daniel 12:1-2, Luke 14:14 and John 11:24-25.) Those who belong to YHWH will receive eternal life when they pass from this world; but the unbelievers and "lukewarm" and ungodly will die once here on Earth, *and a second time* on Judgment Day when they will be cast from YHWH's Presence forever. This, then, is the "second death". In Revelation 21, we get an in-your-face glimpse of the type of person who will

167

experience the second death and be eternally separated from YHWH:

Revelation 21: 6. *And he said to me: I am Alap and the Taw, the Beginning and the Completion: to him who thirsts, will I give of the fountain of living water, freely. 7. He that overcomes will inherit these things; and I will be his Elohim, and he will be my son. 8. But to the timid and the unbelieving, and to the sinful and polluted, and to manslayers and whoremongers, and sorcerers, and idolaters, and to all false persons, their portion will be in the lake that burns with fire and sulfur, which is the second death.*

This is quite a contrast to what happens to those who will enter eternal life:

Revelation 2: 17. *He that has ears, let him hear what the Spirit says to the assemblies. To him that is victorious, will I give to eat of the hidden manna; and I will give him a white counter, and upon the counter a new name written which no one knows but he that receives it.*

Revelation 2: 26. *And to him that is victorious, and to him that observes my works to the end, to him will I give authority over the nations; 27. and he will rule them with a rod of iron; and like vessels of pottery, will they be broken: as I also have received of my Father. 28. And I will give him the morning star. 29. He that has ears, let him hear what the Spirit says to the assemblies.*

Revelation 3: 5. *He that is victorious will be so clothed in white robes; and I will not blot out their name from the book of life; and I will confess their name before my Father and before his Messengers. 6. He that has ears, let him hear what the Spirit says to the assemblies.*

Revelation 3: 12. *Him that is victorious, will I make a pillar in the temple of my Elohim; and he will not again go out: and I will write*

168

upon him the name of my Elohim, and of the new Urishlim
(Jerusalem) *which descends from heaven from my Elohim, and my*
own new name. 13. He that has ears, let him hear what the Spirit
says to the assemblies.

Revelation 4: 20. Behold, I have been standing at the door, and I
will knock: if any man hear my voice and open the door, I will come
in to him, and will dine with him, and he with me. 21. And to him
that is victorious, to him will I give to sit with me on my throne,
even as I was victorious and sat down with my Father on his
throne. 22. He that has ears to hear, let him hear what the Spirit
says to the assemblies.

Through John's vision, we receive a glimpse into Heaven.
In Revelation 4 which follows, note how the descriptions
of YHWH and Yeshua ultimately end up flowing together,
not denoting separate Entities, but **ONE** Elohim. Notice
also how the four creatures cited resemble our Savior in
various ways: As a lion (the Lion of Yehudah); a calf (our
Final Sin Sacrifice); and one that had a "face like a man"
(His human side); and "an eagle when flying" (symbolizing
strength and freedom from "the world" - or, perhaps this is
Yeshua speaking through the eagle mentioned in
Revelation 8:13).

Revelation 4: 1. After these things, I looked and behold, a gate
opened in heaven. And the first voice which I heard was as of a
shofar talking with me. It said, Come up here; and I will show you
the things that must occur afterwards. 2. Instantly, I was in the
Spirit: and behold, a throne was placed in heaven; and there was
(one) seated on the throne. 3. And he who sat, was like the
appearance of a jasper-stone, and of a sardonyx (sard), and of a
rainbow of the clouds, round about the throne, in form as the
appearance of emeralds. 4. Around the throne were twenty and four
seats; and upon those seats sat twenty and four Elders, who were
clothed in white robes, and on whose heads were crowns of gold. 5.

169

And from the throne proceeded flashes of lightning, and the sound of thunders; and seven lamps of fire were burning before his throne, which are the seven Spirits of Elohim. 6. And before the throne, as it were a sea of glass like crystal; and in the midst of the throne, and around it, and before the throne were four creatures full of eyes in their front and in their rear. 7. And the first creature resembled a lion; and the second creature resembled a calf; and the third creature had a face like a man; and the fourth creature resembled an eagle when flying. 8. And these four creatures had, each of them, six wings around it: and within they were full of eyes: and they have no cessation, day or night, from saying: Kadosh, Kadosh, Kadosh, (Holy, Holy, Holy) *the Master YHWH, Elohim, the Omnipotent, who was, and is, and is to come. 9. And when these creatures give glory and honor and praise to him that sits on the throne, to him who lives forever and ever, 10. the twenty and four Elders fall down before him who sits on the throne, and they worship him who lives forever and ever; and they cast their crowns before the throne, saying, 11. Worthy are you, our Master (Y'shua) and our Elohim, the Set Apart, to receive glory and honor and power; for you have created all things, and by you they exist; and because of your pleasure they had being and were created.*

YHWH's wrath begins with the Seal Judgments:

Revelation 5: 1. And I saw, at the right hand of him who sat on the throne, a book which was written within and on the back side, and which was sealed with seven seals. 2. And I saw a strong Messenger who proclaimed with a loud voice, Who is worthy to open the book, and to loose the seals here? 3. And no one either in heaven above, or on the earth, or beneath the earth was able to open the book, or even to look upon it. 4. And I wept greatly because no one was found who was able to open the book or to look on it. 5. And one of the Elders said to me, Weep not; behold, the Lion of the tribe of Yehuda, the Root of Dawid, has been victorious: He will open the book and its seven seals. 6. And I looked, and in the midst of the Elders stood a lamb, as if slain; and it had seven horns and seven eyes which are the seven Spirits of Elohim that are sent into

170

all the earth. 7. And he came, and took the book from the right hand of him who sat on the throne. 8. And when he took the book, the four Creatures and the twenty and four Elders fell down before the Lamb, each of them having a harp, and cups of gold full of aromas which are the supplications of the Set Apart believers. 9. And they sung a new song, saying: Worthy are you, to take the book, and to open the seals; because you were slain and have redeemed us to Elohim by your blood, out of every tribe and tongue and people and nation; 10. and you have made them kings and priests to our Elohim; and they reign on the earth. 11. And I looked, and I heard, as it were the voice of many Messengers around the throne, and the creatures and the Elders; and the number of them was a myriad of myriads, and thousands of thousands 12. who said, with a loud voice; Worthy is the Lamb that was slain, to receive power and riches, and wisdom and strength, and honor and glory and blessing; 13. and (to be over) every created thing that is in heaven or on earth, or under the earth, or in the sea; and all that are in them. And I heard him who sat on the throne say: To the Lamb be given blessing and honor, and glory and power, forever and ever. 14. And the four creatures said: Amen. And the Elders fell down, and adored.

…And then, suddenly, we are introduced to "four horsemen" – one riding a white horse; one a red horse; another a black horse; and the last, a pale horse….

Revelation 6: 1. And when the Lamb had opened one of the seven seals, I looked, and I heard one of the four Creatures say, as with a voice of thunder, Come, and see. 2. And I looked, and there was a white horse: and he who sat on it had a bow; and a crown was given to him, and he went forth conquering, that he might conquer.

There are myriad suggestions as to what the "four horsemen" might represent (and we will only know for sure once we have left this world and received our eternal bodies). Traditionally, they have been described as Pestilence, War, Famine and Death. The German-language

171

Lutheran *Stuttgarter Erklärungsbibel*, for instance, sees the first horseman as war and internal strife. However, I tend to believe that the first horseman is "religion/religiosity" as it mimics Yeshua on a white horse, as we see later on in Revelation 19: *11. And I saw heaven opened: and lo, a white horse; and he that sat on it is called Faithful and True: and in righteousness he judges, and makes war.*

"Religion and religiosity" have been bitter enemies of YHWH. Millions have been killed in the name of "religion" over nonexistent gods that in no way resemble the Creator, YHWH, who sent His Son to become our Final Sin Sacrifice. Instead, the world's religions have masqueraded as "good" and holy while, in reality, catering to *haSatan* and wreaking tremendous havoc with their false teachings.

This, in my opinion, includes Christianity which claims to worship the God of Abraham, Isaac and Jacob, but has categorically denied the need for **obedience** to His Torah, even going so far as to call Torah "a curse!" Instead of following the teachings of our Torah observant Jewish Messiah, Yeshua, "the church" insists on adhering to the misunderstood writings of the mere mortal, Paul who - although they keep overlooking this fact - was completely Torah observant, himself!

It's the rare person who has been astute enough to ask how **any commands** our Creator ever put forth concerning holy behavior could end up being a "curse." How could the laws YHWH had Moshe **write upon stone** end up being a curse? After all, the Ten Commandments are part of Torah! How could the Seventh Day Sabbath end up as a curse, when YHWH Himself rested on the Seventh day, and then later told mankind the seventh day was to be a **sign** between Him and His people **forever** (Ezekiel 20:1112; Isaiah 66:23; Isaiah 58:13)....

172

Instead of recognizing that YHWH did not make His New Covenant with the Gentiles, but with the Torah observant Houses of Israel and Judah (Jeremiah 31:32), "the church" decided not only to ignore His commanded Seventh Day Sabbath and the Feasts, but they've changed the Name of our Savior (from Yeshua to "Jesus" which detracts from the original meaning of His Name: "YHWH is Salvation") along with the dates of His birth, death and resurrection - and all the while, dining on swine and shellfish and other "unclean foods," simply because they *believe* Paul taught this! Somehow, they believe that YHWH would treat His adopted children differently from His natural ones - never mind that YHWH, over and over, reiterated that ALL who worship Him are to obey His Torah. (Example: Numbers 15:13-16)

Moving on, in Revelation 6 we see the "red" and "black" and "pale" horses, which denote wars, famines, agony and death - all things mankind has already suffered, and will continue to suffer until the end comes!

*Revelation 6: 3. And when he had opened the **second seal**, I heard the second Creature say, Come. 4. And there went forth another, a red horse; and to him who sat upon it, it was given to take peace from the earth; and that they should kill one another; and there was given to him a great sword.*

Who has taken "peace from the earth" since the beginning? Satan, of course! Who has caused man to experience unholy emotions such as the murderous rage and jealousy Cain exhibited towards Abel (Genesis 4)? Satan! And he has never let up, as is evidenced in the never-ending wars and terrorist acts perpetrated by man.

*Revelation 6: 5. And when he had opened the **third seal**, I heard the third Creature say, Come, and see. And I looked, and behold, a black* *horse; and he that sat upon it, had a balance in his hand. 6. And I heard a voice in the midst of the four Creatures, saying: A quart of wheat for a denarius, and three measures of barley for a denarius; and hurt not the oil and the wine.* (In other words, these things will be extremely hard to come by one of these days!) *7. And when he had opened the **fourth seal**, I heard the fourth Creature say: Come, and see. 8. And I looked, and behold, a pale horse; and the name of him who sat on it was Death; and Gehenna followed after him. And there was given him authority over the fourth part of the earth, to slay with the sword, and by famine, and by death, and by the ravenous beast of the earth. 9. And when he had opened the **fifth seal**, I saw under the altar the souls of them who were slain on account of the Word of Elohim, and on account of the testimony to the Lamb which was with them.*

How many times in history has mankind experienced famine and plagues? How many people have been violently murdered in one way or another (including "by the sword" as is the Muslim way)? How often have we heard of "ravenous beasts" (bears, mountain lions, sharks and all types of wild animals that have been forced out of the wild to become household pets, such as apes and pythons) killing humans, or of locust swarms eating entire fields of precious grains? Many diseases were and still are caused by "beasts" - such as the Plagues of Frogs (Exodus 8:1-15), insects (Exodus 8:1-15), flies (Exodus 8:20-32) and locusts (Exodus 10:1-20). In the Middle Ages flea infested rats were the cause of millions of deaths through the Bubonic Plague. More recently, we have seen *"Bovine spongiform encephalopathy commonly known as mad-cow disease, is a fatal, neurodegenerative disease in cattle....caused by cattle, who are normally herbivores, being fed the remains of other cattle in the form of meat and bone meal, which caused the infectious agent to spread"* (Source: Wikipedia).

We can only surmise that these events, thanks to man's ignorance and unwillingness to heed YHWH, will increase greatly before Yeshua's return....

Revelation 6: 10. And they cried with a loud voice, saying: How long, O Master YHWH, you Set Apart and True, do you not Judge and avenge our blood on them that dwell on the earth? 11. And to each one of them was given a white robe; and it was told them that they must be quiet yet a little while, until the consummation of their fellow-servants and Brothers who were to be killed as they had been. 12. And I looked when he had opened the sixth seal, and there was a great earthquake; and the sun became black, like sackcloth of hair; and the whole moon became like blood. 13. And the stars of heaven fell on the earth as a fig-tree casts its unripe figs, when it is shaken by a strong wind. 14. And the heavens separated, as a scroll is rolled up: and all mountains and islands were removed out of their places. 15. And the kings of the earth, and the nobles, and the captains of thousands, and the rich men, and the men of valor, and every servant and free man hid themselves in caves, and in the clefts of the mountains; 16. and they said to the mountains and to the clefts, Fall over us, and hide us from the face of him who sits on the throne, and from the wrath of the Lamb: 17. For the great day of their wrath is come; and who is able to stand?

I firmly believe we are entering the sixth seal right now! Man has already endured famines, sickness, death, wars and violence, and untold horrors, etc., but we have not yet seen the sun turning black or the moon becoming like blood, nor witnessed the stars falling to earth by the thousands or even millions. We have not yet witnessed the heavens separating or the mountains and islands removed from their places. From Revelation 6:10-17 above, you can see mankind will have gone through all kinds of horrendous tribulations by the time the sixth seal is opened. And we're nowhere near the "last shofar" yet! The things that happen *after* the sixth seal is opened are nothing short of terrifying!   And it's only just the beginning of man's woes....

Revelation 7: 1. And after these things I saw four Messengers who stood on the four corners of the earth; and they held the four winds of the earth, so that the wind blew not on the earth, nor on the sea, nor on the trees. 2. And I saw another Messenger, and he came up from the rising of the sun; and he had the seal of the living Elohim; and he called out with a loud voice to the four Messengers to whom it was given to hurt the earth and the sea, saying: 3. Hurt you not the earth, nor the sea, nor the trees, until we will have sealed the servants of our Elohim upon their foreheads. 4. And I heard the number of them that were sealed a hundred and forty and four thousand, sealed from every tribe of Israelites.

Jehovah's Witnesses insist "only a little flock of 144,000 go to heaven to rule with Christ" - and, naturally, they believe these to be Jehovah's Witnesses. One wonders why Jehovah's Witnesses would be "the" anointed flock because, as is espoused at Watchtower.org: (1) Jehovah's Witnesses are not Torah observant; (2) they believe "Christ is God's Son and is inferior to him"; and that (3) "Jesus Christ is Michael the Archangel." Furthermore, apparently, no one has ever told them that, by using the name "Jehovah", they *cannot* be referring to the God of Abraham, Isaac and Jacob, because there is no "J" in Hebrew and YHWH never said His Name was or would be pronounced "Jehovah"; it's pronounced "Yahweh." As a matter of fact, if you were to dissect the word Jehovah, you would come up with "Je" (for Yah) and *hovah* in Hebrew, which means "mischief, ruin, disaster"!

YHWH revealed his exact Name to Moshe (Moses) in Exodus 3:

Exodus 3: 13 Moshe said to God, "Look, when I appear before the people of Isra'el and say to them, 'The God of your ancestors has sent me to you'; and they ask me, 'What is his name?' what am I to tell them?" God said to Moshe, "Ehyeh Asher Ehyeh [I am/will be what I am/will be]," and added, "Here is what to say to the people of Isra'el: 'Ehyeh [I Am or I Will Be] has sent me to you.'" God said further to Moshe, "Say this to the people of Isra'el: 'Yud-Heh-Vav-Heh [יהוה], the God of your fathers, the God of Avraham, the God of Yitz'chak and the God of Ya'akov, has sent me to you. This is my name forever; this is how I am to be remembered generation after generation.

Since He gave us His proper Name, why aren't we using it? Who said we could add or subtract to any part of the Bible, including the changing of YHWH's Name?

Neither Jehovah's Witnesses nor most who proclaim to believe in God seem to realize that **Torah is the Covenant and Seal** that YHWH progressively revealed to mankind through Adam, Noach, Avraham and all His chosen prophets and people! Therefore, those who will be "sealed" are none other than those who have the testimony of Yeshua AND obey His Torah.

Revelation 7: 4. And I heard the number of them that were sealed a hundred and forty and four thousand, sealed from every tribe of Israelites. 5. Of the tribe of Yehuda, twelve thousand were sealed: of the tribe of Reuben, twelve thousand: of the tribe of Gad, twelve thousand: 6. of the tribe of Ashur, twelve thousand: of the tribe of Naphtali, twelve thousand: of the tribe of Manasseh, twelve thousand: 7. of the tribe of Simeon, twelve thousand: of the tribe of Levi, twelve thousand: of the tribe of Issachar, twelve thousand: 8. of the tribe of Zebulon, twelve thousand: of the tribe of Yosip, twelve thousand: of the tribe of Benjamin, twelve thousand. 9. And after these things, I looked, and lo, a great multitude which no one could number, from all kindreds and nations and tribes and tongues;

who stood before the throne and before the Lamb, clothed in white robes, and palms in their hands; 10. and they cried with a loud voice, saying: Salvation to our Elohim, to him who sits on the throne, and to the Lamb. **11. And all the Messengers stood around the throne and the Elders and the four Creatures; and they fell upon their faces before his throne, and worshipped Elohim,** *12. saying: Amen. Blessing and glory, and wisdom and thanksgiving, and honor and power and might, (be) to our Elohim, forever and ever. Amen. 13. And one of the Elders turned and said to me: These who are clothed in white robes, who are they and whence came they? 14. And I said to him: My Master (Y'shua), you know. And he said to me: These are they who came from great affliction; and they have washed their robes and made them white in the blood of the Lamb. 15. Therefore are they before the throne of Elohim; and they serve him day and night in his temple; and he who sits on the throne will protect them: 16. they will not hunger, nor thirst anymore; nor will the sun fall on them, nor any heat. 17. Because the Lamb which is in the midst of the throne, will feed them; and will lead them to fountains of living water; and Elohim will wipe every tear from their eyes.*

As we move through the chapters of Revelation, we can almost feel the horrors unfurling on the horizon....And still no sign of the "last shofar"!

Revelation 8: 1. And when he had opened the seventh seal, there was silence in heaven for about half an hour. 2. And I saw the seven Messengers who stood before Elohim; **and to them were given seven shofars.** (Please note, there are seven shofars and here the first one hasn't even been sounded yet....) *3. And another Messenger came and stood by the altar; and he held a golden censer: and much incense was given him so that he might offer, with the prayers of all the Set Apart believers, upon the golden altar before the throne. 4. And the smoke of the incense of the prayers of the Set Apart believers went up before Elohim from the hand of the Messenger. 5. And the Messenger took the censer, and filled it with* *fire from the altar and cast it upon the earth: and there were thunders, and flashes of lightning, and voices, and an earthquake.*

YHWH's wrath continues to grow as we enter the seven Trumpet/shofar Judgments – no special explanation needed:

*Revelation 8: 6. And the seven Messengers who had the seven shofars, prepared themselves to sound. 7. **And the first sounded;** and there was hail and fire which were mingled with water: and these were thrown upon the earth; and a third part of the earth was burned up, and a third part of the trees were burned, and all green grass was burned. 8. And the **second Messenger sounded** and, as it were a great mountain burning with fire, was cast into the sea; and also a third part of the sea became blood. 9. And a third part of all the creatures in the sea that had life, died; and a third part of the ships were destroyed. 10. And the **third Messenger sounded,** and there fell from heaven a star burning like a lamp; and it fell upon a third part of the rivers and upon the fountains of water. 11. And the name of the star was called Wormwood; and a third part of the waters became wormwood; and many persons died from the waters because they were bitter. 12. And the **fourth Messenger sounded,** and a third part of the sun was smitten, and the third part of the moon, and the third part of the stars; so that the third part of them were dark, and they became dark; and the day did not give light for the third part of it, and the night in like manner. 13. **And I saw and heard an eagle which flew in the midst, and it had a tail of blood, while it said with a loud voice: Woe, woe, to them who dwell on the earth because of the remaining sounds of the trumpets of the three Messengers, who are to sound.***

Please pay special attention to all the things that happen after each Messenger sounds! Our God is not kidding around!

179

Revelation 9: 1. And the fifth Messenger sounded; and I saw a star which fell from heaven upon the earth. And there was given to him the key of the pit of the abyss (Yeshua!). *2. And he opened the pit of the abyss; and smoke issued from the pit, like the smoke of a furnace that is in blast; and the sun and the air were darkened by the smoke of the pit. 3. And out of the smoke came locusts upon the earth: and power was given them, like that which scorpions have on the earth.* **4. And it was commanded them that they should not hurt the grass of the earth, nor any herb, nor any tree; but (only) the persons who had not the seal of Elohim upon their foreheads.** *5. And it was given them, that they should not kill them, but should torment them five months: and their torment was like the torment of a scorpion when it strikes a person. 6. And in those days, men will desire death and will not find it; and they will long to die, and death will fly from them. 7. And the appearance of the locusts (was this); they were like the appearance of horses prepared for battle; and on their heads was, as it were a crown, resembling gold; and their faces were like the faces of men. 8. And they had hair, like the hair of women: and their teeth were like those of lions. 9. And they had breastplates, like breastplates of iron: and the sound of their wings was like the sound of the chariots of many horses rushing into battle. 10. And they had tails like those of scorpions, and stings; and with their tails they had the power of hurting men five months. 11. And they had a king over them, the Messenger of the abyss; and his name, in Hebrew, is Abaddon; and in Greek, his name is Apollyon. 12. One woe is past; behold, there come yet two woes after them.*

There has been much speculation about the locusts. Some have speculated that these "locusts" represent various kinds of military equipment, including bombers and tanks and helicopters. But, again, who is to say these things have to be man-made? Perhaps they will be exactly as described – evil beings from the pit; maybe even the nephillim, the fallen angels. After all, they came out of the pit, preceded by thick smoke that darkened the sun, and their master was Abaddon, a word you can look up in

Strong's Concordance, with the meanings of ruin; destruction; the place of destruction; the name of the angel-prince of the infernal regions; the minister of death and the author of havoc on the earth. They were allowed by YHWH to emerge to torture the unbelievers of this world! This is not man doing something to man; this is GOD's wrath to show the stubborn exactly *who* is in charge!

*Revelation 9: 13. And the sixth Messenger sounded; and I heard a voice from the horns of the golden altar which was before Elohim, 14. that said to the sixth Messenger having a trumpet: Loose the four Messengers that are bound at the great river Euphrates. 15. And the **four Messengers were loosed; who are prepared, for an hour, and a day, and a month, and a year, to slay the third part of men.** 16. And the number of the warrior horsemen was two myriads of myriads: and I heard their number. 17. And while I looked on the horses in the vision, and on them who sat on them (I saw) that the breastplates were of fire and of jacinth and of sulfur. And the heads of the horses were like the heads of lions; and from their mouths issued fire and smoke and sulfur. 18. And **by these three plagues, a third part of the men were slain; (namely,) by the fire, and by the smoke, and by the sulfur which issued from their mouths.** 19. For the power of the horses was in their mouth and in their tails; for their tails were like serpents, having heads to strike with. 20. And the remnant of men who were not slain by these plagues repented not of the works of their hands and worshipped demons, and idols of gold, and of silver, and brass, and stone, and wood, which cannot see nor hear. 21. And they repented not of their murders nor of their sorceries, nor of their sexual sins, nor of their thefts.*

Again, it is unclear as to whether these will be actual horses with supernatural powers, or whether they represent tanks of some kind. Regardless, it is undeniable that these things are dangerous and *will* kill – and even then, most people will *not* "get it" and repent before

YHWH! By now, surely everyone on earth will have heard that the worldwide disasters are a result of the end times prophesied in the Bible. Yet, most will ignore the warnings and continue to label believers as "religious kooks"....

John was shown that things would get so bad by the time that last shofar sounded, that "a voice from heaven" commanded the horrors to be sealed up:

Revelation 10: 1. And I saw another mighty Messenger that descended from heaven, clothed with a cloud; and a cloud-bow was over his head, and his face was like the sun, and his feet like pillars of fire. 2. And he had in his hand an open little book and he placed his right foot upon the sea, and his left upon the land: 3. and he cried with a loud voice, as a lion roars: and when he had cried, the seven thunders shouted their voices.

Nothing man-made here! As you have probably realized by now, there are a lot of strange, unusual and unfamiliar things going on in the spiritual realm. The end times will surely leave the world stunned with creatures and events that can only be described as "other-worldly." Apparently we humans here on Earth will not be able to see the messengers who are sent and commanded to perform various acts; but we will definitely see the end results of the wrath that will unfold.

Revelation 10: 4. And when the seven thunders had spoken, I was about to write. And I heard a voice from heaven, saying: Seal up the things which the seven thunders have spoken, and write them not. 5. And the Messenger whom I saw standing upon the sea and the land, raised his right hand to heaven, 6. and swore by him who lives forever and ever, who created heaven and the things in it, and the earth and the things in it, and the sea and the things in it, that the time should be no longer; 7. but, in the days of the voice of the seventh Messenger, when he will sound and the mystery of Elohim will be consummated; as he announced to his servants the prophets. 8. And the voice which I heard from heaven spoke to me again, and said: Go, take the little open book in the hand of the Messenger that stands on the sea and on the land. 9 And I went to the Messenger, telling him to give me the little book. And he said to me, Take, and eat it: and it will make your bowels bitter, but in your mouth it will be sweet as honey. 10. And I took the little book from the hand of the Messenger, and ate it: and it was in my mouth sweet like honey: and when I had eaten it, my bowels were bitter. 11. And he said to me, You must again prophesy upon many nations and peoples, and princes, and kings.

It's anybody's guess as to what "the little book" is. Perhaps it represents Torah, which is sweet in our mouths, but can have dire consequences when ignored because, unless we know YHWH's Torah, we cannot ever have a true connection with Him.

Anyway, before that last shofar sounds, John shares with us the last few prophecies he was given concerning the things that will happen before YHWH finally puts an end to Man's nonsense. Among them are John's vision about the Third Temple which we've already discussed in Chapter 7 (and which is also outlined in Appendix 5):

Revelation 11: 1. And a reed was given to me, like a rod; and the Messenger stood, saying, Arise and measure the temple of Elohim, and the altar, and them that worship inside it. (Those who are worshipping are measured/judged, along with the Temple - see Matthew 7; 1 Peter 4:17.) *2. But the court which is without the temple, leave out, and measure it not, because it is given to the Gentiles; and they will tread down the Set Apart city forty and two months.* (Again, this reveals that the Third Temple will be on Earth during the Millennium, because there will be no "Jew" or "Gentile" in heaven, as we are

ONE in Messiah!) *3. And I will give my two witnesses; and they will prophesy a thousand and two hundred and sixty days, clothed in sackcloth. 4. These are the two olive-trees and the two menorahs which stand before Master YHWH of the earth.*

Note that the two witnesses are the two olive-trees and the two menorahs – more on this later. Who are they in human terms? Many "two-house" or "two-stick" types (who believe that Ephraim and Yehudah will become "one stick" in the end times) insist that the two witnesses are the two Houses of Israel. The thing is, we are told there are only TWO witnesses, not thousands! YHWH will allow these *two* to prophesy in Jerusalem for a thousand two hundred and sixty days, clothed in sackcloth, and then be killed….

Therefore, a good guess as to who these "two witnesses" are is derived from the following:

The prophet Zechariah first mentions the two witnesses in Zechariah 4:

Zechariah 4: 11 I replied by asking him, "What are those two olive trees on the right and left sides of the menorah?" 12 Then I asked the question again: "What are those two olive branches discharging gold[-colored oil] through the two gold spouts?" 13 He replied, "Don't you know what they are?" I answered, "No, my Lord." 14 He said, "Those are the two who have been anointed with oil; they are standing with the Lord of all the land."

According to Numbers 35:30 and Deuteronomy 17:6; 19:15, YHWH requires two or more witnesses to obtain His Judgment. This is a legal requirement that establishes and ensures YHWH's authority, rather than man's. (See also 1 Cor. 14:27-29; 2 Cor. 13:1; 1 Tim 5:19; Hebrews 10:28.) The individuals YHWH raises up are well qualified to do His bidding according to HIS laws!

The two witnesses referred to in Revelation 11:3 above (who could be any of the prophets of old such as Moses and Elijah), will boldly declare YHWH's judgments and deliver His messages and condemnation the whole time they are on earth - just before all hell breaks loose upon those who have continuously rejected Him (Isaiah 41:27; 30:27)!

Today Israel's national symbol is a menorah flanked by two olive branches. The Menorah, which has always been used to light the Temple, represents Israel (and the only symbol YHWH Himself ever ordered man to make – Exodus 25:31-32), which will, in the future, become a "light to all nations." Olive trees symbolize strength, peace, wisdom, glory, fertility, power and pureness; they are tough and rugged and able to handle any kind of climate. Therefore, **the two menorahs and two olive trees of Revelation 11 will represent the YHWH's Land, the State of Israel and the Torah observant believers in Messiah Yeshua located around the world.** The witnesses will loudly and boldly proclaim the warning from the streets of Jerusalem, which will spark international controversy and cause uproar on Earth – until Zion finally fulfills her calling (Isaiah 62:6-7)!

Revelation 11: 5. *And if any person will harm them, fire comes out of their mouth and consumes their adversary; and if any one will harm them, thus must he be slain. 6. They have power to shut up heaven so that the rain will not fall in those days: and they have power over the waters, to turn them into blood; and to smite the earth with all plagues as often as they please. 7. And when they will have completed their testimony, the beast of prey that came up from the abyss will make war upon them and will overcome them. 8.*

And their dead bodies (will be) in the open street of that great city which is spiritually called Sodom and Egypt, where also their Master (Y'shua) was executed on the stake. 9. And (they) of the nations and tribes and peoples and tongues will look upon their dead bodies, three days and a half; and will not suffer their dead bodies to be laid in the grave. 10. And they who dwell on the earth will rejoice over them and will be merry, and will send presents to one another; because those two prophets tormented them who dwell on the earth.

Can't you just imagine how "the world" will rejoice over the death of YHWH's prophets who stood and proclaimed Truth? Right now, we are as decadent as people were "in the days of Noah," just before YHWH struck the earth with a flood. (Case in point, singers over the last couple of decades – including Madonna who kissed another woman on the lips while on stage, and Michael Jackson who saw fit to grab his crotch during performances; while Adam Lambert took it a step further, glorifying bondage, and pushing a chained man's face against his own groin – for some reason have decided they must entertain audiences with weird, lewd and lascivious sexual behavior on national television under the guise of "expressing themselves.")

Today, in our "politically correct" world, the Ten Commandments have been trampled on by the ungodly who were instrumental in having them removed from our government buildings and schools and many homes. YHWH's Torah is considered by many – if not most - to be a "curse"....How much worse it will surely be as these future events unfold, by the time these two "witnesses" are killed!)

Revelation 11: 11. And after these three days and a half, the Spirit of Life from Elohim entered into them, and they stood upon their

186

feet: and great fear fell on those who saw them. 12. And they heard a great voice from heaven, which said to them: Come up here. And they ascended to heaven in a cloud; and their enemies saw them. 13. And in the same hour there was a great earthquake, and the tenth part of the city fell: and the persons killed in the earthquake were seven thousand names: and they who remained were afraid and gave glory to Elohim. 14. The second woe is passed: behold, the third woe comes quickly.

The world has been shaken in unimaginable ways, and so finally, we have arrived at the "last shofar"! Here's a quick recap of what happens when it sounds:

1 Corinthians 15: 51. Behold, I tell you a mystery; we will not all sleep, but we will all be changed, 52. Suddenly, as in the twinkling of an eye, at the last shofar, when it will sound; and the dead will arise, without corruption; and we will be changed. 53. For this which is corruptible, is to put on incorruption; and that which dies, will put on immortality. 54. And when that which is corruptible, will put on incorruption, and that which dies, immortality; then will take place the Word that is written, "Death is absorbed in victory."

...And finally, here it is, the moment of truth:

Revelation 11: 15. And the seventh Messenger sounded; and there were voices and thunders which said: The kingdom of the world has become (the Kingdom) of our Master (Y'shua) and of his Mashiyach; and he will reign for ever and ever. 16. And the twenty and four Elders who are before the throne of Elohim, (and) who sit upon their seats, fell upon their faces and worshipped Elohim, 17. saying: We praise you, O Master YHWH Elohim, Omnipotent, who is and who was, because You have assumed your great power, and have reigned. 18. And the nations were angry; and your anger is come, and the time of the dead, that they should be judged: and that You should give a reward to your servants, the prophets, and the Set Apart believers, and to them that Fear Your Name, the small and

187

the great; and that You should destroy them who destroyed the earth. 19. And the temple of Elohim in heaven was opened; and the ark of His Covenant was seen in his temple: and there were flashes of lightning and thunders, and voices and an earthquake, and great hail.

Now, please think about this: Since the world has already experienced countless atrocities, death, plagues, famine, disease and so forth; and we can expect all of the above to *yet happen* in the proverbial "Biblical proportions," what makes so many believe that they will "be raptured out of here" BEFORE the "Great Tribulation" occurs?

Adam and Eve didn't escape; Abel didn't escape; Noah didn't escape; Lot didn't escape; Joseph didn't escape; Shadrach, Meshach and Abednego didn't escape; none of the Apostles escaped....Not even our Divine Savior escaped His "tribulation"! The Bible teems with examples of people who had to go *through* their tribulations; so, what makes today's people arrogant enough to think THEY will escape - especially the ones who don't bother to adhere to YHWH's Torah?

It doesn't matter what people choose to "believe". The Bible tells us what is ahead; and, according to the Scriptures, *nobody* escapes! Therefore, the ONLY thing we need to concentrate on is that we "get ourselves right with God."

And how do we do that? By discovering exactly who YHWH is (see the first five Books of the Bible) and then learning and doing our best to follow His Divine Instructions to mankind....

Before I end this chapter, did you, by any chance, notice *who* is with Elohim after the seventh shofar in Revelation 11:15-19? Listed are 24 elders, the servants and the

Prophets. Since we are not any of these - what assures *us* we will be with Elohim after the seventh shofar sounds? The answer is in Revelation 11:18: The "Set Apart Believers"! We become "set apart believers" when we obey and observe the *mitzvot* of YHWH.

Halleluyah!

And There Was War in Heaven!
Surviving the End Times

Chapter 12

The Wine Press

As we continue unraveling the Book of Revelation, we can see that it is not always easy to figure out the meaning of a particular passage, or the references and nuances; or, in the case of the following, the particular time lines. In Revelation 12, the entire passage seems to jump back and forth between past and future:

Revelation 12: 1. And a great wonder was seen in heaven; a woman clothed with the sun, and the moon under her feet, and on her head a crown of twelve stars. 2. And, being with child, she cried and labored, and had the pangs of giving imminent birth. 3. And there appeared another wonder in heaven; and behold, a great fiery dragon which had seven heads and ten horns, and upon his head seven diadems. 4. And his tail drew along the third part of the stars of heaven, and cast them on the earth. And the dragon was standing before the woman, who was about to bring forth so that, when she should bring forth, he might devour her child. 5. And she brought forth a male child who was to rule all nations with a rod of iron. And her child was caught up to Elohim and to his throne. 6. And the woman fled into the wilderness where she had a place which was prepared for her by Elohim; so that they might nourish her there a thousand and two hundred and sixty days.

The "woman" is Israel, about to give birth to the Messiah, with Satan lying in wait to devour Him at His birth. This refers to evil people such as King Herod who was so enraged over the birth of Yeshua (Matthew 2:1-23), that he ordered the deaths of all the children aged two years and under, in hopes that among them would be Yeshua. In the meantime, an angel appeared to Joseph and told him to take his wife Mary and their son into Egypt and to stay until Herod died.

In verse 5, Yeshua has already died and is with YHWH and Israel is scattered into the nations. Verse 6 is has elicited many differing opinions as to where the "woman" would be nourished for 1,260 days. According to Roth, it is possible this place will be Midian, in Arabia, because Midian is the only known wilderness with an oasis.

Roth noted it is imperative to understand that the wandering in the wilderness of the Israelites in the Book of Exodus was not all "wild"; it wasn't all desert, as they came across settled cities as they traveled. It is tempting to think the woman will be nourished (like Moses and his people) "close to the action" in Jerusalem and Zion - until we realize that the vision is not bound by geographical concerns. An echo of this idea was expressed by Rav Shaul:

Galatians 4: 22. For it is written that Awraham had two sons, one from a servant woman and one from a freewoman. 23. But he who was from the servant woman is by the flesh (and) he who was from the freewoman was by the promise. 24. Therefore, these things were symbolic of two covenants, the one from Mount Sinai gave birth to bondage, which is Hagar. 25. For Hagar is the mountain that is in Arabia, and it surrenders to this Urishlim which is now in bondage with her children. 26. But that Urishlim is the freewoman who is the mother of us all. 27. For it is written: Take delight, O barren one. Rejoice and cry, you who cannot travail with birth pains, for the sons of those who are forsaken outnumber the sons of the favored. 28. Now we, my brothers, are as Yitz'chak was, sons of the promise. 29. And just as he who was born through the flesh was persecuted by he who was (born) through the Spirit, so it also is now. 30. But what does the Scripture say? Cast out the bondwoman and her son, for he who is of the bondwoman will not inherit along with the son of the freewoman. 31. Therefore, my brothers, we are not sons of the bondwoman, but sons of the freewoman.

Meanwhile, continuing in Revelation 12, verse 7 (following), we are ported back in time to the beginning, before man was created, when the beautiful angel, Lucifer, decided to challenge YHWH - who, in turn, promptly kicked Lucifer and his followers (messengers/angels) out of heaven.

Revelation 12: 7. And there was war in heaven: Michael and his Messengers fought against the dragon, and the dragon and his Messengers fought, 8. and did not prevail; nor was their place found any more in heaven. 9. And the great dragon was cast out, the old serpent who is called the Deceiver, and Satan, who seduces all the inhabited world: he was cast upon the earth and his Messengers were cast out with him. 10. And I heard a great voice in heaven which said: Now is there deliverance, and the power and the Kingdom of our Elohim, and the dominion of his Mashiyach: because the Accuser of our Brothers is cast out, who accused them day and night before our Elohim. 11. And they overcame him, because of the blood of the Lamb, and because of the word of their testimony: and they loved not their life, even to death. 12. Therefore, be joyful, O heaven and you that dwell there. Woe to the earth, and to the sea; for the Deceiver has come down to you, being in great wrath since he knows that his time is short.

Next, in verse 13 we once again see the serpent pursuing Israel, spewing water from his mouth in hopes of drowning her in a flood.

Revelation 12: 13. And when the dragon saw that he was cast out upon the earth, he persecuted the woman who brought forth the male child. 14. And to the woman were given the two wings of the great eagle, that she might fly into the wilderness, to her place; where she is nourished a time and times and half a time, from the face of the serpent. 15. And the serpent spewed from his mouth waters like a river after the woman, that he might cause her to be carried away by the flood. 16. And the earth helped the woman: and the earth opened its mouth and drank up the flood which the serpent ejected from his mouth. 17. And the dragon was enraged against the woman; and he went to make war upon the remnant of her seed who keep the Commandments of Elohim and have the testimony of Y'shua. (Please take note of the "and" in between those last two thoughts: If you want eternal life, you cannot separate one from the other!)

I believe this refers not to an actual flood, or only to the time when Yeshua walked the earth but, rather, to the world as a whole, where Jews have been persecuted, tormented and killed since time immemorial, while Satan placed obstacle after obstacle into their paths.

Some of the more heinous persecution and extermination attempts were The Crusades, the Spanish Inquisition, the pogroms and the Holocaust in which Adolf Hitler tried to exterminate the Jews from the face of the earth. (For an in-depth study on these issues, please Google an article by the International Director of Bridges for Peace, Clarence H. Wagner, Jr., entitled "The Error of Replacement Theology.") As Mr. Wagner wrote, "*Hitler is gone, Nazi Germany has ceased to exist, the apple of God's eye, the Jewish people are here and Israel is a fact.*" Many empires have fallen over the millennia, but "the Jews" are still here because YHWH made a covenant with Abraham, as we remember from Genesis 12:1-3 and Deuteronomy 7:6-8....exactly as YHWH promised:

Isaiah 43: 10 "You are my witnesses," says ADONAI, "and my servant whom I have chosen, so that you can know and trust me and understand that I am he - no god was produced before me, nor will any be after me. 11 I, yes I, am ADONAI; besides me there is no deliverer. 12 I have declared, saved and proclaimed - not some alien god among you. Therefore you are my witnesses," says ADONAI. "I am God. 13 Since days began, I have been he. No one can deliver from my hand. When I act, who can reverse it?"

Note that in Revelation 12:16 you read, *"the earth helped the woman."* If you think about it, "the earth" HAS helped Israel in many ways. Remember, YHWH dispersed the Jews into the nations (Leviticus 26:13-16; Deuteronomy 30:1-5; Nehemiah 1:8-9). If He hadn't dispersed them and they had remained in Israel, they surely would have seen total annihilation by now. (Not to mention that no one outside of Israel would ever have heard of YHWH or Yeshua!) And, despite the many efforts by evil men to destroy the Jews, there were always those who helped them out in some way, as evidenced in the life stories of people like Anne Frank and Corrie ten Boom. This is why in Revelation 12:17 we see that "the dragon was enraged against the woman; and he went to make war upon the remnant of her seed who keep the Commandments of Elohim *and* have the testimony of Y'shua."

Now, please read the next verses carefully because it gets really interesting as we dig deeper into the end times events:

Revelation 13: 1. And he stood on the sand of the sea. And I saw a beast of prey come up from the sea, having ten horns and seven heads; and upon his horns ten diadems, and upon his heads names of blasphemy. 2. And the beast of prey which I saw, was like a leopard; and his feet like (those) of a wolf, and his mouth like the mouth of lions: and the dragon gave to him his own power and his throne, and great authority. 3. And one of his heads was wounded as it were to death; and his deadly wound was healed. (Islam's deadly wound was healed, as it is on the rise again today.) *And all the earth wondered after the beast of prey. 4. And they worshipped the dragon, because he had given authority to this beast of prey, and (they said), who can make war upon him?*

Remember, at the beginning of this book I said that nobody can proclaim they are able to perfectly interpret the symbols of the Book of Revelation; it simply cannot be done. All we can do is to use common sense while consulting the Holy Spirit about these things. So, from what I can tell, the "beast of prey" refers to the Antichrist and the ungodly system of worldly beliefs he institutes, including the use of Islam to subdue the masses.

Satan, if you'll recall, received the first blow to his wicked ego when he, as the angel Lucifer, was kicked out of heaven when he attempted to usurp the throne of YHWH (Isaiah 14:12). The second blow was when Yeshua defeated him and overcame death at the cross/stake. And so now, in these end times, he is doing his level best to do whatever he can to deceive and confuse the whole world so he can take as many as possible to hell with him. He has been doing this for millennia already, but by the time the events of Revelation 13 begin to unfold, he has begun to pull out all the stops as he uses the Antichrist, a very charismatic man who caters to his every whim. We previously examined the description of this man in Chapter 7 (via Daniel 11:21-45), but here are some quick highlights:

The characteristics of the Antichrist are as follows:

- A despicable man not entitled to inherit the majesty of the kingdom, but he will come without warning and gain the kingdom by intrigue.

- Alliances will be made with him, but he will undermine them by deceit.

- Although he will have but a small following, he will emerge and become strong.

- Armed forces will come at his order and profane the sanctuary and fortress. They will abolish the daily burnt offering and set up the abomination that causes desolation.

- Those who act wickedly against the covenant he will corrupt with his blandishments, but the people who know their God will stand firm and prevail.

- He will do as he pleases, exalt himself and consider himself greater than any god, uttering monstrous blasphemies against the God of gods. He will prosper only until the period of wrath is over, for what has been determined must take place.

- He will show no respect for the gods his ancestors worshipped, or for the god women worship - he won't show respect for any god, because he will consider himself greater than all of them.

- He will honor the god of strongholds; with gold, silver, precious stones and other costly things he will honor a god unknown to his ancestors.

- He will deal with the strongest fortresses with the help of a foreign god. *(Stands to reason that this refers to Allah!)*

- Finally, when he pitches the tents of his palace between the seas and the mountain of the holy Glory, he will come to his end, with no one to help him.

Besides Islam, the "beast of prey" in Revelation 13:1 may also represent the godless world government systems/ideologies which have sprung up and died over the millennia while man continuously struggled to find his peace with God via religions and religiosity. It could also be referring to the growing decadence of "the world" in which Satan is becoming ever more glorified. For instance, if you've ever studied the "Goth" subculture, you'll notice Satan's dark influence with their often morbid, eroticized fashion and style of dress complete with dyed black hair, dark eyeliner, black fingernails, black period-styled clothing, tattoos and/or body piercings. What "Goths" have done, in effect, is to "erect an image" of Satan, as their culture reflects an unholy, anti-Christ lifestyle. Goth is a type of "beast" because it is wreaking havoc among our young people, leading them straight into the pits of hell....

Revelation 13: 5. And there was given to him a mouth speaking great things, and blasphemies: and authority was given him to operate forty and two months. 6. And he opened his mouth in blasphemy towards Elohim, to blaspheme his name and his tabernacle, and them who dwell in heaven. 7. And authority was given him over every tribe and people and tongue and nation: and it was given him to wage war with the Set Apart believers, and to overcome them. 8. And all that dwell on the earth whose names are not written in the book of life of the Lamb slain from the foundation of the world, will worship him.

Whose names are "not written in the book of life of the Lamb"? Those who have chosen "religion" and various other gods over the worship of YHWH, the Creator of the universe and all that is in it: Atheists, Satanists, witches, sorcerers, whoremongers and/or those who believe themselves to be godly, yet never bother to obey YHWH's commands.....

Revelation 13: 9. If any one has ears, let him hear. 10. If (anyone) carries into captivity, he will himself go into captivity; and if anyone slays with the sword, he must be slain with the sword: here is the patience and the faith of the Set Apart believers.

Since we studied Revelation 13:11-18 earlier in Chapter 4 in our "mark of the beast" discussion, we don't need to belabor the topic here because, by now, you have a pretty good idea of what to watch our for.

But, as you can see, it is extremely difficult to determine exactly what the Apostle John was attempting to describe in what came to be known as the Book of Revelation. Many insist the passages above describe Catholicism and the Pope, but there is a major flaw with that theory, and it is this: The Pope is *not* "anti-Christ" (against-Christ). Catholicism *believes* in "Jesus." The problem is, Catholics give more credence to Mary than to her Son, and thus, their theology, riddled with idols and idolatry, resembles nothing that Yeshua actually taught. But Catholics are definitely not "anti Christ." Nor does the Catholic Church "behead" people today....

Revelation 14: 1. And I looked, and behold, a Lamb stood on mount Tsiyon; and with him the number of a hundred and forty and four thousand, having his name and the name of his Father written upon their foreheads. 2. And I heard a sound from heaven, as the sound of many waters, and as the sound of great thunder; and the sound which I heard was like that of harpers striking on their harps. 3. And they sang a new song before the throne, and before the four Creatures and the Elders: and no one was able to learn that song except the hundred and forty and four thousand who were redeemed from the earth. 4. These are they who have not defiled themselves with women, for they are virgins. These are they who followed the Lamb, wherever he went. These have been redeemed by Y'shua from among men, the first fruits to Elohim and the Lamb. 5. And in their mouth was found no deceit; for they are without faults.

And now consider this: In the Torah (first five Books of the Bible, also called the Books of Moses) YHWH allowed us a glimpse into who He is and how He expects to be worshipped and obeyed. In the Tanach (the Books of Moses plus the rest of the "Old Testament" – the Prophets and the writings), He gave us examples of human behavior and the results of disobedience. In the *B'rit Chadasha* (the "New Testament"), YHWH introduced the ultimate in Grace and Mercy by sending His only Son - the "arm" of YHWH Himself (Isaiah 53:1) - who personally taught mankind about Torah and the necessity of obedience, and then martyred Himself to become our Final Sin Sacrifice. And in the Book of Revelation, He provides a hard glimpse of the end times in which most of mankind ultimately chooses to hang onto their sinful ways, even though YHWH and His messengers warned us over and over again....

Revelation 14: 6. And I saw another Messenger flying in heaven: and with blood, he had the everlasting Good News to proclaim to dwellers on the earth, and to every nation and tribe and tongue and people; 7. saying with a loud voice, Worship Elohim, and give glory to Him; because the hour of his judgment is come; and adore you Him, who made heaven and earth, and the sea, and the fountains of water. 8. And another, a second Messenger followed him, saying: Fallen, fallen is Babylon the great, which made all nations drink of the wine of the rage of her whoredom. 9. And another, a third Messenger followed them, saying with a loud voice: If any man will worship the beast of prey and its image, and will receive its mark upon his forehead or on his hand, 10. he also will drink of the wine of the wrath of Elohim, which is poured undiluted into the cup of his indignation and will be tormented with fire and sulfur, before the Set Apart Messengers, and before the throne. 11. And the smoke of their torment ascends up for ever and ever; and there is no rest, by day or by night, to those that worship the beast of prey and its image. 12. Here is the patience of the Set Apart believers who keep the commandments of Elohim, and the faith of Y'shua.

Revelation 14: 13. And I heard a voice from heaven, saying: Write, Blessed are the dead that die in Master YHWH from now on: yes, says the Spirit, that they may rest from their toils; for their deeds do accompany them. 14. And I looked, and lo, a white cloud; and upon the cloud sat one who was like the Son of man; and on his head was a crown of gold, and in his hand a sharp sickle (Yeshua!). *15. And another Messenger came out of the temple, crying with a loud voice to him that sat on the cloud. 16. And he thrust his sickle over the earth; and the earth was reaped* (the "rapture" of believers). *17. And another Messenger came out of the temple that is in heaven, having also a sharp sickle. 18. And another Messenger came out from the altar, having authority over fire. And he cried with a loud voice to him who had the sharp sickle, saying: Thrust in your sickle which is sharp, and gather the clusters of the vineyard of the earth, because the grapes of the earth are ripe. 19. And the Messenger thrust in his sickle on the earth and gathered the vintage of the earth, and cast (it) into the wine-press of the wrath of the great Elohim. 20. And the wine-press was trodden, up to the horses' bridles, for a thousand and six hundred furlongs.*

Did you question by "wine-press" in verse 19? The "wine-press of the wrath of the great Elohim" refers to time when YHWH's patience has come to an end and He reaps the sinful *unbelievers* - all those who have denied Him in one way or another and lived lives fraught with willful sinning, which includes Christians who were under the erroneous impression that their adultery or homosexuality and all manner of carnal sins were forgiven just because they "believed in Jesus!" The "vintage" are these sinners and the "wine-press" is the Earth. Billions will die once the battles begin, from famine, disease and the weaponry of man, as you will see in Revelation 15 and 16. This does not mean they will be "raptured" to stand before YHWH right away. That comes later, at the end of the millennium....

*Revelation 15: 1. And I saw another sign in heaven, great and wonderful; seven Messengers having seven plagues, the last in order, because with them the wrath of Elohim is completed. 2. And I saw as it were, a sea of glass mixed with fire: and they, who had been innocent over the beast of prey and over its image, and over the number of its name, were standing on the sea of glass; and they had the harps of Elohim. 3. And they sing the song of Moshe the servant of Elohim, and the song of the Lamb, saying: Great and marvelous are your deeds, Master YHWH Elohim Almighty; just and true are your ways, O King of worlds. 4. Who will not Fear you, O Master YHWH, and glorify Your Name? Because You only are Set Apart and just: Because all nations will come and worship before you, since your righteousnesses have been revealed. 5. And after this I beheld, and the temple of the tabernacle of the testimony in heaven was opened. 6. And the seven Messengers who had the seven plagues went forth from the temple, clothed in clean splendid linen, and girded about their breast with girdles of gold. 7. And one of the four Creatures gave to those seven Messengers **seven cups of gold full of the wrath of Elohim who lives forever and ever.** 8. And the temple was filled with smoke from the glory of Elohim and from his power; and no one was able to enter the temple until the seven plagues of the seven Messengers were accomplished.*

Chapter 13

Behold the Savior

The last few chapters of Revelation set the stage for Yeshua's return. Apostle John tells us those "who had been innocent" and stood strong against the beast and remained faithful would survive the wrath; but, what happens to the rest? Hold on to your hats as it is revealed in the sequence of events outlined in the seven cup/bowl judgments!

Revelation 16: 1. And I heard a voice which said to the seven Messengers: Go forth and pour those seven cups of the wrath of Elohim upon the earth. 2. ***And the first went and poured his cup upon the earth;*** *and there was a malignant and painful sore upon those men who had the mark of the beast of prey, and who worshipped its image.* (Those who bowed down to Allah and/or various other gods and/or the godless world system.) *3.* ***And the second Messenger poured his cup upon the sea;*** *and it became blood, like that of a dead person; and every living soul of things in the sea, died. 4.* ***And the third Messenger poured his cup upon the rivers and the fountains of water;*** *and they became blood. 5. And I heard the Messenger of the waters say: Righteous are you, Who is and Who was and are Set Apart; because You have done this judgment. 6. For they have shed the blood of Set Apart believers and prophets; and you have given them blood to drink, for they deserve it. 7. And I heard (one from) the altar say: Yes, Master YHWH, Elohim Almighty: true and righteous is your judgment. 8.* ***And the fourth poured his cup upon the sun:*** *and it was permitted him to scorch men with fire. 9. And men were scorched with great heat; and men blasphemed the name of Elohim who has authority over these plagues; and they did not repent, to give glory to Him.*

Can you believe the arrogance of man? Even in those days when the final prophecies are unfolding before their very eyes, and the entire earth is being systematically destroyed after four bowl judgments, man *still* refuses to recognize that YHWH is in charge! Instead of repenting while they still have a chance to gain eternal life on Judgment Day, mankind continues to remain stubborn and proud. The first to perish are those who took the "mark" (verse 16:2) and turned to the ways of the beast.

Revelation 16: 10. And the fifth poured his cup on the throne of the beast of prey; and his kingdom became darkness; and they gnawed their tongues from pain; 11. and they blasphemed the Elohim of heaven on account of their pains and their ulcers, and did not repent of their deeds. 12. And the sixth poured his cup upon the great river Euphrates; and its waters dried up so that a way might be prepared for the kings from the rising of the sun (Kings of the East). *13 And I saw (issuing) from the mouth of the dragon, and from the mouth of the beast of prey, and from the mouth of the false prophet, three unclean spirits like frogs: 14. (for they are the spirits of demons who work signs;) and they go forth to all the kings of all the habitable world, to gather them to the battle of the great day of Elohim Almighty.* (Man is arrogant and *dumb* enough to think he can beat God Almighty in battle!)

Amazingly, as the wrath grows, instead of repenting for their sins and asking YHWH for mercy upon their souls, men continue to BLASPHEME Him! Isn't this just like people to be "lukewarm" towards God? They want and want, and pray fervently for Him to give them whatever *they* want; and when they don't get it, they become angry because things didn't go their way. Hardly anyone stops to think that YHWH often refuses to answer prayers because men's desires may not necessarily line up with HIS will. Many are quick to blame Him for the ills in their lives, but very slow to remember to thank Him when things go well! And in these times of terror, instead of asking themselves

"What have I done? Why did I follow the ways of the world?" they will blame YHWH and fail to repent.

Revelation 16: 15. *(And lo, I come as a thief. Blessed is he that watches and keeps his garments; or else he walk naked and they see his shame.)* 16. *And they collected them together in a place called, in Hebrew, Armageddon.* 17. **And the seventh poured his cup on the air; and there issued a loud voice from the temple, from the throne, which said: It is done! 18. And there were flashes of lightning, and thunders, and voices; and there was a great earthquake, the like of which there was never, since men were on the earth, such an earthquake, and so great. 19. And the great city became three parts. And the city of the nations fell; and Babylon the great was remembered before Elohim, to give her the cup of the wine of the heat of his wrath.** 20. *And every island fled away; and the mountains were not found.* 21. *And a great hail, as it were of a talent weight, fell from heaven upon men: and the men blasphemed Elohim on account of the plague of hail; for the plague of it was very great.*

Revelation 17: 1. *Then came one of the seven Messengers who have the seven cups, and talked with me, saying: Come, I will show you the judgment of the great harlot who sits upon many waters;* 2. *with whom the kings of the earth have practiced illicit sexuality, and the inhabitants of the earth have been intoxicated with the wine of her harlotry.*

We are told later that the "waters" in Revelation 17:1 "are peoples and multitudes, and nations, and tongues" (see Revelation 17:15, below) - meaning multitudes are enthralled with debauchery (described as a woman/harlot who represents all manner of sin and decadence), and the way of the world which is full of sin. We see this *now*! Everything YHWH has ever considered "bad" is now considered "good" by "the world" - homosexuality, adultery, sexual affairs of all kinds, lying, cheating, stealing, abortion (murder), etc. - these things are all justifiable according to today's lawlessness. (Remember, *sin/lawlessness* is the transgression of Torah - Leviticus 4:13 and 1 John 3:4.)

There was a poster in the Seventies that featured a turtle having sex with an Army helmet and its caption read: "If it feels good, DO IT!" That, all by itself, sums up the way of the world today....

Revelation 17: 3. And he led me in spirit into the wilderness: and I saw a woman sitting on a red beast of prey, which was full of names of blasphemy and had seven heads and ten horns. 4. And the woman was clothed in purple and scarlet, and gilded with gold and precious stones and pearls; and she had a cup of gold in her hand which was full of the pollutions and impurity of her whoredoms of the earth. (This sentence explains our "worldliness" in a nutshell!) *5. And upon her forehead was the name written: Mystery: Babylon the great; the Mother of Harlots, and of the contaminations of the Earth. 6. And I saw that the woman was intoxicated with the blood of the Set Apart believers, and with the blood of the witnesses of Y'shua* (YHWH's Torah observant believers who kept themselves from the world and all its enticements and decadence). *And when I saw her, I wondered with great amazement.*

The woman *"clothed in purple and scarlet, and gilded with gold and precious stones and pearls; and she had a cup of gold in her hand which was full of the pollutions and impurity of her whoredoms of the earth"* (verse 17:4*)* – could very well be referring to the Catholic Church; the entity that originally twisted the Word of YHWH and forbade the mention of anything "Jewish" in its services, thus, effectively doing away with the Seventh Day Sabbath command and the *mo'edim* (Feasts), while instituting the pagan "holy days" of Christmas and Easter.

Revelation 17: 7. And the Messenger said to me, Why do you wonder? I will tell you the mystery of the woman and of the beast of prey that bears her, which has the seven heads and the ten horns. 8. The beast of prey which you saw, was and is not; and he will ascend from the abyss and go into perdition: and the dwellers on the earth whose names are not written in the book of life from the foundation of the world, will wonder when they see the beast of prey which was, and is not, and approaches. 9. Here is intelligence for him who has wisdom. Those seven heads are the seven mountains on which the woman sits.

By the way, Rome is the only city on Earth that boasts of sitting on seven hills. The Catholic Encyclopedia states: "It is within the city of Rome, called the city of seven hills, that the entire area of Vatican State proper is now confined." [Robert Broderick, *The Catholic Encyclopedia,* Thomas Nelson Inc., 1976].

In the Bible we see many references to "waters"; each having a deeper meaning than just the word itself. "Waters" represents total immersion into something, filling every crack and crevice of the earth and of the very fibers of our humanity. Examples: Living waters (John 4:10-15), healing waters (John 5), drinking waters, baptism in flowing waters, the waters from which the earth was born (2 Peter 3:6-7), and the waters by which Noah and his family were kept alive:

*1 Peter 3: 18. For the Mashiyach also once died for our sins, the righteous for sinners; that he might bring you to Elohim. And he died in body but lived in spirit. 19. And he preached to those souls which were detained in Sheol (Hades) 20. which were formerly disobedient in the days of Noah when the long suffering of Elohim commanded an ark to be made, **in hope of their repentance**; and eight souls only entered into it and were **kept alive in the waters.***

Having mentioned 1 Peter 3, it is imperative to discuss 2 Peter 3:1-18, which is also extremely prophetic:

2 Peter 3: 1. This second letter, my beloved, I now write to you; in (both of) which I stir up your honest mind by admonition: 2. that you may be mindful of the words which were formerly spoken by the Set Apart prophets, and of the commandment of our Master and Redeemer by the hand of the Shlichim: 3. knowing this previously, that there will come in the last days scoffers who will scoff, walking according to their own lusts 4. and saying, Where is the promise of his coming? for, since our fathers fell asleep, everything remains just as from the beginning of the creation.

Note the words, *"that there will come in the last days scoffers who will scoff, walking according to their own lusts and saying, Where is the promise of his coming?"* Scoffers (the self-absorbed and decadent) are everywhere these days, telling believers there is no God and that those who believe are deluded and have hung their hope on a mythical being. Scoffers include people such as atheists, our unbelieving media and the "humanists" and "pro-choice" abortionists who either don't believe in God, or prefer to think of Him as "love" - someone who condones everything they think, say and do....

2 Peter 3: 5. For this they willingly forget, that the heavens were of old; and the earth rose up from the waters, and by means of water, by the Word of Elohim. 6. (And), by means of these (waters), the world which then was, (being submerged) again perished in the waters. 7. And the heavens that now are, and the earth, are by His Word stored up, being reserved for the fire at the day of judgment and the perdition of wicked men. 8. And of this one thing, my beloved, be not forgetful: That one day to Master YHWH, is as a thousand years; and a thousand years, as one day. 9. Master YHWH does not delay His promises as some estimate delay; but He is long suffering for your sakes, being not willing that any should perish, but that everyone should come to repentance.

Verses 5-9 above are powerful in that they reveal two very important matters: The fact that the scoffers don't recognize YHWH as the all-knowing, all-powerful Entity who created everything, and who also has the ability to destroy it all in seconds; and that the only reason He has chosen to hold off judgment is to give *all* mankind a chance to repent and accept Him before Judgment Day....when there will be no more chances.

2 Peter 3: 10. And the day of Master YHWH will come like a thief; in which the heavens will suddenly pass away; and the elements, being ignited, will be dissolved; and the earth and the works in it will not be found. 11. As therefore all these things are to be dissolved, what persons should you be, in Set Apart conduct and in the Fear of Elohim, 12. expecting and desiring the coming of the day of Elohim in which the heavens being tried by fire will be dissolved and the elements being ignited will melt? 13. But we, according to his promise, expect new heavens and a new earth in which righteousness dwells.

The message in verses 10-13 is that YHWH is not kidding around! If we want to enter eternal life, we *must* be "Set Apart"! Remember, "set apart" means not only accepting Messiah Yeshua as our Final Sin Sacrifice, but also to OBEY His commands!

*2 Peter 3: 14. Therefore, my beloved, as you expect these things, strive that you may be found by him in peace, without spot and without blemish. 15. And account the long suffering of Master YHWH to be redemption; **as also our beloved brother Paul** (Every Christian needs to pay special attention to this!), **according to the wisdom conferred on him, wrote to you; 16. as also in all his letters speaking in them of these things in which there is something*** *difficult to be understood; (and) which they who are ignorant and unstable pervert, as they do also the rest of the Scriptures, to their own destruction. 17. You therefore, my beloved, as you know (these things) beforehand, guard yourselves or else, by going after the error of the Torahless, you fall from your steadfastness. 18. But be you growing in grace and in the knowledge of our Master and Redeemer Yshua the Mashiyach and of Elohim the Father: whose is the glory now and always and to the days of eternity. Amen.*

Here, we have Peter suggesting we be careful to NOT misunderstand the writings of the Apostle Paul! *"...as also our beloved brother Paul, according to the wisdom conferred on him, wrote to you; as also in all his letters speaking in them of these things in which there is something difficult to be understood; (and) which **they who are ignorant and unstable pervert, as they do also the rest of the Scriptures, to their own destruction.** You therefore, my beloved, as you know (these things) beforehand, guard yourselves or else, by going after the error of the Torahless, you fall from your steadfastness."*

Could it be any clearer? Paul never spoke against Torah, as the "church" insists, and neither did any of the other Apostles....Only the "ignorant and unstable" would dare to pervert the Words of YHWH and the teachings of His Messiah and the Apostles!

The Bible truly outlines *everything* we need to know about YHWH, His expectations of mankind and these things that will take place. Yet most people see the Bible as a smorgasbord, something to pick and choose from to build their own belief system....

Revelation 17 goes on to prophesy about world leaders during the end times who have chosen to ignore YHWH's commands and rule according to the druthers of the beast:

Revelation 17: 10. *And there are seven kings: of whom five have fallen, one exists, and the other has not yet come; and when he comes he must continue for a short time. 11. And the beast of prey which was and is not, is the eighth, and is from the seven, and is for perdition (eternal damnation). 12. And the ten horns which you saw, are ten kings. These persons have not yet received royalty; but they receive authority as if kings, with the beasts of prey, for one hour. 13. They have one mind; and they will give their power and authority to the beast of prey. 14. They will make war upon the Lamb; and the Lamb will vanquish them; because he is Master of Masters and King of Kings, and these with him (are) called and chosen and faithful. 15. And he said to me:* **The waters which you saw, where the harlot** (metaphor for sin and decadence) **sits, are peoples and multitudes, and nations, and tongues.** *16. And the ten horns which you saw, and the beast of prey, will hate the harlot; and they will make her desolate and naked, and will eat her flesh, and burn her with fire. 17. For Elohim has put into their hearts to do His will and to execute one purpose, and to give their kingdom to the beast of prey until these Words of Elohim will be fulfilled. 18. And the woman whom you saw is the great city which has dominion over the kings of the earth.*

As mentioned before, "the harlot" in verse 15 represents sin and decadence. Please note this is not the "woman" of 17:3 which is identified in verse 18 as the place from which the beast-system is administered. But the Harlot is hated (verse 16)! Who is the most verbal about sinning today? (Hint: It's NOT Christians because many of them are themselves entrenched in "the world" and don't even view some sins as "sins"!) Who hates explicit sexuality and even cause their women to cover themselves from head to foot? Who hates democracy and the "western" way of life? It's Islam! Between the twisted theologies of Catholicism and Islam, Satan has done a superb job of confusing the masses about who God is and how to properly worship Him!

Self-proclaimed "prophecy expert" Jack Van Impe of Jack Van Impe Ministries, wants people to believe Revelation 17 somehow refers to the European Union and the Vatican, etc. And, while that may be (who truly knows?), he also insists the "mark of the beast" is the Radio Frequency Identification (RFID) microchip implant - but the question remains: Who says the spiritual world will employ *human devices* as the end times play out? As mentioned in Chapter 2, the "mark" will represent and reflect the spiritual battle going on behind the scenes; it will have something to do with the struggle between YHWH and His main enemy, *haSatan* - the one who has been attempting to lead people away from YHWH's holy Torah since the day man was created!

The bottom line is this: No one can know for sure exactly how the events of the Book of Revelation will unfold, or what the meanings of each symbol is, until it happens. The one thing we *can* know is that, since nearly 400 Bible prophecies have already come true, the remaining will also come to pass - and it won't be pretty! Therefore, it is imperative that mankind starts to "get right" with YHWH and becomes vigilant about our unholy environment, speaking out against the sin in our midst that has become "the norm." We need to stop electing leaders who act against what Torah teaches! For instance, President Obama proclaims to be a Christian, yet he is FOR abortion, FOR homosexual marriage, and AGAINST Israel. (Please Google Obama's June 4, 2009 speech in Cairo wherein he insisted Israel must be divided.) It's a sad commentary on America when the President of the United States, the most powerful nation in the world, dares to go up against YHWH Himself:

Genesis 12: 1 Now ADONAI said to Avram, "Get yourself out of your country, away from your kinsmen and away from your father's house, and go to the land that I will show you. 2 I will make of you a great nation, I will bless you, and I will make your name great; and you are to be a blessing. 3 I will bless those who bless you, but I will curse anyone who curses you; and by you all the families of the earth will be blessed."

Continuing in the Book of Revelation:

Revelation 18: 1. After these things, I saw another Messenger come down from heaven; and he had great authority and the earth was illuminated by his glory. 2. And he cried with a strong voice, saying: Fallen, fallen is Babylon the great: and has become a cavern of demons, and the home of every unclean spirit, and the home of every unclean and hateful bird and the home of every unclean and hateful beast of prey. 3. For all the nations have drunken of the wine of her wrath; and the kings of the earth have practiced whoredom with her; and the merchants of the earth have been enriched by the abundance of her luxuries.

Revelation 18: 4. And I heard another voice from heaven, saying: Come out of her my people; that you may not participate in her sins, and may not partake of her plagues. 5. For her sins have reached up to heaven; and Elohim has remembered her iniquities. 6. Recompense you to her, as she also has recompensed; and render to her double, according to her deeds; in the cup which she has mixed, mix you to her two fold. 7. As much as she pleased herself with lusting, so much of anguish and sorrow give you to her. Because she says in her heart, I sit a queen, and am no widow, and I will see no sorrow; 8. therefore, in one day, will these her plagues come, death, and mourning, and famine; and she will be burned with fire: for strong is Master YHWH, Elohim, who judges her. 9. And the kings of the earth who committed whoredom and were lustful with her will weep and mourn and bewail her when they will see the smoke of her burning, 10. standing afar off, from fear of her torment, (and) saying, Alas, alas! that great city Babylon, that powerful city; for in one hour is your judgment come!

"Her" in verse 4 refers to spiritual Babylon represented by all religious organizations which invalidate Torah and speak against Yeshua. All earthly governments and religious institutions will have patterned their structures and values after her; she is the "harlot system" of materialism, relativism, humanism and paganism. She has installed her own religious "priesthood" by replacing YHWH and His Mashiyach with her own "messiahs." "Come out of her" means to abandon the harlot system and to turn to YHWH, observe His Torah and walk in Mashiyach according to the image of Elohim.

Revelation 18: 11. And the merchants of the earth will mourn over her, because no one purchases their cargo; 12. no more, the cargo of gold, and silver, and precious stones, and pearls, and fine linen, and purple, and silk, and scarlet, and every aromatic wood, and all vessels of ivory, and all vessels of very precious wood, and of brass, and of iron, and of marble, 13. and cinnamon, and amomum, and aromatics, and unguents, and frankincense, and wine, and oil, and fine flour, and wheat, and beasts of burden, and sheep, and horses, and chariots, and the bodies and souls of men. 14. And the fruits which your soul desired, have departed from you; and all things delicious and splendid have perished from you; and the traders in them will obtain them no more.

Although Babylon could possibly represent huge, wealthy and influential places such as New York City, Los Angeles, Tokyo, Shanghai, Sidney, Frankfurt, Beirut or any other powerful city on Earth, "Babylon" in verse 10 does not refer to just one city. It represents all places on Earth that are steeped in sin; those that are engaged in the import and export of human, carnal "stuff" which keeps the world enslaved with the desire for more sex, more money, more power, more jewelry, more possessions - all the "me-oriented" attributes that make YHWH cringe. These places, this "Babylon", will all be, in one way or another, wiped off the face of the Earth because, when Yeshua returns, mankind will be forced to **concentrate on our Creator,** and to finally learn to obey His Will!

Revelation 18: 15. And they who were enriched from her, will stand far off, for fear of her torment; and will weep and mourn, 16. saying: Alas, alas! that great city, which was clothed in fine linen, and purple, and scarlet, and gilded with gold, and precious stones, and pearls; because, in one hour, such riches are laid waste. 17. And every pilot, and every navigator to the place, and the sailors, and all who do business by sea stood afar off 18. and cried when they saw the smoke of her burning, saying: What (other) is like this great city! 19. And they cast dust on their heads, and cried, weeping, and mourning, and saying: Alas, alas that great city, in which all that have ships in the sea became rich, by her preciousness; for in one hour she has become desolate. 20. Rejoice over her, O heaven, and you (heavenly) Messengers, and Shlichim (Apostles), and Prophets; because Elohim judges your cause with her.

Next, we see what will happen to the "Babylons" of the world:

Revelation 18: 21. And a Messenger took up a stone like a great millstone and cast it into the sea, saying: So will Babylon, the great city, be thrown down with violence, and will no more be found: 22. and the voice of harpers and musicians and pipers and trumpeters will no more be heard in you; and no artificer of any trade will be found any more in you. 23. And the light of a candle will not be seen in you; and the voice of a bridegroom and bride will no more be heard in you: for your merchants were the great men of the earth, because all nations were seduced by your sorceries. 24. And in her was found the blood of prophets and Set Apart believers, and of all those that have been slain on the earth.

How succinctly these scriptures describe the total destruction of "Babylon"! The message is completely clear:

"Babylon", the collection of humanity mired in decadence and sin, will be destroyed. Obedience is all YHWH has ever asked of us, and most have failed...and most will perish. Note in verse 24 that many of the Set Apart believers are also killed, slain during the destruction of Babylon. This might instill fear in many reading this who may wonder why the Set Apart might also be destroyed. But that is just the point! The Set Apart are *not* destroyed for they have eternal life! Many will lose their earthly bodies and earthly existence in the horrors of the events, but they die with the knowledge that they will be with YHWH at the first resurrection (referring back to Chapter 5).

Revelation 19: 1. And after these things, I heard a loud voice of a great multitude in heaven, saying: Hallelu-YAH: Deliverance, and strength, and glory, and honor, to our Elohim: 2. for, true and righteous are his judgments; for he has judged that great harlot who corrupted the earth with her harlotry; and has avenged the blood of his servants at her hand. 3. And again they said: Hallelu-YAH: and her smoke ascends up forever and ever. 4. And the twenty-four Elders fell down, and the four Creatures, and worshipped Elohim who sits on the throne, saying: Amen: Hallelu-YAH! 5. And a voice came forth from the throne, saying: Praise our Elohim, all you his servants; and such as Fear Him, small and great.

*Revelation 19: 6. And I heard, as it were the voice of a great multitude, and as the voice of many waters, and as the voice of heavy thunders, saying: **Hallelu-YAH; for our Master (Y'shua) Elohim, Omnipotent, reigns. 7. Let us rejoice and exult, and give glory to him: for the marriage supper of the Lamb has come, and his bride has made herself ready.** 8. And it was granted her to be clothed in fine linen, bright and clean: for fine linen is the righteousnesses of the Set Apart believers. 9. And he said to me, Write: Blessed are they who are called to the supper of the marriage feast of the Lamb. And he said to me, These my (sayings) are the true Words of Elohim.*

HalleluYah! At this point Yeshua reigns on Earth and people are finally going to learn to do things HIS way! Does that mean the requirement for "obedience" negates our free will and free choice? No, not at all. Obedience *brings* freedom and leads to a more fruitful life and a more cohesive community. Physical actions of obedience come after spiritual convictions (faith) are written upon the heart; and physical actions of obedience guide the spiritual man away from carnal lifestyles. According to an appendix in the AENT entitled, "Deliverance Through Obedience" (page 763), obedience is central to judgment:

> Obedience to the Word of YHWH is evidence of true deliverance. Mashiyach says that those who do not do the will of his Father will not partake of the Kingdom of Elohim (Matt. 7:21). The judgment of all peoples and nations is according to the same Standard which is revealed in the Word of YHWH and that the Set Apart believers obey: *"And the temple of Elohim in heaven was opened; and the ark of His Covenant was seen in his temple: and there were flashes of lightning and thunders, and voices and an earthquake, and great hail."* (Rev. 11:18). There is a clear and future judgment on the horizon. The ark of His Covenant contains all of the Ten Commandments that are to be "written upon the hearts" of YHWH's people. Those who don't have Torah written upon their hearts will not be able to excuse themselves by suggesting that "Jesus did it all for them" or that their Rabbi or Pastor promised them that they would be in heaven.
>
> Deliverance is won when there is an active pursuit of righteousness, and this is also a good definition of Faith; this is beyond just belief or

intellectual acknowledgement of righteousness or the knowledge of good and evil. If this were not the case, then Adam and Eve would never have been expelled from Gan (Garden) Eden as their "knowledge" about the Tree of Life would have been sufficient to keep them in! Instead, it was their direct disobedience to YHWH, that changed their status. The fact remains that Adam and Eve's story originates in the oldest part of the *Tanakh*, but their fall from grace because of their disobedience remains very much a current problem today and for the Good News writers (Romans 5:12-21, 1 Corinthians 15:22, 45)! So, if the earliest part of the Torah remains relevant, binding and in need of resolution for every current believer, how then can later parts of Torah become irrelevant?

The enemy attempts to micro-manage souls into doing his bidding; therefore, it is imperative to remember that Torah sets the Standard by which all flesh shall be judged. Torah observance protects us from becoming prey for the enemy. Although many religious people may claim that Torah observance "doesn't matter," the evidence shows that lack of trust, faith and disloyalty towards the Word of YHWH is what is waging war against the Unity of the Body. Those who say it "doesn't matter" are simply relying on their own religious traditions to carry them through. But Mashiyach says, "*All who loosen, therefore, from one (of) these small commandments and teach thus to the sons of man, will be called little in the Kingdom of Heaven, but all who do and teach this will be called great in the Kingdom of Heaven. For I say to you that unless your righteousness exceeds more than that of the scribes and the Pharisees, you will not enter the Kingdom of Heaven."* (Matthew 5:19, 20)

Returning to John's vision as he beholds our Savior, Yeshua:

Revelation 19: 10. And I fell at his feet to worship him. And he said to me, See that you do not do this; I am your fellow-servant and of those your Brothers who have the testimony of Y'shua. ***Worship you Elohim: for the testimony of Y'shua is the Spirit of Prophecy.*** *11. And I saw heaven opened: and lo, a white horse; and he that sat on it is called Faithful and True: and in righteousness he judges, and makes war. 12. His eyes (were) like a flame of fire, and on his head (were) many diadems; and he had names inscribed; and the name which was written on him, no one knew, except himself. 13. And he was clothed with a vesture sprinkled with blood; and his name is called, The Word of Elohim. 14. And the army of heaven followed him on white horses, clad in garments of fine linen, pure (and) white. 15. And from his mouth issued a sharp two-edged sword, that with it he could strike the nations; and he will rule the nations with a rod of iron; and he will tread the wine-press of the wrath of Elohim Almighty. 16. And he has upon his vesture and upon his thigh the words written: King of Kings, and Master of Masters.*

A little reminder that the words written upon Yeshua's thigh are not a tattoo but, rather, the *tzit-tzits* (braids, knots, tassels) that fall across His thighs. These knots spell out the Name of YHWH. (Each letter of the Hebrew alphabet has a numerical value and, consequently, the number of knots on the tzit-tzits on the four corners of a tallit, tied properly, infer the name of YHWH.)

Revelation 19: 17. And I saw a Messenger standing in the sun; and he cried with a loud voice, saying to all the fowls that fly in the midst of heaven: Come you, assemble to this great supper of Elohim; 18. that you may eat the flesh of kings, and the flesh of captains of thousands, and the flesh of valiant men, and the flesh of horses and of those who sit on them, and the flesh of all the free-born and of slaves, and of the small and the great.

Revelation 19: 19. And I saw the beast of prey and the kings of the earth and their warriors, that they assembled to wage battle with him who sat on the (white) horse, and with his warriors. 20. And the beast of prey was captured, and the false prophet that was with him, who did those prodigies before him, whereby he seduced them who had received the mark of the beast of prey and who worshipped his image. And they were both cast alive into the lake of fire which burns with sulfur. 21. And the rest were slain by the sword of him that sat on the horse, by that (sword) which issues from his mouth: and all the fowls were satiated with their flesh.

The judgment has begun!

Chapter 14

The Victory!

**And now for the moment for which we have all been
waiting:** Yeshua's rule and reign for one thousand years!

*Revelation 20: 1. And I saw a Messenger that descended from
heaven, having the key of the abyss and a great chain in his hand. 2.
And he seized the dragon, the old serpent, who is the Deceiver and
Satan, who seduced the whole habitable world: and he bound him a
thousand years. 3. And he cast him into the abyss and closed and
sealed upon him; so that he might deceive the nations no more until
these thousand years will be completed: but after that, he will be
released for but a short time.*

Now, re-read carefully the end of verse 3. Have you ever
wondered why YHWH would allow Satan to be released
from his bonds towards the end of the Millennium? The
answer is: Unbelievably, even though the world will have
been ruled by Yeshua personally for a thousand years,
there will *still* be those who will rebel against Him, and
YHWH will allow them to make their choice to side with
Satan! As mind-boggling as this is, it is exactly what we
are told will come to pass.

There is a tradition called "Rumspringa" (Pennsylvania
German meaning, "running around") in some Amisch
circles, whereby children who turn 16 have an opportunity
to go into the secular cities to experience "the world" after
which they can decide to remain there, or return to the
Amisch church and be baptized. YHWH affords all human
beings the same choice: He turns us loose to give us the
latitude to come back to HIM, or to spend eternity with
His enemy, Satan; there is no gray area. YHWH wants to

surround Himself only with those who truly love Him and wish to be in His Presence forever!

Revelation 20: 4. And I saw thrones, and (persons) sat on them, and judgment was given to them, and to the souls that were beheaded for the testimony of Y'shua and for the Word of Elohim: and these are they who had not worshipped the beast of prey nor its image; neither had they received the mark upon their forehead or on their hand; and they lived and reigned with their Mashiyach those thousand years. 5. This is the first resurrection. 6. Blessed and Set Apart is he that has part in this first resurrection: over them the second death has no dominion; but they will be, (and) are, priests of Elohim and of his Mashiyach; and they will reign with him the thousand years.

This chapter of Revelation also reveals a very important fact: Contrary to popular opinion, the "rapture"/first resurrection (verse 5) does *NOT* take place before the Mark of the Beast! No one is going to be "left behind" for seven years as the "pre-tribbers" suggest, because *nobody* is going anywhere until the seven years are finished! Furthermore, according to verse 6, the SECOND resurrection (second death) is a thousand years *after* the "dead and alive in Christ" have risen.

This is the very same event Paul described in I Thessalonians 4:16-17 - *"...and the dead who are in the Mashiyach will first arise; 17. and then we who survive and are alive will be caught up together with them to the clouds to meet our Master (Y'shua) in the air; and so will we be ever with our Master."*

Revelation 20: 7. And when these thousand years will be completed, Satan will be released from his prison; 8. and will go forth to seduce the nations that are in the four corners of the earth, Gog and Magog; and to assemble them for battle, whose number is as the sand of the sea. 9. And they went up on the breadth of the earth and encompassed the camp of the Set Apart believers and the beloved city. And fire came down from Elohim out of heaven and consumed them. 10. And the Accuser who seduced them, was cast into the lake of fire and sulfur, where also were the beast of prey and the false prophet: and they will be tormented, day and night, forever and ever.

Please take notice of verse 20:7 where we are told that Satan would be released from his prison so he can "seduce the nations" and assemble them for battle. Wow! Why in the world would Yeshua do that? By that time Yeshua - YHWH's holy Messiah - has been ruling and reigning on the earth for a thousand years, and there have been no human rulers to confuse anyone, so - *why* bother to release man's mortal enemy for ANY reason? And, after all that time, we are told, Satan will be able to find so many that they number "as the sand of the sea! What is going on?

The answer is: Man is inherently evil. Thanks to the Fall of man in Genesis 3, we are born into sin. If you have a hard time accepting this, just take a look at what happens to innocent babies once they become toddlers and realize they don't have to be completely dependent on Mom and Dad anymore; they constantly get into trouble doing things they aren't supposed to, and the first word they learn to use is **"NO!"** We want what we want, and in the end, even though people will have had a thousand years under Yeshua's rule, there will still be those who simply don't agree with Him.

Revelation 20:7-8 is proof positive that man is inherently evil. This scripture indicates, beyond a shadow of a doubt, that there *will* be major rebellion on Earth, regardless of the fact that YHWH-in-the-Flesh, at that point, will have been in charge for a thousand years! Those who managed to make it through the terrible trials of that initial seven year period before Yeshua's return to Earth, kept on living and dying, marrying, and perpetuating the human race. Their children and grandchildren and great-grandchildren, etc., will have known no other ruler during their generations, yet their carnal nature prevailed and many end up rebelling.

YHWH who is holy (Leviticus 11:44) cannot and will not be in the presence of evil, and so all those who receive eternal life and get to live in heaven with Him, will be those *who truly love and want to be in His Presence*. That is why, on Judgment Day, He will separate the "sheep from the goats" for the last time in the history of man (Matthew 25:31-46). He doesn't want ANYONE in His heaven who doesn't completely belong to Him! When Satan is released from prison, that will be the final time man gets to choose. After that, those who chose YHWH will receive eternal life; and those who didn't (there's no gray area!) will receive death, eternally separated from Him....

In verse 20:10 above, we saw what becomes of Satan, the false prophet and the beast of prey as they are unceremoniously "cast into the lake of fire and sulfur...and they will be tormented, day and night, forever and ever." The rest of the world who followed these entities will *not* be tormented forever; they will simply be separated from God throughout eternity – the worst punishment imaginable.

Please pay special attention to what happens next, because it signifies the end of humanity as we know it: Judgment Day!

Revelation 20: 11. And I saw a great white throne and Him who sits upon it; from whose presence the earth and heaven fled away, *and this their place was not found. 12. And I saw the dead, great and small, standing before the throne; and the books were opened; and another book was opened, which is (the book) of life. And the dead were judged from the things written in the books, according to their deeds. 13. And the sea gave up the dead in it; and death and Sheol gave up the dead in them. And they were judged, each one according to his deeds. 14. **And death and Sheol were cast into the lake of fire.** This is the second death, (namely,) this lake of fire. 15. And if any one was not found enrolled in the book of life, he was cast into this lake of fire.*

The Lake of Fire is the "second death". The *first* death, remember, is the resurrection of the righteous (Revelation 20:5-6); and the second death is for those who never bothered to become believers in YHWH, much less, attempt to live holy lives. They died while on earth, only to die again when they receive eternal death (separation from YHWH forever) once they are "raptured" to stand before YHWH on Judgment Day.

AND NOW PRESENTING: A "new heaven and a new Earth"!

Revelation 21: 1. And I saw new heavens and a new earth: for the former heaven and the former earth had passed away: and the sea was no more. 2. And I saw the Set Apart city, the New Urishlim, descending from Elohim out of heaven, prepared like a bride adorned for her husband. 3. And I heard a great voice from heaven, which said: Behold, the tabernacle of Elohim is with men; and he dwells with them: they will be his people; and Elohim will be with them, an Elohim to them.

Revelation 21: 4. And every tear will be wiped from their eyes; and there will no more be death, nor mourning, nor wailing; nor will pain be any more; because the former things are passed away. 5. And He who sat on the throne, said: Behold, I make all things new. And he said: Write; because these are the faithful and true Words of Elohim. 6. And he said to me: I am Alap and the Taw, the Beginning and the Completion: to him who thirsts, will I give of the fountain of living water, freely. 7. He that overcomes will inherit these things; and I will be his Elohim, and he will be my son. 8. But to the timid and the unbelieving, and to the sinful and polluted, and to manslayers and whoremongers, and sorcerers, and idolaters, and to all false persons, their portion will be in the lake that burns with fire and sulfur, which is the second death.

Please look at verse 8 again. How anyone can possibly believe that unholy people will enter heaven, is beyond me! Many of today's priests, pastors and rabbis are actually teaching that "God is love" and that "He will accept you as you are" and "forgive anything." They tend to omit the fact that God will forgive your **PAST** sins only (see Hebrews 10:26 below); YHWH will *not* tolerate lukewarm, halfhearted attempts to clean up your life once you've accepted Yeshua and have the *Ruach haKodesh* (Holy Spirit) "in your heart"; it's all, or nothing! Yes, He will forgive your occasional **unintentional** sins in your walk with Him whenever you repent and ask forgiveness, but He will absolutely NOT pardon willful rebellion. No "God is love, God is grace" theology can change this fact!

Hebrews 10: 26. For if a man sin voluntarily after he has received a knowledge of the truth, there is no longer a sacrifice which may be offered for sins: 27. but the fearful judgment impends, and the zeal of fire that consumes the adversaries. 28. For if he who transgressed the Torah of Moshe, died without mercies at the mouth of two or three witnesses; 29. how much more, do you think, will he receive capital punishment who has trodden upon the Son of Elohim and has accounted the blood of his covenant by which he is sanctified, as the blood of all men and has treated the Spirit of grace in an insulting manner?

226

If you fall into any of the categories in Revelation 21:8, make no mistake, YHWH is **NOT** kidding around! He is not going to be "tolerant" or "understanding" or "forgiving" of your willful sins on Judgment Day. You've had your chance to seek Him and His ways, and if you chose to ignore Him, you've lost your chance forever. He couldn't have been any clearer about who will be denied eternal life, and again - no amount of scripture twisting and obfuscation of the truth will change that fact!

Revelation 21: 9. And there came one of those seven Messengers who have the seven cups filled with the seven last plagues, and talked with me, saying: Come, I will show you the bride, the wife of the Lamb. 10. And he bore me away in the spirit to a mountain great and high, and he showed me the Set Apart city, Urishlim, descending out of heaven from Elohim; 11. in which was the glory of Elohim, as a brilliant light, and resembling a very precious gem; like a jasper stone, resembling crystal. 12 And it had a wall great and lofty, which had twelve gates, and names inscribed on them, which are the names of the twelve tribes of the children of Israel. 13. On the east, three gates; on the north, three gates; (on the south, three gates; and on the west, three gates).

Revelation 21: 14. And the wall of the city had twelve foundations, and upon them the twelve names of the twelve apostles of the Lamb. [Amazingly, TWELVE apostles are honored, even though one of them, Judas, betrayed Yeshua in the end!] *15. And he that talked with me had a measure, a golden reed; so that he could measure the city and its gates, and its wall. 16. And the city stood up four square; and its length was the same as its breadth. And he measured the city with the reed to twelve furlongs of twelve thousand; and the length and the breadth and the height of it were (all) equal. 17. And he measured its wall, a hundred and forty and four measures of the cubits of a man, that is, of the Messenger. 18. And the structure of its wall (was of) jasper; and the city was of pure gold, like pure glass.*

Revelation 21: 19. And the foundations of the wall of the city were adorned with every precious stone. The first foundation, a jasper; the second, a sapphire; the third, a chalcedony; the fourth, an emerald; 20. the fifth, a sardonyx; the sixth, a sardius; the seventh, a chrysolite; the eighth, a beryl; the ninth, a topaz; the tenth, a chrysoprasus; the eleventh, a jacinth; the twelfth, an amethyst.

*Revelation 21: 21. And the twelve gates (were) twelve pearls; each (pearl) one gate, and each (gate) one pearl: and the broad street of the city was pure gold, like brilliant glass. 22. And I saw no temple in it; for Master YHWH Almighty is its temple, and the Lamb. 23. And the city has no need of the sun or of the moon to enlighten it; for the glory of Elohim enlightens it, and the Lamb is the lamps of it. 24. **And the nations that were saved will walk by means of its light, and the kings of the earth will bring their glory and the wealth of the nations into it. 25. And its gates will not be shut by day; for there is no night there. 26. And they will bring the glory and honor of the nations into it. 27. And there will not enter it anything polluted, or that practices impurity and falsehood; but they who are registered in the Lamb's book of life.***

Notice after the description of the new Jerusalem just who occupies the "city". Verses 24-27 reiterate that only the righteous, the holy and those who "bring glory and honor" to YHWH are in the new kingdom. He is very clear about this - *"there will not enter it anything polluted, or that practices impurity and falsehood."*

Revelation 22: 1. And he showed me a river of living water, transparent (as) crystal, which proceeded from the throne of Elohim and the Lamb. 2. And in the middle of its broad avenue and near the river, on this side and on that, (was) the tree of life; which bore twelve (sorts of) fruits yielding one of its fruits each month: and the leaves of the tree (were) for the healing of the nations. 3. And there will be no blight anymore: and the throne of Elohim and the Lamb will be in it; and his servants will minister to him. 4. And they will see his face, and his name (will be) on their foreheads. 5. And there will be no more night; and they have no need of the light of a lamp or of the light of the sun; because Master YHWH, Elohim, gives them light: and they will reign forever and ever.

Revelation 22: 6. And he said to me: These words (are) faithful and true. And the Master YHWH, Elohim of the Spirit of the prophets, has sent me, his Messenger, to show to his servants the things that must soon occur. 7. And, lo, I come quickly: Blessed is he that keeps the words of the prophecy of this book. 8. And moreover I am Yochanan, the hearer and the seer of these things. And when I heard and saw, I fell down to worship at the feet of the Messenger who showed me these things. 9. And he said to me: See, that you do not do this: I am your fellow-servant and of your Brothers the prophets, and of them that observe the words of this book. Worship Elohim. 10. And he said to me: Do not seal the words of the prophecy of this book; for the time is near. 11. He that does evil, let him do evil still; and he that is filthy, let him be filthy still; and he that is righteous, let him practice righteousness still; and he that is sanctified, let him be sanctified still.

*Revelation 22: 12. **Behold, I come quickly; and my reward is with me to recompense everyone according to his work. 13. I am Alap and the Taw, the First and the Last, the Beginning and the Completion.** 14. Blessed are they who do His (Master YHWH's) Mitzvot, that they may have a right to the tree of life and may enter through the gates into the city. 15. **Without (will be) dogs** (refers not necessarily to literal dogs, but to those who behave like animals) **and sorcerers, and whoremongers and manslayers and idolaters, and everyone that loves and does falsehood.***

*Revelation 22: 16. **I Y'shua have sent my Messenger to testify to you these things before the assemblies.** I am the root and offspring of Dawid: like the splendid star of the morning. 17. And the Spirit and the bride say, You come. And let him that hears, say, You come. And let him who thirsts, come; and he that is inclined, let him take*

229

the living water freely. 18. I testify to every one who hears the words of the prophecy of this book, that if anyone will add to them, Elohim will add to him the plagues that are written in this book. 19. And if any one will take away from the words of the book of this prophecy, Elohim will take away his portion from the tree of life and from the Set Apart city, which are described in this book. 20. He who testifies these things, says: Yes, I come quickly. Amen. Come, Lord Y'shua! 21. The grace of our Master (Y'shua) Y'shua the Mashiyach, (be) with all the Set Apart believers. Amen.

And so we finally come to the end of the Book of Revelation...and the end of our study on the end times.

Now the question remains: Have you determined the key to surviving the end times? What are YOU doing to prepare? There are so many "conspiracy theories" today, especially on the Internet, along with suggestions for us to prepare by stocking up on canned goods and bottled water. But the thing is, canned goods and bottled water aren't going to save you if you are killed by an airborne disease or swallowed up by an earthquake, trapped in a burning building, or drowned in the rising waters of a hurricane.

The most important thing you can do for yourself is to prepare yourself *spiritually*. Even those of solid faith and righteous lives and those living with Torah in their hearts must still experience the events of the end times, and many of these righteous will lose their earthly lives as these events unfold. It is not so important how or why or who meets what fate. What is important is what you have done during *your* life to ensure *your* place as a "Set Apart" believer in the new kingdom (Revelation 22:14).

This means, you need to:

- Admit in your mind and heart that there is a Creator who made you, and that His Name is YHWH.

- Admit your mind and heart that, without His will, you wouldn't be here today and then repent for your sins, asking YHWH to help you break all bad habits and "quirks."

- Admit and *believe* with all your mind and heart that He sent His Son Yeshua who died a horrible death on the cross/stake on your behalf to become the Final SIN Sacrifice for *you*.

- Recognize the *fact* that nearly 400 Bible prophecies have already come true, and that there are just a few more to go before Yeshua returns to rule and reign on Earth for a thousand years.

- Stop playing around with the Word of YHWH by letting everyone else's theology or opinions confuse you; and start spending time getting into the Bible yourself to see what it actually says about obedience.

- Be obedient by learning what YHWH asks of you and begin to apply it in your life!

Thank you for reading this book. May YHWH richly bless you, and may you find the way to surviving the end times and winning the victory:

Revelation 2: 7. He that has ears, let him hear what the Spirit says to the assemblies. To him who is victorious, will I give to eat of the tree of life which is in the paradise of my Elohim

Appendix 1

48 Important Bible Prophecies

Nearly 400 Bible prophecies have come to pass, which means we will soon get to witness the final few. Yeshua has fulfilled many of them, as indicated in the following list of just 48 prophecies that are directly linked to Him.

Interestingly, the probability of 48 prophecies being fulfilled in one person is the incredible number 10 to the 157th power (10 followed by 157 zeros), according to Professor Peter Stoner (June 16, 1888 – March 21, 1980), former Chairman of the Departments of Mathematics and Astronomy at Pasadena City College until 1953; Chairman of the science division, Westmont College, 1953-57; Professor Emeritus of Science, Westmont College; Professor Emeritus of Mathematics and Astronomy, Pasadena City College. He is probably best known for his work *Science Speaks* that discusses, among other things, Bible prophecies *vis a vis* probability estimates and calculations. (Wikipedia).

Prophecy	Old Testament (Torah & Haphtarah)	New Testament Fulfilled
1. Messiah's pre-existence.	Micah 5:2	John 1:1, 1:14
2. To be from the seed of a woman.	Genesis 3:15	Matthew 1:18
3. To be from the seed of Abraham.	Genesis 12:3	Matthew 1:1-16
4. To be from the seed of David.	Isaiah 11:10	Matthew 1:1
5. Abraham's descendant would bless all nations.	Genesis 12:3; 18:18	Matthew 1:2
6. To be from the tribe of	Genesis 49:10	Matthew 1:1-3

Judah.		
7. To be a prophet like Moses.	Deuteronomy 18:15,19	John 5:45-47
8. To be the Son of God.	Isaiah 9:6-7	Luke 1:32
9. To be called Lord	Jeremiah 23:5-6	John 13:13
10. To be called Mighty God	Isaiah 9:6	Matthew 1:23
11. To be God within a man	Zechariah 12:10-11	John 10:30
12. To be presented with gifts.	Psalm 72:10	Matthew 2:10
13. To die before the 2nd Temple is destroyed.	Daniel 9:24-27	Temple destroyed in 70 A.D.; Jesus killed between 30-33 A.D.
14. To enter Jerusalem between 30-33 A.D.	Daniel 9:24-27	Jesus enters Jerusalem between 30-33 A.D.
15. To be born in Bethlehem.	Micah 5:2	Luke 2:4-2:7
16. To perform miracles.	Isaiah 35:5-6	Matthew 11:4-6
17. To enter Jerusalem on a donkey.	Zechariah 9:9	Matthew 21:6-9
18. To enter Jerusalem as a King.	Zechariah 9:9	Matthew 21:5
19. To suffer.	Isaiah 53:10-11	Mark 15:34-37
20. To bring salvation.	Isaiah 59:16-20	Luke 19:10
21. When God establishes His new covenant, Israel will come to know the Lord; not just His laws.	Jeremiah 31:31-34	Matthew 11:29-30
22. To be raised from the dead.	Psalm 16:10, Isaiah 53:10	Mark 16:9-10
23. To sit at the right hand of God.	Psalm 110:1	Mark 16:19
24. To be a priest forever.	Psalm 110:4	Hebrews 5:5-6
25. To be an intercessor between man and God.	Isaiah 59:16	Matthew 10:32
26. To be called wonderful counselor	Isaiah 9:5-6	Luke 4:22
27. To be called everlasting	Isaiah 9:5-6	Matthew 1:23

father.		
28. To be called prince of peace.	Isaiah 9:5-6	John 16:33
29. To be a guide to Jews and Gentiles.	Isaiah 42:1; Isaiah 49:1-8	Luke 2:32
30. To be accepted by Gentiles.	Isaiah 11:10	Acts 13:47-48
31. To be preceded by a messenger.	Isaiah 40:3	Matthew 11:10-11
32. To bring light to Galilee.	Isaiah 9:1-2	Matthew 4:15
33. Would be rejected.	Isaiah 53:3; Daniel 9:24-26	John 1:11
34. Would be tried and condemned.	Isaiah 53:8	Acts 8:31-35
35. Would be pierced.	Isaiah 53:5	John 20:25
36. Would be wounded.	Isaiah 53:5	John 19:17-18
37. Would be considered a criminal.	Isaiah 53:12	Luke 22:37
38. Would pray for criminals.	Isaiah 53:12	Luke 23:34 (in reference to the soldiers)
39. Would have no broken bones.	Psalm 34:20/21, Exodus 12:46, Numbers 9:12)	John 19:33
40. Would be silent before His accusers.	Isaiah 53:7	Matthew 27:14
41. Would be buried in a rich man's tomb.	Isaiah 53:9	Matthew 27:57-60
42. Would heal the blind.	Isaiah 61:1-2	John 9:25-38
43. Would preach to the poor.	Isaiah 61:1-2	Matthew 11:5
44. Would die for the sins of Israel & the World.	Isaiah 53:5-6	Matthew 20:28
45. Israel would see, but not see; hear, but not hear.	Isaiah 6:9-10	Matthew 13:13-15
46. His message would spread world-wide.	Isaiah 49:6	Acts 15:15-18
47. Would be a priest after the order of Melchizedek.	Psalm 110:4	Hebrews 5:10

48. Darkness would fall over Israel at 12:00 P.M. on a day where the Lord would have Israel mourn for an only Son.	Amos 8:9-10	Matthew 27:45

INTERESTING NOTE: Outside of the prophecies Yeshua has fulfilled, two others came to pass on May 14, 1948, right after the Holocaust, when "the world" briefly felt sorry for "the Jews" and returned Israel to them. This fulfilled Isaiah's predictions that Israel would become a nation once more and it was to happen in *one day*!

Isaiah 66: 7 *Before going into labor, she gave birth; before her pains came, she delivered a male child. 8 Who ever heard of such a thing? Who has ever seen such things? Is a country born in one day? Is a nation brought forth all at once? For as soon as Tziyon went into labor, she brought forth her children.*

Appendix 2

YHWH's "Forever" Commands

YHWH provided many rules and commands that can be found scattered throughout the Torah, the first five Books of the Bible. We must understand, however, that the "numbering" of the original commandments was done by *man*, not by YHWH Himself, which means there is no reason to worry about trying to "keep all 613 commands." Many of the "613" commands were directed at the *cohens* (priests) and not at the general population. Furthermore, some commands are only for men, while others only for women.

The "numbering" of the commands is a tradition that can be found in the Talmud which says there are 613 bones in the human body and, when a person practices the 613 commandments, he affects each one of the 613 bones and vessels.

While YHWH eventually gave *ten* commandments to Moses that every believer was to keep, we must remember, these ten are just part of the larger picture taken from YHWH's Torah which He said would stand *forever*. The ten were etched in stone, but when YHWH says "do" or "don't", whether or not it is cast in stone, it is still a "commandment". Many Christians balk at this idea because they are under the erroneous impression that they don't even have to bother keeping the TEN Commandments anymore (let alone the "613"). Rather, they argue there are just *two* - and they cite the following as "proof":

237

*Matthew 22: 36. "Teacher, which Commandment in Torah is the greatest?" 37. And Y'shua said to him, that "You should love Master YHWH your Elohim with all your heart and with all your soul and with all your might and with all your mind." 38. This is the first and the greatest Commandment. 39. And the second is like it. That "You should love your neighbor as yourself." 40. **On these two commandments hang Torah and the prophets.**

See? Matthew 22:37-38 says we only have to "love God and love our neighbors." Two commands. I would ask those who insist they only need to keep these two commandments to please re-read these verses in Matthew but include verse 40, with the help of the *Ruach haKodesh* (Holy Spirit). Does verse 40 imply that all of God's original instructions or commands have been "done away with" because *"All of the Torah and the Prophets are dependent on these two mitzvot"* (words/commands)? **NO!** Verse 40 says that these two commandments are only the "tip", the "greatest" of all the commandments. That was the question of Yeshua. "Which are the GREATEST?" By including the words of verse 40 in His reply, Yeshua was saying Torah, and Torah embodied in the future as revealed by the prophets, is still *all* important! Nobody, including Yeshua, has the right to negate any of the Father's original commands!

Please note also in verse 40 that, Torah and Prophets hang or "hold on by" these two "Greatest Commandments" is expressed as Love. One expresses one's love of YHVH by obeying the Commandments, (Matt 19:17; 1 John 5:2-3). ALso without love of neighbor, observance of Torah is vanity, and without Torah, "love" of one's self is vanity.

The verses below from Numbers pronounce that EVERYONE who accepts the God of Abraham, Isaac and Jacob is to be Torah observant:

Numbers 15: 13 "Every citizen is to do these things in this way when presenting an offering made by fire as a fragrant aroma for ADONAI. 14 If a foreigner stays with you - or whoever may be with you, through all your generations - and he wants to bring an offering made by fire as a fragrant aroma for ADONAI, he is to do the same as you. 15 For this community there will be the same law for you as for the foreigner living with you; this is a permanent regulation through all your generations; the foreigner is to be treated the same way before ADONAI as yourselves. 16 The same Torah and standard of judgment will apply to both you and the foreigner living with you."

The "aliens" both then and now include anyone who wasn't born through Abraham's lineage. "Jewish" or not, *anyone* who is "grafted-in" through the blood of Messiah belongs to YHWH and is therefore obligated to obey His Torah! Yeshua Himself was Torah observant and He showed mankind how to do it yet, for some reason, Christians have decided that God treats His adopted children differently from His natural ones...

But Yeshua abolished the need for Torah! No, He didn't! Why would He? He came to proclaim the Kingdom of YHWH, perfectly performing the duties of Torah Himself – as did all His Apostles, and every believer throughout the First Century before Catholicism came to remove anything "Jewish" from the Word of God! The ONLY thing that changed was the need to kill innocent animals as *sin* sacrifices, because the Divine Yeshua was the FINAL Sin Sacrifice who martyred Himself on our behalf. What Yeshua attempted to "do away with" was *not* the Father's divine instructions, but the rabbinical, man-made, added-on "stuff" that had crept into the worship of YHWH. Even Paul verified this when he said:

Romans 3: 31. Do, we then nullify Torah by faith? May it never be! On the contrary, we establish Torah.

You will find YHWH's original commandments sprinkled throughout Torah in places like Genesis 26:2-5; Exodus 15:25-27, 16, 20:6; Leviticus 22, 26, 27; Numbers 15 and 36; and Deuteronomy 4, 5, 6, 7, 8, 10, 11, 13, 26, 27, 28, 30, 31. Please study these scriptures thoroughly and then ask yourself, "What is this telling me?" If you don't conclude that Torah consists of YHWH's instruction for life, then perhaps you have missed the point! Yeshua taught that sin keeps you from the Kingdom (Matthew 5:20) and that you will be judged according to Torah (Matthew 5:19). Without Torah as a measure, we cannot know what constitutes sin (Romans 3:20).

As mentioned before, many of the Torah commandments cannot be kept today because they were for the priests and kings of the day; and some are only for men, some only for women. However, there were some commandments YHWH gave to everyone to last throughout eternity, and these include:

- **The Ten Commandments** (Exodus 20 and 34 - which included several "forever" commandments).

- **The Seventh Day Sabbath** (Exodus 31:13; Exodus 31:16-17; Leviticus 23:3). YHWH told us that the Sabbath would *forever* be a *sign* between Him and the children of Israel (which includes *every* believer, grafted-in or otherwise!) In the end times (which we are in now) the seventh day Sabbath will distinguish TRUE believers from the "lukewarm" - especially when the Antichrist starts putting pressure on people to conform to his rules:

Exodus 31: "Tell the people of Isra'el, 'You are to observe my Shabbats; for this is a sign between me and you through all your generations; so that you will know that I am ADONAI, who sets you apart for me.

- *Exodus 31: 16 The people of Isra'el are to keep the Shabbat, to observe Shabbat through all their generations as a perpetual covenant. 17 It is a sign between me and the people of Isra'el forever; for in six days ADONAI made heaven and earth, but on the seventh day he stopped working and rested.'"*

- **The Feasts** (YHWH's Appointed Times with mankind) are outlined in places like Leviticus 23 which includes wording such as: "*do this forever*" or "*this is to be a permanent ordinance throughout your generations.*"

- **Keeping kosher.** Yes, eating "clean" foods was a "forever" commandment. Pigs and shellfish and crows, etc., are still unclean, as they are basically "garbage disposals" that eat other dead and diseased things which can kill us if we choose to eat them! For a complete outline, see Deuteronomy 14:1-21 and Leviticus 11.

The above is by no means a complete list, but it will give you a good start and a lot to think about. Yeshua even said He did NOT come to abolish/loosen Torah, but to fulfill. "Fulfill" never meant He was abolishing it!

Matthew 5: 17. Do not think that I have come to loosen Torah or the prophets, I have not come to loosen but to fulfill. 18. For truly I say to you that until heaven and earth pass away not one Yodh or one stroke will pass from Torah until everything happens. 19. All who loosen, therefore, from one (of) these small commandments and teach thus to the sons of man, will be called little in the Kingdom of

Heaven, but all who do and teach this will be called great in the Kingdom of Heaven. 20. For I say to you that unless your righteousness exceeds more than that of the scribes and the Pharisees, you will not enter the Kingdom of Heaven.

Has everything happened that must happen? Have heaven and earth passed away yet?

*Revelation 12: 17. And the dragon was enraged against the woman; and he went to make war upon the remnant of her seed who keep the Commandments of Elohim **and** have the testimony of Y'shua.*

*Revelation 14: 12. Here is the patience of the Set Apart believers who keep the commandments of Elohim, **and** the faith of Y'shua.*

Some versions use "saint" as opposed to "Set Apart Believers." But who exactly is a "saint"? Certainly not someone who refuses to be Torah observant! Who are those who hold to the testimony of Yeshua **and** remain faithful to Him? The Torah observant believers in Messiah Yeshua! Jews don't believe in Yeshua and Christians don't believe in being Torah observant. Until both sides "get it", they remain incomplete.

Appendix 3

YHWH's Appointed Times

YHWH designed His *mo'edim* - Appointed Times/Feasts for His people to come together for corporate worship. They are strategically spaced throughout the year so that we can remain in constant communion with Him.

These Feasts are specifically outlined in **Leviticus 23** which describes the whole annual cycle of special convocations. They are as follows:

- **Passover (Pesach):** Passover (Nisan 14) falls in the March/April time frame on the Gregorian calendar. Leviticus 23:5 tells us*: "'In the first month, on the fourteenth day of the month, between sundown and complete darkness, comes Pesach for ADONAI."* This Feast celebrates the deliverance of the Hebrew slaves from Egypt; a tale of redemption through the killing of the Passover Lamb whose blood was to be applied to the doorposts of their houses - an act which would spare their firstborn from the Tenth Curse against Pharoah. YHWH promised that the Angel of Death would "pass over" those houses with the blood on the doorposts, and spare the first born (Exodus 12:1-13). Foreshadowed Yeshua, YHWH's "Passover Lamb" who fulfilled Passover when he was crucified and willingly allowed His own blood to be shed on our behalf in order to become our redemption.

- **Unleavened Bread (Hag HaMatzot):** Celebrated on Nisan 15, it marks the beginning of a seven day period during which the eating of leavened Bread is forbidden as leaven is a symbol of sin (I Cor. 5:6-8). Messiah Yeshua fulfilled this Feast when he was buried and became our righteousness (Rom. 6:4, II Cor. 5:21).

- **Firstfruits (Yom HaBikkurim):** Fulfilled when Yeshua, the Firstruits of Creation, rose from the dead (I Corinthians 15:-20-23). Celebrated on Nisan 16, Firstfruits falls during the March/April timeframe. This Feast celebrates the bringing of the firstfruits of the winter harvest to the Temple - indicating there would be more to come. Please note, the first three Feasts were fulfilled through the crucifixion, burial and resurrection of Yeshua haMashiach!

- **Feast of Weeks (Shavuot):** Known by Christians as "Pentecost", is celebrated during the May/June timeframe. Exodus 34:22 tells us: *"Observe the festival of Shavu'ot with the first-gathered produce of the wheat harvest, and the festival of ingathering at the turn of the year.* Torah directs the seven-week Counting of the Omer (which begins on the second day of Passover and culminates after seven weeks, the next day being Shavuot). The counting of the days and weeks conveys anticipation of and desire for the Giving of the Torah. In other words, at Passover, the Israelites were freed from their lives of slavery in Egypt; and 50 days later on Shavuot they accepted YHWH's Torah which made them a nation committed to serving God. This Feast was fulfilled by the coming of the promised Ruach HaKodesh (Holy Spirit) on the disciples of Yeshua in the Temple. It represents the beginning of the body of Messiah on Earth, in which ALL believers, redeemed through the blood of Messiah, are lifted up before ADONAI and set apart as holy (Acts 2, John 14:15-18, Ephesians 2:11-22).

- **Feast of Trumpets (Rosh Hashanah):** YHWH's New Year; the anniversary of the creation of Adam and Eve and their first actions toward the realization of man's role in the world; of the first sin that was committed and resulting repentance; a day when YHWH takes stock of all of His Creation, which includes all of humanity. This Feast on Tishri 1 falls in the September/October timeframe. Leviticus 23:23-25 says: *23 ADONAI said to Moshe, 24 "Tell the people of Isra'el, 'In the seventh month, the first of the month is to be for you a day of complete rest for remembering, a holy convocation announced with blasts on the shofar. 25 Do not do any kind of ordinary work, and bring an offering made by fire to ADONAI.'"*

- **Day of Atonement (Yom Kippur):** Celebrated ten days later; represents the need for the sacrifice/sin offering that must be made for the sins of the nation. Yeshua WAS that Sacrifice and He will be recognized for it at the Marriage Supper of the Lamb which will take place immediately after Rosh Hashana/the "rapture" just BEFORE we all return with Him to fulfill the Feast of Tabernacles, wherein Yeshua will "tabernacle" among us for the next thousand years! Celebrated on Tishri 10, this Feast falls in the September/October timeframe. Leviticus 16:29 tells us: *"It is to be a permanent regulation for you that on the tenth day of the seventh month you are to deny yourselves and not do any kind of work, both the citizen and the foreigner living with you.*

245

- **Feast of Tabernacles (Sukkot):** Celebrated five days later; Yeshua, our Savior, was born during the Feast of Sukkot and circumcised eight days later. The idea that He was born on "Christmas" in December is a lie! This Feast also serves as a reminder of the days in the wilderness when YHW's people were forced to reside in tents/huts or temporary dwellings - a reminder of our temporary lives on Earth. It will be fulfilled by the ingathering of the "Final Harvest" of souls just prior to the setting up of the Kingdom of the Messiah on Earth. Celebrated on Tishri 15, this Feast falls in the September/October timeframe. It is outlined in Deuteronomy 16:13-15, where YHWH tells the Israelites: *13 "You are to keep the festival of Sukkot for seven days after you have gathered the produce of your threshing-floor and winepress. 14 Rejoice at your festival - you, your sons and daughters, your male and female slaves, the L'vi'im, and the foreigners, orphans and widows living among you. 15 Seven days you are to keep the festival for ADONAI your God in the place ADONAI your God will choose, because ADONAI your God will bless you in all your crops and in all your work, so you are to be full of joy!*

PLEASE NOTE that the first three major events for believers in Yeshua - His death, burial and resurrection - fell <u>exactly</u> on the first three Feasts, and the symbolism of the Feasts appears to be beyond coincidence:

- While Passover was being celebrated - which included the slaying of an unblemished Lamb – Yeshua was being slain on the cross (1 Cor 5:7).

- The feast that followed, Unleavened Bread, is a picture of sanctification, as Yeshua was buried.

246

Leaven is representative of sin, of which Yeshua had none.

- And then the Feast of Firstfruits, to be celebrated on the morning AFTER the first Sabbath following the Feasts of Unleavened Bread (Sunday) (Lev 23:10-11) is symbolic of Yeshua being the first of the Firstfruits (1 Cor 15:23).

- The next big event for believers was the coming of the Holy Spirit, and it fell *EXACTLY* on the next Feast 50 days later, on what Christians call Pentecost.

Since the first four major events of the "New Testament Church" happened on the first four Biblical Feasts, the next big event – the so-called "Rapture" – should fall on the next one – the Feast of Trumpets or *Rosh Hashanah*, when YHWH calls his people together. Again the symbolism is seemingly beyond coincidence as this is to be a day of regathering and rejoicing.

There is, of course, much more to YHWH's Feasts, but the bottom line is: Judging from the importance that HE placed on them, why would anyone think "Jesus abolished them"?

Appendix 4

Torah explained in simple terms

Many Christians who have been taught that "Jesus nailed it to the cross" don't seem to understand exactly WHAT was nailed to the cross. For some reason they are under the mistaken impression that "Torah" – YHWH's Divine teaching and instruction - was somehow abolished on the cross, which is a dangerously off-the-mark assertion which, on Judgment Day, will render "lukewarm" many who thought they had the "market cornered" on Truth..

Many insist, "all that Old Testament stuff was just for the Jews" - while not realizing *there actually were no "Jews"* before Jacob begat the Tribe of Judah! Adam and Eve (Gen. 2) weren't Jews; Cain and Abel (Gen. 4) who offered sin sacrifices weren't Jews; and neither was Noah (Gen. 6) who knew the difference between "clean and unclean" animals; and neither were Abraham, Isaac and Jacob. And yet, *all* believers in the God of Abraham, Isaac and Jacob were Torah observant!

Please stop and ask yourself why that was! The answer is: *Because God said so.* He gave rules for us to live by, and man's job was not to question but to obey because, without God's Torah, man would have *no blueprint* for moral, holy living (1 Peter 1:16)!

No one is suggesting that YHWH's love is conditional. He loves us, no matter what. But why would that negate obedience to His rules? Where are we given permission to ignore His "forever" commands, just because "Jesus died"? Where did Jesus personally ever say that His death was to negate His Father's Torah? Paul even agreed:

Romans 10: 12. And in this, it discriminates neither Jews nor Gentiles. For there is one, Master YHWH, over them all, who is abundantly generous towards every one that calls on him. 13. For everyone that will call on the name of Master YHWH, will have life.

In view of this, it would seem that those who claim to "love" God would **WANT** to obey His "forever" commands instead of coming up with their own rules, as did "the church." Christianity has blatantly ignored YHWH's commands and categorically denies Torah because they erroneously believe "Jesus nailed it to the cross" *without realizing that what was nailed to the cross was **not** God's Divine Instructions*, but rather the rabbinical and legalistic "man-made stuff" that had crept into worship.

Yeshua was our Final SIN Sacrifice, and since Yeshua Himself was Torah observant, doesn't that suggest He was showing **US** how to do it? Did He *ever* say, "After my death you don't have to do anything but 'believe'?"

Let's view this from another, simpler perspective:

Your children "believe" in you, too, and you love them unconditionally. But does that mean that they don't have to mind you anymore just because they "believe" in you? Does "believing in you" give them a blanket authority to forget your teachings on right and wrong, good and bad? Can they touch that hot stove, now that they believe in you? Does it mean they can now cross the freeway without first making sure there are no cars coming, or to kill someone at will if they're angry? That's what Christians are implying when they insist they are not obligated to obey YHWH's "forever" commands (such as the Seventh Day Sabbath and the Feasts)....Sure, you love your children unconditionally, but the rules you set out for them are

FOREVER because those rules will keep them safe from harm. They don't have the right to ignore your rules just because they "believe" in you.

Pets are another example. They are safe and sound as long as they stay within the boundaries of your fenced-in property. But, from the moment they decided to climb over that fence, there is no guarantee they won't get hit by a car or shot by a mean neighbor. Life has rules we simply cannot ignore – especially the rules YHWH gave us!

The Torah is full of rules - how to worship YHWH, how to treat each other according to Him, what we can and can't eat (have you ever noticed that all the animals that God considers "unclean" are the carnivores who eat anything including disease-laden garbage and roadkill?)....Yet the church decided all "old" stuff that was just for "the Jews"....

Back to the beginning:

YHWH, as our Creator, is our Father. From the very beginning, He tried to teach us right from wrong; He had rules for man to live by: (Paraphrased from Gen. 2:15-17) *"Adam, work the garden, but do not eat from the tree of the knowledge of good and evil in the middle of the Garden; you will die if you do!"* "Do's" and "Don'ts" - TORAH! - from the very beginning!

Divine law and priesthood have ALWAYS been around, as far back as Adam. And when Adam and Eve sinned and were banished from the Garden (banished and not killed - because of God's grace!), YHWH imposed even more rules on mankind because, now that man had partaken from tree of the knowledge of good and evil, he was destined to reap the consequences. And the consequences required sacrifices and offerings to God....which was His prerogative as our Creator.

The sacrifice for sin was always the shedding of innocent blood. Why blood? Because it is life-giving! Without it, we die. Why an innocent animal? To make man *feel* the anguish over the loss of an innocent life on his behalf! Something had to die so that Mr. and Ms. Sinner could live! YHWH demanded the blood of an innocent animal to impress upon man the importance of knowing the consequences for sin, and for total obedience. The first account of an animal sacrifice is when YHWH personally killed an animal to make coverings for the naked Adam and Eve after they ate from the fruit of the tree (Genesis 3).

The Bible doesn't tell us how, but YHWH obviously taught Adam and Eve about sacrifices because we know that Cain and Abel offered sacrifices in Genesis 4:3-5. At that time, while the population of the earth was still fairly small, a high priest was not required to handle the sacrifices. Every obedient man offered his own sacrifice and, in essence, was his own priest, as appears in the case of Abel, Noah, Melchizedek, Job and Abraham.

The need for a high priest - an intercessor between YHWH and man - arose when Israel's population began to grow. (The duties of the high priest and his special vestments are outlined in the books of Exodus and Leviticus, the chief references being Ex. 28: 6-42; Ex. 29: 6; Ex. 39: 27-29; Lev. 6: 19-23; Lev. 21: 10.) Yeshua Mashiyach ultimately became our High Priest! He was not a "new god" or someone who came to replace YHWH, the Father! He was the SON who came to do His Father's Will, and who martyred Himself on our behalf in order to abolish the need for SIN sacrifices by allowing us the privilege to simply "believe" on the blood shed at the cross. (Remember, this in no way negated the need for OBEDIENCE!)

*Luke 4: 43. And Y'shua said to them that, It is necessary for me to preach to other cities **the Kingdom of Elohim, for because this reason I have been sent.***

*Acts 28: 23. And they appointed him a day; and many assembled, and came to him at his lodgings. **And he explained to them respecting the Kingdom of Elohim, testifying and persuading them concerning Y'shua, out of the Torah of Moshe, and out of the prophets, from morning till evening.***

Acts 24: 14. But this indeed I acknowledge, that in that same doctrine of which they speak, I do serve the Elohim of my fathers, believing all the things written in Torah and in the prophets.

But unlike the other high priests, Yeshua offered Himself on our behalf and thus bore the sins of *ALL* of us permanently. The only thing required of us, in return, was to acceot that and believe in His shed blood at the cross/stake (Hebrews 3:1; John 3:15-18; 1 Peter 1:18-19; John 10:8-9; John 10:10; 2 Cor. 5:17-18; Matthew 1:21, Isaiah 7:14); thereby becoming new creatures in Messiah who *desire* to follow YHWH in every respect.

We need to remember that, just because Moses was the first one to present YHWH's Divine Instruction to mankind as "Torah" - *YHWH*, not Moses, is the author of the Torah. It is *not* the "MOSAIC Law! YHWH allowed Moses to see His wisdom and commanded him to share that knowledge with the Hebrews and to all those who had followed the Hebrews out of Egypt and chosen to accept their God.

Torah includes the keeping of the Seventh Day Sabbath (Genesis 2:3) which YHWH commanded in places such as Exodus 31:13-16, Isaiah 66:23 and Isaiah 58:13, among others. Torah also includes the seven *mo'edim* (Feasts/Appointed Times - as outlined in Leviticus 23. To illustrate the importance of the Feasts, one must understand that Yeshua has so far only fulfilled the first four of the seven, with three more to go - and the next one is the "Rapture" (see Appendix 3)!

YHWH wasn't "cursing" man when He gave us rules to live by. His rules taught man right from wrong and how to obey God and to worship Him properly.

Most Christians don't mind adhering to the Ten Commandments (even though they don't bother to keep even the Fourth Commandment concerning the Seventh Day Sabbath) which are part of Torah. But man has always liked to "pick and choose" when it comes to God's Word, and it's time to realize that seventh-day Sabbath command, along with His Feasts were *never* abolished - on the cross, or anywhere else!

2 Timothy 3: 16. All Scripture that was written by the Spirit is profitable for instruction and for decisive refutation, and for correction, and for deep extensive learning in righteousness; 17. that the man of Elohim may become perfect and complete for every good work.

So, exactly what was it that Yeshua's death abolished?

Yeshua attempted to show us that *man-made* traditions and teachings had twisted YHWH's Word. The teachings of the rabbis in "Biblical times" (just as the teachings of today's pastors!) had clouded the things YHWH had actually said! This is backed up by the teachings of Paul, who wrote, though often misunderstood as condemning Torah:

Colossians 2: 14. *and, by his mandates, he blotted out the handwriting of our debts which (handwriting) existed against us, and took (it) from the midst and affixed (it) to his stake.*

What does the above refer to? Our SINS! Did Rav Sha'ul (Paul) say **Torah** was nailed to the cross? No! Yeshua was our SIN Sacrifice; that is all. YHWH sent an aspect of Himself (an "arm"; see Isaiah 53:1) to earth in the form of a man with whom we could better identify and understand the things He taught. Yeshua personally taught us about the things of God, how to live with each other according to God's will; and then to offer Himself as the Final Sin Sacrifice. Yeshua wiped away the documented opinions of men (bill of charges) against us and took them from our midst....He even said He came NOT to abolish Torah, but to fulfill it. "Fulfill" did not mean "put an end to, or negate!

The Torah is holy, righteous and good (Romans 7:12). To suddenly have it "nailed to the cross" as Christians would have us believe, suggests that the things of God were originally evil, something to be done away with.

The bottom line is: Torah contains exactly what God wanted us to know about Himself, how to worship Him, and how we are to live together in harmony according to HIS commands.

In Numbers 15:13-16 we are shown four times in a row that ALL are to observe His *Mitzvot* (Words/Commands), while other scriptures reveal that *we will be keeping the Feasts and the Seventh Day Sabbath* for *all eternity*....

Ezekiel 20: 10 So I had them leave the land of Egypt and brought them into the desert. 11 I gave them my laws and showed them my rulings; if a person obeys them, he will have life through them. 12 I gave them my shabbats as a sign between me and them, so that they would know that I, ADONAI, am the one who makes them holy.

Ezekiel 20:10-12 tells us the Sabbath was to be a **SIGN** between YHWH and His creation, yet Christians have changed the Seventh Day Sabbath to Sunday (the first day) because they are under the mistaken impression that Jesus rose on a Sunday. Where is the scripture to support the idea that YHWH's Day of Rest was to change to the first day after Yeshua's death? Did Yeshua ever suggest we do that?

Now, please pay close attention to this one:

*Isaiah 66: 22 "For just as the new heavens and the new earth that I am making will continue in my presence," says ADONAI, "so will your descendants and your name continue. 23 "Every month on Rosh-Hodesh and every week on Shabbat, **everyone living** will come to worship in my presence," says ADONAI. 24 "As they leave, they will look on the corpses of the people who rebelled against me. For their worm will never die, and their fire will never be quenched; but they will be abhorrent to all humanity." ["Every month on Rosh-Hodesh and every week on Shabbat, everyone living will come to worship in my presence," says ADONAI.]*

YHWH said His Torah would stand *forever* (2 Chronicles 7:14-22). Forever didn't end when Christianity came onto the scene! On Judgment Day He will ask you why you chose to ignore His Torah, why you changed His seventh-day Sabbath, and why you didn't keep the Feasts that He commanded to be kept forever, and which will be continued in heaven:

Exodus 31: 13 "Tell the people of Isra'el, "You are to observe my Shabbats; for this is a sign between me and you through all your generations; so that you will know that I am ADONAI, who sets you apart for me.

Exodus 31: 16 The people of Isra'el are to keep the Shabbat, to observe Shabbat through all their generations as a perpetual covenant. 17 It is a sign between me and the people of Isra'el forever; for in six days ADONAI made heaven and earth, but on the seventh day he stopped working and rested. "'

Again, *who* are the children of Israel? Anyone who believes in the God of Abraham, Isaac, and Jacob! As a grafted in Gentile believer **YOU** are ONE in Messiah, which means you have to obey God! Torah is not a "tradition"; it is YHWH's commandments - without which the world would not have a blueprint for holy behavior.

Appendix 5

The Third Temple

There are endless theories about the future Temple. Some say it will be a literal Temple on earth, while others insist it will be in heaven, and still other suggest that, once Yeshua died, our bodies became the Temple and there is no longer a need for a physical temple.

The thing is, the Bible says otherwise. Since the "Antichrist" will pass himself off as God and claim the Temple for his own three and a half years after he "makes a strong covenant with the leaders" (Daniel 9:27; Revelation 11:1-2), he will go into a *physical* temple to desolate it (Daniel 12:11). This, all by itself, reveals that the Temple *has* to be a Temple on Earth – because the Antichrist will definitely not be enjoying a single day in Heaven (Revelation 19:20)!

Here's more proof:

It is true that Yeshua was our Final *Sin* Sacrifice; however, He did not remove the need for some of the other Temple sacrifices (offers of thanksgiving, burnt and guilt offerings, etc.). These sacrifices were stopped after the Second Temple was destroyed, only because YHWH requires a proper Temple for anything sacrificed to Him (Exodus 20:19-26; I Kings 6). That will change with the erection of the Third Temple in Jerusalem!

Revelation 11: 1. And a reed was given to me, like a rod; and the Messenger stood, saying, Arise and measure the temple of Elohim, and the altar, and them that worship inside it. 2. But the court which is without the temple, leave out, and measure it not, because it is given to the Gentiles; and they will tread down the Set Apart city forty and two months.

Let's ask ourselves this: Since all believers are ONE in Messiah (Ephesians 3:5-6), why would there be Gentiles in heaven who have to remain outside the Temple proper?

Scriptures tell us there will be a literal Third Temple because sacrifices will be taking place prior to the second coming and even during the thousand year reign. For this to occur, there must be an altar and some sort of structure - be it a stone temple or a tent similar to Moses' or David's tabernacle. In the scriptures which follow, we see that Ezekiel clearly describes a future *physical* temple (given to him in a vision from YHWH (Ezekiel 40:1-4) because, how else could we explain the fact that Levites and descendents of Aaron will be ministering there to offer *sin* sacrifices? Will there be SIN in heaven?

Ezekiel 40: 45 He said to me, "This room facing south is for the cohanim in charge of the house; 46 while the room facing north is for the cohanim in charge of the altar; these are the descendants of Tzadok, who are the descendants of Levi designated to approach ADONAI and serve him."

Ezekiel 43: 18 He said to me, "Human being, Adonai ELOHIM says, 'These are the regulations for the altar when the time comes to construct it, offer burnt offerings on it and splash the blood against it: 19 you are to give to the cohanim, who are L'vi'im descended from Tzadok and who approach to serve me,' says Adonai ELOHIM, 'a young bull as a sin offering. 20 You are to take its blood and put it on the four horns of the altar, on the four corners of the ledge and on the molding all the way around; this is how you will purify it and make atonement for it. 21 You are also to take the bull which is the sin offering and have it burned up at the designated place [on the grounds] of the house, outside the sanctuary. 22 On the second day you are to offer a male goat without defect as a sin offering, and they are to purify the altar as they purified it with the bull.

In light of Yeshua being the Sin sacrifice and the Great High Priest after the order of Melchizedek (Psalm110:4, Hebrews 7:17), why bother reverting back to a priesthood based on the descendents of Aaron? Because, as you will see below, it's the only way to interpret the verses that describe the Levitical priesthood ministering in the temple described by Ezekiel and Zechariah!

Now, check out the following:

Ezekiel 43: 23 When you have finished purifying it, you are to offer a young bull without defect and a ram from the flock without defect. 24 You are to present them before ADONAI, and the cohanim will throw salt on them and offer them as a burnt offering to ADONAI. 25 Every day, for seven days, you are to prepare a goat as a sin offering; they are also to prepare a young bull and a ram from the flock without defect. 26 For seven days, they are to make atonement for the altar and cleanse it; in this way they are to consecrate it. 27 When these days are over, then, on the eighth day and afterwards, the cohanim will present your burnt offerings on the altar and your peace offerings; and I will accept you,' says Adonai ELOHIM."

Again, there are no days and nights in heaven, so this could NOT refer to a heavenly temple. Furthermore, why would YHWH require offerings in heaven, when the purpose of the offerings was to atone for man's guilt, shame, sins, etc.? There will be NO SIN, no guilt and no shame in heaven!

Ezekiel 44: 9 Here is what Adonai ELOHIM says: 'No foreigner, uncircumcised in both heart and flesh, is to enter my sanctuary - no foreigner living among the people of Isra'el. 10 "'Rather, the L'vi'im, who went far away from me when Isra'el went astray, going astray after their idols - they will bear the consequences of their guilt, 11 but they are to serve in my sanctuary. They will have charge of the gates of the house and of serving in the house; they will slaughter the burnt offering and the sacrifice for the people; and they will attend and serve them.

There is no such thing as a "foreigner" in heaven. *All* who believe are grafted in to the Olive Tree, and YHWH treats His adopted children exactly the same as His natural ones (no matter what some "intellects" insist; those who adhere to the misunderstood writings of Paul, over and above what Yeshua taught!)

We also need to ask ourselves: If this is a temple in heaven, how could the Levites "bear the consequences of their guilt" there? Whose guilt are they bearing since everyone in heaven after Judgment Day is there because they are sin and guilt-free!

Ezekiel 44: 12 Because they served them in the presence of their idols and became an occasion of sin for the house of Isra'el, I am raising my hand against them,' says Adonai ELOHIM, 'and they will bear the consequences of their guilt. 13 They will not approach me to serve me in the office of cohen or approach any of the holy things or the especially holy things; but they will bear their shame for the disgusting practices they committed. 14 Yet I will put them in charge of the house and all its maintenance and everything to be done in it. 15 "'However, the cohanim, who are L'vi'im and descendants of Tzadok, who took care of my sanctuary when the people of Isra'el went astray from me - they are the ones who will approach me and serve me; it is they who will attend me and offer me the fat and the blood,' says Adonai ELOHIM. 16 They will enter my sanctuary, approach my table to minister to me and perform my service. 17 "'Once they enter the gates of the inner courtyard, they are to wear linen clothing; they are not to wear any wool while serving at the gates of the inner courtyard or inside it. 18 They are to wear linen turbans on their heads and linen underclothes on their bodies, and they are not to wear anything that makes them sweat. 19 Before going out to the people in the outer courtyard, they are to remove the clothes in which they minister, lay them in the holy rooms, and put on other clothes; so that they won't transmit holiness to the people by means of their clothing. 20 They are not to shave their heads or let their hair grow long, but must keep their hair carefully trimmed. 21 No cohen is to drink wine when he enters the inner courtyard. 22 They may not marry a widow or a divorcee but must marry virgins descended from the house of Isra'el or a widow whose deceased husband was a cohen.

Isn't everyone who is in heaven **holy**? And **marriage** in heaven? Not according to Yeshua who said: *"30. For in the resurrection of the dead, men do not marry women, nor are women given to husbands. Rather, they are as the Messengers of Elohim in Heaven."* (Matthew 22:30).

Ezekiel 44: 23 "They are to teach my people the difference between holy and common and enable them to distinguish between clean and unclean.

If this is in heaven, wouldn't we already know the difference between holy and common?

Ezekiel 44: 24 They are to be judges in controversies, and they are to render decisions in keeping with my rulings. At all my designated festivals they are to keep my laws and regulations, and they are to keep my shabbats holy.

Controversies in heaven?

Ezekiel 44: 25 They are not to come to any dead person, because this would make them unclean; however, for father, mother, son, daughter, brother or sister who has had no husband they may make themselves unclean.

A dead person or a corpse in heaven?

Malachi 3: 1 "Look! I am sending my messenger to clear the way before me; and the Lord, whom you seek, will suddenly come to his temple. Yes, the messenger of the covenant, in whom you take such delight - look! Here he comes," says ADONAI-Tzva'ot. 2 But who can endure the day when he comes? Who can stand when he appears? For he will be like a refiner's fire, like the soapmaker's lye. 3 He will sit, testing and purifying the silver; he will purify the sons of Levi, refining them like gold and silver, so that they can bring offerings to ADONAI uprightly. 4 Then the offering of Y'hudah and Yerushalayim will be pleasing to ADONAI, as it was in the days of old, as in years gone by. 5 "Then I will approach you for judgment; and I will be quick to witness against sorcerers, adulterers and perjurers; against those who take advantage of wage-earners, widows and orphans; against those who rob the foreigner of his rights and don't fear me," says ADONAI-Tzva'ot. 6 "But because I, ADONAI, do not change, you sons of Ya'akov will not be destroyed.

Will there be widows and orphans in heaven, or those who take advantage of them and the wage-earners, or those who rob the foreigner of their rights?

There are plenty of other references that could be discussed, but you get the picture....

The Bible tells us there will come a time when sacrifices will be offered again. It says so in Ezekiel, and it is also mentioned by Daniel 8:9-11, when referring to the evil ruler - "the little horn" - who does away with the daily sacrifices and casts YHWH's sanctuary down. For sacrifices to be abolished and YHWH's sanctuary to be cast down, there needs to be a *physical* temple where sacrifices are being offered....

YHWH came to Solomon's temple after it was built (1 Kings); and through Yeshua He came to the Second Temple built by Zerubbabel (Ezra 5:2). Therefore, it stands to reason that Yeshua will enter the Third Temple, as well!

Ezekiel 43: 1 After this, he brought me to the gate facing east. 2 There I saw the glory of the God of Isra'el approaching from the east. His voice was like the sound of rushing water, and the earth shone with his glory. 3 The vision seemed like the vision I had seen when I came to destroy the city; also the visions were like the vision I had seen by the K'var River; and I fell on my face. 4 ADONAI's glory entered the house through the gate facing east. 5 Next, a spirit took me up and brought me into the inner courtyard, and I saw ADONAI's glory fill the house. 6 I heard someone speaking to me from the house, and a man was standing by me. 7 He said, "Human being, this is the place for my throne, the place for the soles of my feet, where I will live among the people of Isra'el forever. The house of Isra'el, both they and their kings, will never again defile my holy name by their prostitution, by [burying] the corpses of their kings [on] their high places, 8 or by placing their threshold next to my threshold and their door-frames next to my door-frames, with only a common wall between me and them. Yes, they defiled my holy name by the disgusting practices they committed; which is why I destroyed them in my anger. 9 So now, they should put their prostitution at a distance and the corpses of their kings far away from me; then I will live among them forever. 10 "You, human being, describe this house to the house of Isra'el, so that they will be ashamed of their crimes. And let them measure accurately. 11 If they become ashamed of all they have done, show them the elevation and plan of the house, its exits and entrances, all its details and decorations, and all its specifications, its design and its Torah. Sketch it for them to see, so that they can observe the entire design with its specifications, and carry them out. 12 This is Torah for the house: the whole surrounding area on the mountaintop will be especially holy. This is Torah for the house."

There will come a time when we will need no temple at all because YHWH Himself is our Temple in heaven:

Revelation 21: 21. And the twelve gates (were) twelve pearls; each (pearl) one gate, and each (gate) one pearl: and the broad street of the city was pure gold, like brilliant glass. 22. And I saw no temple in it; for Master YHWH Almighty is its temple, and the Lamb. 23. And the city has no need of the sun or of the moon to enlighten it; for the glory of Elohim enlightens it, and the Lamb is the lamps of it. 24. And the nations that were saved will walk by means of its light, and the kings of the earth will bring their glory and the wealth of the nations into it. 25. And its gates will not be shut by day; for there is no night there. 26. And they will bring the glory and honor of the nations into it. 27. And there will not enter it anything polluted, or that practices impurity and falsehood; but they who are registered in the Lamb's book of life.

Appendix 6

The Aramaic English New Testament

Below is a short explanation as to why I chose to use New Testament scriptures from the Aramaic English New Testament (AENT) by Andrew Gabriel Roth:

The AENT is a is a compilation, annotation and translation of the Aramaic New Testament Peshitta Text, which includes the translation of the Khabouris Codex, the oldest known New Testament ever discovered. Some scholars suggest it dates back to between 120-160 CE. The AENT was compiled, edited and translated with consultation to both Ancient and Modern Authorities including not only the Khabouris Codex, but also the 1905 Edition of the Syriac New Testament by the British and Foreign Bible Society.

It is important to note that these documents, as a collective whole, prove that the original New Testament writings were *in Aramaic, not Greek*. This makes sense because, why would the Jewish Apostles, whose native tongue was Hebrew and Aramaic, write the Gospels in a foreign language, even if they might have been fluent in Greek?

The AENT serves not only to return the original writings to their proper context, but also to correct any mistranslated words, thoughts and concepts, especially those contained within the writings of Paul.

Example: Every Bible version shows that Yeshua said in Matthew 19:24, Mark 10:25 and Luke 18:25 that "it is easier to put a *camel* through the eye of a needle"....when in fact

the Aramaic shows that the word was actually "rope" –
which makes a whole lot more sense.

*Matthew 19: 24. And again I say to you that it is easier for a rope3
to enter into the eye of a needle than for a rich man to enter into the
Kingdom of Elohim.*

Another example:

*Matthew 27: 46. And about the ninth hour, Y'shua cried out with a
loud voice and said, My El! My El! [Lemana shabakthani] Why
have you spared me?4*

---

3 *Gamala* refers to a "heavy rope" rather than a "camel" which is also spelled *gimel-meem-lamed-alap*. Greek scholars puzzled over a camel passing through the eye of a needle, which is a physical impossibility. Y'shua is clearly not saying a rich man can't enter, or he would not "love" this one! The "heavy rope" lesson teaches about a rich man entering into heaven, after he "unravels" his fortune strand by strand as Y'shua instructs. If his wealth was bound tightly and strong like a rope, it is to be unwound like threads which will pass through the eye of the needle! Careful attention is required to thread a needle; so are the rich obligated unto YHWH for how their wealth is acquired and dispersed. Theological attempts to "prove" the eye of the needle to be a geographical location have utterly failed.

4 Y'shua was not necessarily quoting Psalm 22, although the imagery of the Psalm is certainly intended by Matthew. Greek is transliterated *Eli, Eli lama sabacthani*, but Peshitta and Psalm 22 read: *Eli, Eli lama azbatani*. Many Bibles read "forsaken" from which came a false teaching that the Father left Y'shua destitute (Marcionite thinking). Isaiah 53:4 indicates that *"we"* reckoned him smitten of Elohim, but it is not YHWH who tortured His own son, but men motivated by religious tradition. Psalm 22 references those who scorned Y'shua for his Faith in YHWH and called him a worm (detested), but Father YHWH does not forsake the righteous, nor does He at any time "forsake" His own Son – see Psalm 9:9, 10; 37:25; 71:11; Isaiah 49:14-16. Y'shua says "Eli" (my El). He is in great physical pain after being brutally tortured; those around him were confused about whether he was saying "Eli-yah" or "Eliyahu". If Hebrew eyewitnesses were not sure of what he was saying, it shouldn't be a surprise that Greek transliteration was also wrong, putting *"lama sabacthani"* rather than *"lemana shabakthani"*. Perhaps the reason Y'shua says "why are you sparing me" is because he has proven his commitment by laying down his life and has already endured about six hours of the execution! So, it's not a matter of being "forsaken" but that he literally means, "Father, I'm ready, why can't we finish this?" In a matter of moments from saying this, he dies, which fully supports this interpretation.

The bottom line is, the AENT contains YHWH's undiluted TRUTH found not only within the pages that comprise the "New Testament" writings, but also with the extra benefit of copious footnotes and appendices that serve to provide further insight and explanation from the Hebraic viewpoint.

"And There Was War in Heaven!" could *not* have been written without the AENT! Without the wisdom contained within the pages of the AENT, this book would have been just another "Greek" interpretation and mistranslation of the Scriptures.

Made in the USA
Lexington, KY
06 December 2012